The Southern Living® Microwave Cookbook

The Southern Living Microwave Cookbook

MARGARET CHASON AGNEW

© 1988 by Oxmoor House, Inc.
Book Division of Southern Progress Corporation
P.O. Box 2463 Birmingham, Alabama 35201

Library of Congress Catalog Number: 87-061716
ISBN: 0-8487-0725-7

Manufactured in the United States of America
First Printing 1988

Executive Editor: Ann H. Harvey
Production Manager: Jerry Higdon
Associate Production Manager: Rick Litton
Art Director: Bob Nance
Production Assistant: Theresa Beste

The Southern Living *Microwave Cookbook*

Senior Foods Editor: Margaret Chason Agnew
Copy Editor: Mary Ann Laurens
Editorial Assistant: Pam Beasley Bullock
Test Kitchen Director: Laura N. Massey
Test Kitchen Home Economists: Rebecca D. Bryant, Nancy Earhart,
    Julie Fisher, Lisa Glass, Paula Saunders
Senior Photographer: Jim Bathie
Photo Stylist: Kay E. Clarke
Designer: Faith Nance

Cover: *Red Pepper-Citrus Chicken (page 172).*
Back Cover: *Glazed Strawberry Pie (page 82).*
Page ii: *(top) Herbed Green Beans (page 22) and (bottom) Kahlúa Mousse (page 96).*
Page iii: *Garlic-Buttered Shrimp (page 128).*

To find out how you can receive *Southern Living* magazine, write to *Southern Living*®, P.O. Box C-119, Birmingham, AL 35283.

Contents

Microwave Basics and Beyond

You may already have discovered that cooking in a microwave oven can make life simpler and eating more pleasurable. The microwave oven is a sophisticated, modern-day appliance that is extremely easy to operate. In a matter of minutes you can prepare delicious foods—attractive, fresh-tasting vegetables, tender chicken, mouth-watering soups, wonderful candies and desserts, and much more.

We have written *The Southern Living Microwave Cookbook* to help you get the most from your microwave oven. You'll find this cookbook is packed with tempting recipes to prepare for your family and friends. They range from the simplest recipes that are just right for beginning microwave users to those that are more challenging. We've also converted some favorite traditional recipes from conventional to microwave procedures, so now they're easier to prepare than you ever dreamed.

Because we want you to feel confident and get the best possible results, we've taken extra time to refine each recipe in this cookbook. Most of the recipes were prepared at least twice by our test kitchen home economists using 600 to 700 watt, variable-power microwave ovens. If any problems were encountered with a recipe, it was retested until perfected.

We've also included helpful tips and photographs to guide you through the more difficult procedures. But before you get started, review the following basic microwave techniques and terms. These are important to the success of the recipes and will make microwave cooking more fun than ever!

Fresh vegetables are at their best when cooked in the microwave oven. Try (front to back) Snow Peas With Red Pepper (page 241), Cheesy Bacon-Stuffed Potatoes (page 244), Golden Cauliflower (page 230), and Fresh Mexicali Corn (page 233).

How The Microwave Oven Works

The first step to mastering microwave cookery is to understand how the microwave oven works. It is helpful to know what the basic parts and features of the oven are, and how microwaves are produced.

Components of the Microwave Oven   All microwave ovens have five main components. The first is the **magnetron tube,** which converts electricity into microwaves. The second is the **wave guide,** which channels the microwaves into the oven cavity. The third component is a **stirrer,** a **fan,** or an **antenna** that is used to "fan" or distribute the microwaves inside the oven. Fourth is the oven **cavity** which is the area inside the oven where food is placed to absorb the microwaves. The fifth component is the **control system,** or the on and off switches, power settings, timers, etc.

How the Microwave Oven Works   When microwaves are generated by the magnetron tube, they are sent to the oven cavity through the wave guide. There microwaves are fanned out or distributed and enter the food. The microwaves then cause molecules in the food to agitate and rub against each other. This creates heat, which is then conducted throughout the food. This means the food cooks by internal heat rather than by contact with hot air or a hot oven as in conventional cooking.

The Oven Manual   Before using any microwave oven, always read the manufacturer's use and care manual. This will probably help prevent expensive service calls. The manual always contains this important information: the wattage of the oven (which affects how fast it cooks), the cavity size of the oven, and whether the oven can cook by variable power levels.

Oven Wattage   While all microwave ovens have the same basic components, they may vary significantly in power output or wattage. Most newer ovens and most larger ovens yield between 600 and 700 watts of power. Compact models generally yield only 400 to 550 watts. Remember, the lower the wattage, the longer it will take for the food to cook. Compact ovens are ideal for reheating, especially small quantities of food. But because these lower-wattage ovens cook much slower, you will probably need to increase the cooking times suggested in our recipes.

You will notice that our recipes typically offer a range of cooking time—for example, 5 to 7 minutes. If you have a 700 watt oven the food will be done sooner, so you will want to check it at the shorter end of the time range. If your oven is a lower-wattage oven, then you would probably need the longer time range.

If there is no reference to the wattage in the owner's manual, then look on the back of the oven for the label plate and locate the output or wattage figure.

Cavity Size   Even when ovens have the same wattage, the cavity sizes may vary. The cavity size, or the inside dimensions of the oven, is usually stated in cubic feet. You'll want to make sure the oven can hold the size cookware you like to use. For example, can it hold a 13- x 9- x 2-inch baking dish?

But beware—don't go by cubic-foot size alone. Models with the same number of cubic feet can have differing interior dimensions. In a microwave oven, width is more useful than height.

Power Levels   Some microwave oven control systems offer HIGH power level only; some offer HIGH and LOW power levels. Others offer as many as ten different power levels.

The power level reflects the amount of time the oven is making microwaves. For example, at HIGH power the oven is making microwaves the entire time it is on; at MEDIUM (50% power) it is making microwaves for only half the time it is on. Therefore, the higher the power, the longer the oven is producing microwaves, and the faster it cooks.

It's important to understand that just as you control the rate of conventional cooking by turning the temperature knob, you can use power levels to serve the same purpose in microwave cooking.

All of our recipes were tested in variable-power ovens with at least ten different power levels, but four or five power levels are adequate to cook any of the recipes. We refer to the various power levels as:

HIGH   =   100% power
MEDIUM HIGH   =   70% power
MEDIUM   =   50% power
MEDIUM LOW   =   30% power
LOW   =   10% power

Special Features   All microwave ovens cook by time, which is set by an electronic control touch pad or a dial-turn timer, but some models offer additional features. For example, we've already mentioned that some ovens have variable power levels. These power levels usually include a **defrost setting** (MEDIUM LOW or 30% power), which may be considered a special feature of the microwave.

Some units include a **convection-microwave combination** feature which circulates hot air to brown and crispen food when baking, roasting, and broiling. If you have a convection or browning unit in your oven, do not use plastic cookware or plastic utensils when using either of those features.

One of the newest features on some microwave ovens is the **automatic sensor**. Ovens with this feature are programmed to sense the temperature, weight, or humidity of the food that's being microwaved, and the oven automatically stops producing microwaves or turns off when the food is done.

Some ovens feature a built-in **turntable** to rotate the food more evenly through the microwaves. In some models the turntable can be switched off or removed. Keep in mind that wide baking dishes may not have room to rotate in ovens with a turntable. You can also purchase a separate carousel turntable that can be placed in the oven when desired and set to turn automatically; it can be removed when not in use.

Some ovens also feature an **oven shelf** which makes it easier to cook several dishes at the same time. This works better when microwaving small amounts of food; if microwaving large amounts or several dishes, it may be just as quick to use your conventional oven.

A built-in turntable or a separate carousel turntable will rotate food for more even cooking.

Temperature probes, instant-read thermometers, and microwave food thermometers allow you to cook to specific temperatures.

Microwave oven manufacturers also offer computerized ovens that allow for all sorts of **automatic programming.** For example, you may be able to program several different cooking steps and power levels so that the microwave automatically moves on to each step without your presence. Automatic programming can also allow you to set a timer so that the microwave will begin cooking before you get home, turn off at the desired time, and still keep the food warm until serving time. There are even ovens that operate by inserting magnetic "recipe" cards in a special holder; these ovens cook specific foods automatically by "following" the card instructions.

Many ovens routinely include an **oven temperature probe.** Instead of setting the control pad for a specific cooking time, you set it for the desired internal temperature and insert the probe in the center of the food item. When the set temperature is reached, the oven automatically turns off. Of course, an instant-read thermometer or a special microwave thermometer can serve the same purpose.

Approved microwave cookware includes glass or ceramic dishes, some plastic containers, clay cookers, and containers made specifically for microwave cooking.

GUIDE TO MICROWAVE COOKWARE AND UTENSILS

When selecting containers for microwave cooking, consider whether you will be defrosting, heating, reheating, or cooking in them. Some containers work for defrosting or reheating only, while others can be used for any of these cooking methods. The container should be of the proper material and design for each particular method.

The Best Microwave Containers Many kinds of utensils can be used for microwave cooking, but there are some restrictions. **Heat-resistant glass, oven-tempered glass,** or **glass-ceramic cookware** is ideal for microwave cooking. Of course, glass containers have the advantage of allowing you to see through them. And they can be taken from the freezer to the microwave and on to the table without breaking.

Ceramic dishes such as pottery, porcelain, fine china, and stoneware are usually good containers for microwave cooking. They are microwave-safe if they have no metallic trim or glazes.

The guidelines concerning the use of **plastic containers** in the microwave are confusing. Foods with a high fat or sugar content will often become hot enough during microwaving to melt some plastic containers. Old butter or margarine containers and melamine and styrofoam are not recommended for microwave cooking. Heavier storage-type plastic containers can be used for some reheating, but only to a certain temperature; they may begin to melt around 170° to 220°F. Plastic wrap works well when used as a covering, particularly for holding in heat and moisture.

Thermoset polyester and **thermoplastic containers** are designed specifically for use in the microwave oven. However, there are some limitations on temperature and type of heat usage. Thermoset polyester cookware can withstand temperatures up to around 400°F, and can also be used in a conventional oven. Thermoplastic containers are generally recommended for

To determine if a container is microwave-safe, try the water test we have suggested (page 5).

microwave use only. Do not use either thermoset polyester or thermoplastic containers with direct heat, such as a broiler or a browning-type heating element, or for top-of-the-stove cooking.

Paper products may be used for short-term microwave cooking. Wax paper works well as a covering because it prevents spattering yet allows steam to escape. Other paper goods such as paper towels, napkins, and paper plates provide the convenience of easy cleanup.

Be careful not to use paper towels made from recycled paper because they may contain metal fragments that could catch fire.

Wood or **straw products** can be used for quick reheating, but are generally not recommended for long periods of microwave cooking. Straw baskets with metal joints should not be used.

Most **metal containers** reflect microwaves and are not suitable for microwave cooking. Always check your microwave oven owner's manual before using any kind of metal in your oven. Aluminum foil may occasionally be used to shield parts of foods and prevent overcooking. But check your manual before using foil, and be sure to keep it from touching other metals, including the oven walls.

Some special microwave containers have been designed to make safe use of metal, such as browning trays. These containers have been specifically designed for use in the microwave oven and will not cause arcing or sparking if used properly. However, always make sure these dishes are placed in the center of the oven so that they do not touch the sides. *Remember, if metal is close to or touches another metal, it can cause arcing or sparking. The arcing creates heat, which can cause fire.*

Clay pots or **clay cookers, browning dishes,** and **plastic browning bags** may be used for most pleasing results. For example, clay cookers will produce moist results every time when microwaving poultry. Browning dishes are excellent for achieving a toasted brown look on sandwiches or meats. And plastic browning bags are ideal for preparing moist, juicy roasts.

A browning skillet allows you to brown or sear foods much like a conventional skillet.

Is the Container Microwave-Safe? Here's How to Tell   Place a 1-cup glass measure filled with water in the microwave along with the container you are testing. Microwave at HIGH for 1 minute. If the dish remains cool, it is safe for microwaving. If it's slightly warm, it is probably safe for heating or reheating, but not for cooking. If the dish is hot, do not use it in the microwave oven.

The Best Sizes and Shapes   When purchasing microwave cookware, base your selections on the size of your family and whether the container will fit into your microwave oven cavity. If you have a built-in turntable in your oven, be sure the dishes you choose can rotate without hitting the oven walls.

The depth of the container is also important. A shallow container exposes more food surface to the microwaves for faster cooking. Deeper containers are necessary for foods which have a great deal of liquid to bubble and boil, such as sauces or soups. They also allow for the increased expansion of baked goods, such as cakes. A container large enough to hold double the amount of food is usually recommended.

The most efficient shape for microwave containers is the round or doughnut shape. This shape is ideal for foods which cannot be stirred during

Foods cook more evenly when microwaved in round containers.

cooking. A doughnut shape also eliminates the center where food is hard to cook. Food in the corners of square or rectangular dishes sometimes over-cooks because microwaves enter from two sides. We tested some of our recipes in both types of dishes; we found that standing time helps food in the center of a container cook completely.

Oval-shaped containers are also acceptable. Square or rectangular contain-ers are not preferred, but we have called for them occasionally because they are probably the most common containers to be found in kitchens. They can yield better results if they have rounded rather than square corners.

A roasting rack or bacon roaster should be used inside another container when cooking meat. This will elevate the meat and allow juices to drain off as the meat cooks.

Know What Affects Microwave Cooking

With microwave cooking, the decisions you make about cooking time and the microwave techniques you use can make a big difference in the final result. When using our recipes, always check for doneness at the minimum cooking time and add more time, if necessary.

Some of the factors that can affect the cooking time for a recipe include your oven's wattage, the power level you're cooking with, the food itself, and the specific cooking techniques followed.

Wattage   Remember, lower-wattage ovens cook slower than higher-wattage ovens. Also, keep in mind that your oven probably won't cook as fast during certain times of the day that are peak power-use periods.

Using your microwave oven during a peak power-use period will not necessarily result in a poorer product, but you may have to increase the cooking time slightly.

Power Levels   When microwaving at lower power levels you will probably need to increase the cooking time. When microwaving at a higher level, you will probably need to decrease the cooking time. This is because foods microwaved at lower power levels are being exposed to microwaves only part of the time, whereas foods microwaved at HIGH power are being exposed to microwaves 100% of the time.

Size and Shape of Food   The shape of the food will also affect how long it will take to microwave it. Irregularly shaped items like chicken pieces will cook differently than evenly shaped hamburger patties. For chicken, arrange the pieces with the thicker parts towards the outside of the dish to allow for more even cooking.

The size of the food item also affects microwave cooking time. Small pieces cook faster than large pieces; diced or sliced vegetables will cook faster than whole vegetables. Quantity of food also affects cooking time, so if you intend to cook large quantities you will probably discover it is just as quick to cook them conventionally as it is in the microwave.

Diced or sliced vegetables will cook faster than whole vegetables.

Density of Food   Thicker, denser foods such as meatloaf will take longer to cook because microwaves penetrate only up to two inches below the surface. For example, a dense, compact sweet potato will take longer to microwave than a light-textured, porous cake layer.

Quantity of Food   It's not surprising that the quantity of food in the microwave also affects cooking time. Remember, as the quantity of food increases, microwave time increases. That's why one potato cooks quickly while six potatoes take much longer to cook.

Moisture Content   Foods with a high moisture content, such as vegetables, fruits, fish, poultry, and sauces, are ideal for microwaving. Low-moisture foods, such as over-mature vegetables, take much longer and often provide poor results.

Small amounts of food will cook faster than large amounts.

Temperature of Food   Starting temperatures of foods can also make a difference. Foods taken directly from the freezer or refrigerator will take longer to microwave than foods at room temperature.

Fat and Sugar Levels   Foods containing high fat and sugar levels will heat very rapidly in the microwave, while those foods with low fat and sugar levels will heat more slowly. This means that a cup of sweet syrup or butter will come to a boil in the microwave oven much quicker than a cup of water. It is, therefore, a good idea to remove excess fat from the outer edges of meat; otherwise the fat will burn before the meat is cooked.

KNOW THE TECHNIQUES FOR MICROWAVING

Before using our microwave recipes, take time to review the following microwave cooking techniques. These techniques, some as simple as piercing a potato or rotating a dish, will assure better results when preparing food in the microwave oven.

Cover foods with heavy-duty plastic wrap or casserole lids to trap steam; use wax paper to prevent spatters.

Covering Food   Use heavy-duty plastic wrap when you want to trap steam around food to keep it moist and to cook it faster; if the cookware you are using has a lid, you may prefer to use it instead of plastic wrap. Use wax paper to prevent spatters and to help keep some moisture around the food but not so much as to make it soggy. Wrap the food or cover it with paper towels so that the paper towels will absorb moisture or fat, as when heating bread or microwaving bacon.

Venting Plastic Wrap   To protect yourself from steam burns, turn back one corner of plastic wrap coverings or cut several slits in the top to allow steam to escape. Either way, venting the plastic wrap prevents the build-up of steam that can cause burns when the cover is lifted. For further protection, always start by carefully lifting the edge farthest from you when you remove the wrap from the dish.

Remember to vent plastic wrap by folding back an edge; this helps prevent steam burns.

Arrange foods correctly to allow for even cooking.

Piercing allows steam to escape and prevents bursting.

Shielding protects foods in areas where they tend to cook too quickly.

Standing time allows foods to finish cooking.

Arranging Food Arrange food in containers so that the thicker parts are nearest the outside of the dish where they will attract microwaves first. For example, place the tender tips of asparagus or broccoli towards the center of the dish with the tougher stalks near the outside edge.

When placing three or more whole foods, such as potatoes, or dishes, such as custard cups, in the microwave oven, arrange them in a circle. This circular pattern promotes even cooking by giving each food item maximum exposure to the microwaves.

Piercing (or Pricking) Food Piercing or pricking certain foods is another technique used in microwave cooking. This technique is necessary for foods with thick skins, such as potatoes or acorn squash, or foods with membrane coverings, such as chicken livers or egg yolks. Piercing or pricking allows steam to escape and prevents bursting.

Stirring Any food that can be stirred should be stirred to promote even cooking, because the food around the outside of the container will cook faster than the food in the center. Stir from the outside to the center. Some foods like puddings or sauces will need occasional stirring; other foods like soup and diced or sliced vegetables will also require stirring once or twice.

Rotating Rotate foods that cannot be stirred such as cake batters or some casseroles. To rotate means to turn the dish a quarter-turn or half-turn. Like stirring, rotating a dish helps to ensure more even cooking.

Shielding Although it is not used often, shielding can be of great assistance when microwaving unevenly shaped foods like poultry and some meats. Thin, smooth strips of aluminum foil are placed over legs and wing tips or over portions of roasts where they tend to cook too quickly. Food in the corners of square or rectangular dishes may also be shielded, as in the case of a bar cookie, to prevent overcooking. To prevent sparking or arcing, use only small amounts of foil, and be sure the foil doesn't touch any other metal inside the oven cavity or the oven walls themselves. It's a good idea to read the owner's manual for your oven before shielding with foil to be sure the manufacturer approves the use of foil in your oven.

Elevating Cakes and quiches will cook more evenly when the dish they are being microwaved in is placed on top of another dish, such as an inverted pieplate or saucer. This raises the food nearer to the center of the oven's cavity, allowing the microwaves to reach and cook the center and bottom.

Standing Time Some microwaved foods require standing time to finish cooking because cooking continues by heat conduction after the food is removed from the oven. Check for doneness at the earliest suggested time, and then allow for additional cooking to take place during standing time.

Checking for Doneness Judging when foods are done is sometimes difficult. As you prepare our recipes, follow instructions carefully, and remember to check doneness in several places to make sure there are no underdone spots.

MAKE THE MOST OF YOUR MICROWAVE OVEN

Now that you have a pretty good idea of how your microwave oven operates, you should consider using it more and more on a daily basis. By combining microwave cooking and conventional cooking and using the microwave oven to defrost and reheat, you can simplify your daily cooking routines. You will also find it helpful to refer to pages 254 through 258 for our standard microwave cooking times for basic procedures.

Combining Microwave and Conventional Cooking   The microwave oven is a faster and more convenient way to prepare many foods, but don't forget the other time-saving appliances in your kitchen. Combined with the microwave oven these other kitchen appliances will not only save time, but will also give you the best possible results.

Our recipes will help you to use your microwave oven and all your other appliances to their fullest potential. For example, when you prepare pizza, make the sauce in the microwave, but pop the pizza into the conventional oven to give it a crisp crust. We've also offered several pie and quiche pastry shell recipes that you can cook in the microwave, or if you prefer, bake in a conventional oven.

There are several meat recipes that start out in the microwave and are completed on the grill for bold, outdoor flavor. And we've even offered a couple of outstanding ice cream recipes—their custard base is cooked in the microwave before they are churned to perfection in the ice cream freezer.

And there are some instances where the basic recipes are prepared in the microwave, but are served over conventionally prepared rice or pasta. Examples are our gumbo and beef stroganoff recipes.

It is sometimes helpful to combine conventional and microwave cooking. For example, microwave a sauce and cook the pasta conventionally.

Converting a Conventional Recipe to a Microwave Recipe   If you want to turn Grandmother's favorite recipe into a microwave recipe, try these tips:

1. Select a recipe that steams or cooks by moist heat.
2. Look for a microwave recipe that is similar and uses the same amounts of the main ingredients.
3. Reduce liquid by about one-third because less liquid evaporates in microwave cooking.
4. Shorten the cooking time to one-fourth or one-third.
5. Use slightly less seasoning because herbs tend to retain more flavor in microwave recipes since they do not cook as long.
6. Compare the amount of fat or shortening called for in a similar microwave recipe and reduce, if needed.
7. Follow the conventional recipe for dish size and covering, using a round dish when possible. Also, keep in mind that mixtures that must boil and bubble, such as soups and sauces, require a deep dish.

There are conventional recipes which you should not attempt to convert to microwave procedures. Some recipes are those for deep-fat fried foods, popovers, and angel food cake. Pies can be made in the microwave, but some recipes will need alterations. For example, the top pastry, the bottom pastry, and the filling for a double-crust apple pie will have to be cooked separately. Many bread recipes cannot be converted with good results. Also, be aware that while pasta, rice, and dried beans can be cooked in the microwave with good results, you won't save much time over conventional cooking.

Tips for Defrosting and Reheating If you have a busy household, then you can profit from knowing about two important benefits of the microwave oven—defrosting and reheating. The defrost setting makes it simple to reduce thawing time. And reheating in the microwave can save time as well as cleanup because you can reheat and serve food in the same dishes.

Food must be watched carefully while it is **defrosting** in the microwave. Most ovens have a defrost setting. However, the power level assigned to the defrost setting may vary from oven to oven. We've found that the most common defrost setting is MEDIUM LOW (30% power). At reduced power settings the microwave oven will cycle on and off; during the off periods, heat has time to equalize throughout the food. If the power level is too high, food will begin to cook as it defrosts, resulting in a tough, overcooked product.

Lower power levels are best for defrosting. We suggest defrosting at MEDIUM LOW (30% power).

To defrost frozen fruit juice, empty the solid concentrate into a large glass measuring cup or heat-proof pitcher. Microwave for short periods of time over a period of several minutes or until nearly thawed, breaking apart the concentrate several times with a fork. Stir in cold water if using as a beverage.

To defrost meat, place it, in its original plastic- or paper-wrapped package, on a microwave rack in a shallow baking dish. Microwave at MEDIUM LOW (30% power), removing the package and wrappings as soon as it is possible to separate them from the meat. Then cover the meat loosely with wax paper, and turn the meat over on the rack. You can shield the edges of the meat with aluminum foil to help prevent overcooking. If thawing a roast, continue microwaving until a skewer can be inserted in the center.

Test meat often as it defrosts. If warm to the touch, the meat has started to cook and should be prepared immediately. If defrosting for later use, we suggest partially defrosting in the microwave, then placing the meat in the refrigerator where it can defrost completely.

Always place poultry and fish on a microwave rack for defrosting so that the bottom of the food won't start cooking in the liquid that drains off. When partially thawed, immediately plunge poultry or fish into cool water to complete the defrosting process.

Place frozen blocks of soup in a casserole or soup bowl. Cover and microwave until partially thawed; gradually break apart with a fork. Continue this procedure until completely thawed, and then heat briefly at a higher power level.

Defrost frozen foods directly in plastic packages or place in a bowl and cover.

When **reheating** in the microwave oven, care must be taken to avoid additional cooking. Best results can usually be obtained when LOW (10% power) to MEDIUM (50% power) settings are used. Although many foods can be reheated in only a minute or two on HIGH power, others turn out better if reheated gradually on lower settings.

Individual plates of food reheat best at lower power settings. Arrange thick or dense foods to the outside of the plate and softer, more delicate foods towards the center. Cover with wax paper or plastic wrap to hold in heat.

Never reheat meat at HIGH power; this will cause it to toughen. Most refrigerated main dishes should be reheated at MEDIUM (50% power).

Bread can be reheated in just seconds; it will become tough if heated too long. Always wrap bread in a paper towel to absorb moisture.

Dishes that contain eggs, such as wedges of quiche or egg casseroles, can be reheated satisfactorily, but scrambled eggs cook so quickly in the microwave that it is best to start over rather than reheat.

To reheat rice, just add several tablespoons of water, and microwave at MEDIUM HIGH (70% power) for a few minutes. Fluff the hot rice with a fork before serving.

Plan for a Microwave Meal   When it comes to preparing a meal, the microwave oven lends a helping hand. You can use it to prepare side dishes, the main course, or the entire meal.

Begin by getting into the routine of using the microwave oven. Start off with a few of our vegetable side dishes. Then try your hand at some of the meat, seafood, or poultry recipes. After this, you may be ready to consider cooking your whole meal in the microwave oven.

Preparing an entire meal in the microwave makes sense when you take advantage of standing times and consider how simple it is to reheat foods without loss of flavor or quality. The following steps allow for a logical cooking sequence to ensure that dishes are ready when you are.

First, prepare foods which need to be refrigerated or which are served at room temperature. Next, prepare any recipes that require standing time before serving. During the standing time, prepare those foods that cook quickly or reheat any made-ahead dishes. Last minute preparation should be reserved for warming bread or preparing foods that do not reheat well.

You can also prepare a microwave meal by arranging single portions of menu items on individual plates, then heating each plate in the microwave oven. This is especially handy when reheating leftovers. If one food takes longer than the others to heat, then start it off in the microwave by itself and add the other food items later. For example, heat the meat dish until warm, then add the vegetables. Rolls or bread should be added to the plate during the last few seconds.

Some microwave ovens come with a removable shelf in the cavity for when you want to cook the entire meal at the same time. However, this is not always a good way to make a microwave meal because cooking times vary with the types and amounts of foods. If using the shelf, keep these points in mind. First, figure out if you will save any time. Microwaving so many different dishes at once will often take longer than if some of the recipes were cooked conventionally. You also need to be sure that all the dishes fit into your microwave oven at one time. And last, check the foods as they are cooking, and rearrange or remove them from the oven when they are done.

Appetizers, Sandwiches, and Beverages

Most good cooks will tell you that when it comes to appetizers, snack foods, sandwiches, or hot beverages, a microwave oven can be your best friend. We think you will find our recipes in this chapter to be quick, easy, and every bit as tasty as their conventional counterparts.

Many appetizers and snacks can be prepared in advance, refrigerated on microwave-safe serving platters, and microwaved as needed. When possible, save on cleanup time by cooking and serving in the same container.

To prevent sogginess, spread toppings on crackers or toast at the last minute. Placing the appetizers on paper towels during microwaving will help retain a crisper texture.

Our sandwich selections offer enough variety to please everyone. We discovered it was best to microwave some of the fillings separately, then match them with the bun or bread.

Even novice microwave cooks can master our beverage recipes. Other than stirring, no special cooking techniques are used. Just be sure to stir thoroughly before serving for an evenly heated product.

HOT ARTICHOKE-CRAB DIP

1 (14-ounce) can artichoke
  hearts, drained and chopped
1 cup mayonnaise
1 (6-ounce) can crabmeat,
  rinsed and drained
½ cup grated Parmesan cheese
¼ teaspoon garlic powder
1 tablespoon chopped fresh
  parsley
Paprika

Combine first 5 ingredients in a medium bowl, stirring well. Spoon mixture into a lightly greased 1-quart casserole. Cover with wax paper and microwave at MEDIUM (50% power) for 5 to 6 minutes or until thoroughly heated, rotating a half-turn after 3 minutes. Sprinkle with parsley and paprika. Serve immediately with crackers. Yield: 3 cups.

Plan your next party menu to include rich Maison Liver Pâté (page 15) and Cool Cucumber-Shrimp Towers (page 20).

Two-Artichoke Dip

1½ cups (6 ounces) shredded Monterey Jack or Cheddar cheese
1 (8½-ounce) can artichoke hearts, drained and chopped
1 (6-ounce) jar marinated artichoke hearts, drained and chopped
1 (4-ounce) can chopped green chiles
½ cup mayonnaise
2 tablespoons commercial sour cream
⅛ teaspoon red pepper

Combine all ingredients in a 1½-quart casserole. Cover with wax paper; microwave at MEDIUM (50% power) for 6 to 8 minutes or until thoroughly heated, rotating a half-turn after 3 minutes. Serve immediately with chips or crackers. Yield: 3 cups.

Warmed Crab Dip

2 (8-ounce) packages cream cheese
½ pound fresh lump crabmeat, drained and flaked
⅓ cup mayonnaise
1 tablespoon Chablis or other dry white wine
1 teaspoon powdered sugar
½ teaspoon onion juice
½ teaspoon prepared mustard
⅛ teaspoon garlic powder
¼ teaspoon salt
Chopped fresh parsley

Place cream cheese in a 1-quart casserole. Microwave, uncovered, at HIGH for 1 minute to 1 minute and 20 seconds or until softened. Stir in crabmeat, mayonnaise, wine, sugar, onion juice, mustard, garlic powder, and salt. Cover with wax paper and microwave at HIGH for 2 to 3 minutes or until thoroughly heated, stirring after 1 minute. Sprinkle with parsley. Serve dip with crackers. Yield: about 2¾ cups.

Chunky Cheese-Broccoli Dip

1 (10-ounce) package frozen chopped broccoli
½ cup diced sweet red pepper
¼ cup chopped onion
1 tablespoon plus 1 teaspoon butter or margarine
2 (3-ounce) packages cream cheese
1 (8-ounce) carton commercial sour cream
¼ cup grated Parmesan cheese
¼ teaspoon pepper

Remove wrapper from broccoli package; place package in a medium baking dish, and pierce several times with a fork. Microwave at MEDIUM (50% power) for 5 to 6 minutes or until broccoli is thawed, turning package over once. Remove broccoli from package, and press between paper towels to remove excess moisture; set thawed broccoli aside.

Combine red pepper, onion, and butter in a 1-quart casserole. Microwave, uncovered, at HIGH for 2 minutes or until vegetables are crisp-tender; set aside.

CHUNKY CHEESE-BROCCOLI DIP
(continued)

Place cream cheese in a 2-quart casserole. Microwave, uncovered, at HIGH for 40 to 50 seconds or until softened. Stir in sour cream, Parmesan cheese, pepper, broccoli, and red pepper mixture. Microwave, uncovered, at HIGH for 2 to 2½ minutes or until thoroughly heated, stirring after 1 minute. Serve immediately with fresh vegetables or crackers. Yield: about 3 cups.

SPICY CHILI CON QUESO

1 pound hot bulk pork sausage
¼ cup chopped green onions
1 pound process American cheese, cut into 1-inch cubes
¼ cup milk
1 (10-ounce) can tomatoes and green chiles, undrained and chopped

Place sausage and onions in a 1½-quart casserole. Cover with wax paper and microwave at HIGH for 6 to 7 minutes or until sausage is no longer pink, stirring after 3 minutes. Remove sausage mixture from casserole, and drain on paper towels; set aside.

Place cheese and milk in casserole; cover with heavy-duty plastic wrap. Reduce to MEDIUM HIGH (70% power); microwave for 6 to 8 minutes or until cheese melts, stirring every 2 minutes. Stir in sausage mixture and tomatoes and green chiles. Serve immediately with tortilla chips. Yield: 5 cups.

MAISON LIVER PÂTÉ

1 medium onion, chopped
3 tablespoons butter or margarine
1 clove garlic, minced
½ pound chicken livers, cut in half
1 bay leaf
½ teaspoon salt
¼ teaspoon dried whole thyme
¼ teaspoon pepper
¼ cup butter or margarine
1 tablespoon brandy
Green onion strips and green onion curls (optional)
Carrot flowers and carrot curls (optional)
Ripe olives (optional)

Combine chopped onion, 3 tablespoons butter, and garlic in a 1-quart casserole. Microwave, uncovered, at HIGH for 2 to 3 minutes or until onion is tender. Stir in chicken livers and next 4 ingredients. Cover with wax paper and microwave at HIGH for 4 to 5 minutes or until livers are tender, stirring after 2 minutes. Cool; remove and discard bay leaf.

Place ¼ cup butter in a 1-cup glass measure. Reduce to LOW (10% power); microwave, uncovered, for 30 seconds or until softened. Spoon liver mixture, softened butter, and brandy into container of an electric blender or food processor; process until smooth. Spoon mixture into a small bowl or a well-oiled 1½-cup mold; cover and refrigerate at least 8 hours. Unmold pâté; garnish with green onion strips and curls, carrot flowers and curls, and ripe olives, if desired. Serve with crackers. Yield: 1½ cups.

Roquefort Mousse Spread

1 cup whipping cream, divided
2 eggs, separated
1 envelope unflavored gelatin
¼ cup cold water
2 (3-ounce) packages Roquefort
cheese, crumbled
Dash of salt

Place ¼ cup whipping cream in a 1-cup glass measure. Microwave, uncovered, at HIGH for 45 seconds to 1 minute or just until thoroughly heated (do not boil).

Beat egg yolks with a wire whisk in a medium bowl until thick and lemon colored. Gradually stir about 1 tablespoon of hot cream into yolks; add to remaining hot cream, stirring constantly. Reduce to MEDIUM HIGH (70% power); microwave, uncovered, for 1 to 2 minutes or until thickened, stirring every 30 seconds.

Soften gelatin in cold water. Add gelatin mixture, cheese, and salt to egg yolk mixture; beat at high speed of an electric mixer until almost smooth. Let cool completely.

Beat egg whites (at room temperature) until stiff peaks form; set aside. Pour remaining ¾ cup whipping cream into a small bowl; beat at high speed of an electric mixer until soft peaks form. Fold egg whites and whipped cream into cheese mixture.

Pour mixture into a lightly oiled 4-cup mold. Cover and refrigerate 4 hours or until set. Serve with crackers or roast beef. Yield: 3½ cups.

Zesty Horseradish-Beef Spread

½ cup chopped pecans
1 teaspoon butter or margarine
½ cup chopped green onions
2 tablespoons milk
1 (8-ounce) package cream
cheese
½ cup commercial sour cream
⅓ cup mayonnaise
2 tablespoons minced fresh
parsley
2 tablespoons prepared
horseradish
1 teaspoon lemon juice
1 (2½-ounce) jar dried beef,
rinsed, drained, and
shredded

Spread pecans in a pieplate. Microwave, uncovered, at HIGH for 3 to 4 minutes or until lightly toasted; set aside.

Place butter in a 1-quart casserole. Microwave, uncovered, at HIGH for 35 seconds or until melted. Add green onions; microwave, uncovered, at HIGH for 1 minute. Add milk and cream cheese; microwave, uncovered, at HIGH for 1 minute. Stir in sour cream, mayonnaise, parsley, horseradish, lemon juice, and beef. Sprinkle with pecans. Microwave, uncovered, at HIGH for 2 to 4 minutes or until thoroughly heated. Serve immediately with crackers. Yield: about 2½ cups.

PECAN-CHEESE LOG

½ cup chopped pecans
2 tablespoons chopped sweet
  red pepper
2 tablespoons chopped green
  onions
½ teaspoon butter or margarine
1 (8-ounce) package cream
  cheese
2 cups (8 ounces) shredded
  sharp Cheddar cheese
½ (0.6-ounce) envelope Italian
  salad dressing mix
½ teaspoon golden
  Worcestershire sauce
Dash of red pepper

Spread pecans in a pieplate. Microwave, un-covered, at HIGH for 3 to 4 minutes or until lightly toasted; set aside.

Combine sweet red pepper, green onions, and butter in a small bowl. Cover with heavy-duty plastic wrap and microwave at HIGH for 45 seconds or until vegetables are crisp-tender; drain and set aside.

Place cream cheese in a medium bowl. Micro-wave, uncovered, at HIGH for 45 seconds to 1 minute or until softened. Add vegetables, Cheddar cheese, salad dressing mix, Worcester-shire sauce, and red pepper; stir until blended.

Shape mixture into an 11-inch log; roll in pecans. Cover and chill thoroughly. Serve with crackers. Yield: one 11-inch cheese log.

MAPLE-PECAN-TOPPED BRIE

1 (14-ounce) round fully
  ripened Brie
2 tablespoons finely chopped
  pecans
2 tablespoons maple-flavored
  syrup

Remove rind from top of cheese, cutting to within ¼ inch of outside edges. Place cheese on a 12-inch round glass platter. Sprinkle with pecans. Pour syrup over pecans. Cover with wax paper and microwave at HIGH for 1 to 2 minutes or just until Brie is softened, rotating a half-turn after 30 seconds. Serve immediately with crackers. Yield: one cheese round.

Make Maple-Pecan-Topped Brie by removing the rind from the top of the cheese with a sharp knife, leaving a ¼-inch outer edge.

ITALIAN PARTY MIX

3 tablespoons butter or
  margarine
2 (0.6-ounce) envelopes Italian
  salad dressing mix
2 teaspoons Worcestershire
  sauce
¼ teaspoon garlic powder
⅛ teaspoon hot sauce
4 cups bite-size crispy corn or
  wheat square cereal
3 cups pretzel sticks
1 cup mixed salted nuts

Place butter in a 12- x 8- x 2-inch baking dish; microwave, uncovered, at HIGH for 50 seconds or until melted. Stir in salad dressing mix and next 3 ingredients.

Add cereal, pretzel sticks, and nuts to butter mixture; toss gently. Microwave, uncovered, at HIGH for 4 to 5 minutes or until thoroughly heated, stirring after 2 minutes. Let cool; store in an airtight container. Yield: 8 cups.

Sprinkle the cheese with chopped pecans, and top with syrup.

Caramel-Nut Popcorn Mix is the perfect after-school snack.

CARAMEL-NUT POPCORN MIX

2½ quarts freshly popped
   popcorn, unsalted
½ cup butter or margarine
1 cup firmly packed light
   brown sugar
¼ cup dark corn syrup
½ teaspoon salt
¼ teaspoon baking soda
½ teaspoon vanilla extract
1 cup dry-roasted peanuts

Place popcorn in a lightly greased 5-quart casserole; set aside.

Place butter in a 1½-quart casserole; microwave, uncovered, at HIGH for 1 minute or until melted. Stir in brown sugar, corn syrup, and salt; cover with wax paper and microwave at HIGH for 7 to 9 minutes or until mixture reaches hard ball stage (260°), stirring after 4 minutes.

Stir in soda, vanilla, and peanuts. Immediately pour over popcorn, stirring to coat. Let cool, then break into pieces. Store in an airtight container. Yield: 10 cups.

CURRIED NUT MIX

1 tablespoon butter or
   margarine
1 cup whole blanched almonds
1 cup pecan halves
1 cup blanched filberts
2 teaspoons seasoned salt
¾ teaspoon curry powder

Place butter in a 1-cup glass measure; microwave, uncovered, at HIGH for 35 seconds or until melted. Set aside. Combine almonds, pecans, and filberts in a 13- x 9- x 2-inch baking dish; pour butter over nuts, stirring well. Microwave, uncovered, at HIGH for 8 to 9 minutes or until lightly toasted, stirring every 2 minutes. Sprinkle with salt and curry powder; stir well. Microwave, uncovered, at HIGH for 1 to 2 minutes or until thoroughly heated. Drain on paper towels. Serve immediately. Yield: about 3 cups.

CRUNCHY PECAN MUSHROOMS

12 large fresh mushrooms
   (about ¾ pound)
2 tablespoons finely chopped
   onion
2 tablespoons butter or
   margarine
½ cup chopped pecans
½ cup fine, dry breadcrumbs
1 teaspoon lemon juice
½ teaspoon salt

Clean mushrooms with damp paper towels. Remove stems and chop; set caps aside.

Combine mushroom stems, onion, and butter in a 4-cup glass measure; microwave, uncovered, at HIGH for 2 to 3 minutes or until onion is tender. Add pecans, breadcrumbs, lemon juice, and salt; stir well.

Spoon pecan mixture into mushroom caps. Arrange caps in a circle on a 12-inch round glass platter. Microwave, uncovered, at HIGH for 3 to 4 minutes or until thoroughly heated, rotating a half-turn after 2 minutes. Serve immediately. Yield: 1 dozen appetizer servings.

WINE-MARINATED MUSHROOMS

20 medium-size fresh
   mushrooms (about ½ pound)
2 small onions, thinly sliced
⅓ cup vinegar
⅓ cup water
¼ cup Chablis or other dry
   white wine
¾ teaspoon salt
½ teaspoon celery seeds
½ teaspoon mustard seeds
¼ teaspoon whole cloves
¼ cup vegetable oil
1 (2-ounce) jar diced pimiento,
   drained
2 tablespoons chopped green
   onions

Clean mushrooms with damp paper towels; set mushrooms aside.

Combine sliced onions and next 7 ingredients in a 1½-quart casserole. Cover with heavy-duty plastic wrap and microwave at HIGH for 5 minutes. Stir in mushrooms. Cover and microwave at HIGH for 2 to 3 minutes or just until mushrooms are tender.

Remove mushrooms with a slotted spoon, and place in a small bowl. Strain liquid, discarding sliced onions. Add oil, pimiento, and green onions to strained liquid; pour over mushrooms, and toss gently. Cover and refrigerate at least 4 hours. Drain before serving. Yield: 20 appetizer servings.

VEGETABLE-STUFFED MUSHROOMS

16 large fresh mushrooms
   (about 1 pound)
2 tablespoons chopped green
   onions
1 teaspoon butter or margarine
1 small zucchini, shredded
⅓ cup grated Parmesan cheese
1 tablespoon diced pimiento
¼ teaspoon salt

Clean mushrooms with damp paper towels. Remove stems and chop; set caps aside.

Combine mushroom stems, onions, and butter in a 4-cup glass measure; microwave, uncovered, at HIGH for 2 to 3 minutes or until onions are tender. Add zucchini; stir well. Microwave, uncovered, at HIGH for 2 to 2½ minutes or until zucchini is tender. Add cheese, pimiento, and salt, stirring well.

Spoon vegetable mixture into mushroom caps. Arrange caps in a circle on a 12-inch round glass platter. Microwave, uncovered, at HIGH for 3 to 4 minutes or until thoroughly heated, rotating a half-turn after 2 minutes. Serve immediately. Yield: 16 appetizer servings.

COOL CUCUMBER-SHRIMP TOWERS

4 small cucumbers, cut into
   ¾-inch-thick pieces
1 tablespoon plus 1½
   teaspoons butter or
   margarine
¼ cup chopped green pepper
1 tablespoon all-purpose flour
¼ cup half-and-half
¼ cup chopped green onions
⅛ teaspoon salt
⅛ teaspoon white pepper
2 dashes of hot sauce
1 (6-ounce) can tiny shrimp,
   rinsed and drained
1 (2-ounce) jar diced pimiento,
   drained
Paprika

Scoop out center of each piece of cucumber to about halfway down on one end; set aside.

Combine butter and green pepper in a 1-quart casserole and microwave, uncovered, at HIGH for 1 to 2 minutes or until green pepper is crisp-tender. Blend in flour. Gradually add half-and-half, stirring well. Stir in green onions, salt, pepper, and hot sauce. Microwave, uncovered, at HIGH for 1 minute or until thickened. Stir in shrimp and pimiento.

Spoon 1 teaspoon shrimp mixture into each cucumber shell. Cover and chill thoroughly. Garnish with paprika before serving. Yield: 1 dozen appetizer servings.

A platter of delicious Vegetable-Stuffed Mushrooms will draw a crowd.

CHEESY-CHIVE POTATO SKINS

6 slices bacon
3 medium baking potatoes
1 tablespoon butter or
   margarine
⅛ teaspoon hot sauce
½ cup (2 ounces) shredded
   Cheddar cheese
Chopped fresh chives
Commercial sour cream

Place bacon on a rack in a baking dish. Cover with paper towels and microwave at HIGH for 5 to 7 minutes or until crisp. Crumble bacon, and set aside.

Wash potatoes, and pat dry. Prick each potato several times with a fork. Arrange in a circle on paper towels in microwave oven. Microwave, uncovered, at HIGH for 9 to 11 minutes or until tender, turning and rearranging potatoes after 5 minutes. Let stand 5 minutes.

Cut potatoes in half lengthwise. Carefully scoop out pulp, leaving ¼-inch shells (reserve pulp for use in other recipes). Cut shells in half lengthwise.

Place butter in a 1-cup glass measure; microwave, uncovered, at HIGH for 35 seconds or until melted. Stir in hot sauce. Brush butter mixture on both sides of potato quarters. Line a 12- x 8- x 2-inch baking dish with paper towels; arrange potatoes, skin side up, in dish. Microwave, uncovered, at HIGH for 3 to 4 minutes or until desired degree of doneness.

Turn potato skins over, and sprinkle with crumbled bacon, cheese, and chives. Microwave, uncovered, at HIGH for 1½ minutes or until cheese melts. Serve with sour cream. Yield: 1 dozen appetizer servings.

FAVORITE NACHOS

Keep Favorite Nachos crisp by microwaving on a paper towel-lined platter.

2 tablespoons butter or
   margarine
1 medium tomato, chopped
   and drained (about 1 cup)
½ cup finely chopped green
   onions
1 clove garlic, minced
1 (4-ounce) can chopped green
   chiles, drained
1 (16-ounce) can refried beans
½ teaspoon chili powder
½ cup (2 ounces) shredded
   mozzarella cheese
2 (7½-ounce) packages round
   tortilla chips
2 cups (8 ounces) shredded
   sharp Cheddar cheese

Place butter in a 2-quart casserole; microwave, uncovered, at HIGH for 45 seconds or until melted. Tilt casserole to spread butter on sides of dish. Add tomato, onions, garlic, and green chiles to casserole; cover with heavy-duty plastic wrap and microwave at HIGH for 4 to 5 minutes or until onions are tender, stirring after 2 minutes.

Stir beans and chili powder into tomato mixture. Cover and microwave at HIGH for 1 to 3 minutes or until thoroughly heated, stirring after 1½ minutes. Stir in mozzarella cheese; cover and microwave at HIGH for 30 seconds to 1 minute or until cheese melts, stirring after 30 seconds.

Line a 12-inch round glass platter with paper towels. Arrange about 12 tortilla chips on platter. Top each chip with a heaping teaspoonful of bean mixture; sprinkle with Cheddar cheese. Microwave, uncovered, at HIGH for 30 seconds to 1 minute or until cheese melts, rotating a half-turn after 30 seconds. Repeat procedure with remaining chips, bean mixture, and cheese. Yield: 6 dozen appetizer servings.

CHEESE AND BACON CRACKERS

4 slices bacon
½ cup mayonnaise
1 teaspoon Worcestershire sauce
⅛ teaspoon paprika
1 cup (4 ounces) shredded Cheddar cheese
3 tablespoons chopped pecans
2 tablespoons chopped green onions
27 round sesame crackers

Place bacon on a rack in a baking dish. Cover with paper towels and microwave at HIGH for 3½ to 4½ minutes or until crisp. Crumble bacon, and set aside.

Combine mayonnaise, Worcestershire sauce, and paprika in a medium bowl; stir well. Add bacon, cheese, pecans, and green onions, stirring well. Top each cracker with 1½ teaspoons of cheese mixture.

Line a 12-inch round glass platter with paper towels; arrange 9 crackers around outer edge of platter. Microwave, uncovered, at HIGH for 30 seconds to 1 minute or until cheese melts. Repeat procedure with remaining crackers. Serve immediately. Yield: 27 appetizer servings.

BACON-GREEN ONION BITES

1 (8-ounce) loaf sliced party rye bread
½ pound bacon
1 bunch green onions, chopped (about ⅓ cup)
⅓ cup mayonnaise
¼ cup grated Parmesan cheese
¼ teaspoon white pepper
Paprika

Toast bread slices conventionally; set aside.

Place half of bacon on a rack in a baking dish. Cover with paper towels and microwave at HIGH for 5 to 7 minutes or until crisp. Crumble bacon, and set aside. Repeat procedure with remaining bacon.

Combine crumbled bacon and next 4 ingredients; stir well. Spread 1 teaspoon bacon mixture on each slice of toasted bread. Line a 12-inch round glass platter with paper towels; arrange half the slices around outer edge of platter. Microwave, uncovered, at HIGH for 1 minute or until thoroughly heated. Repeat procedure with remaining bread slices. Sprinkle each with paprika. Serve immediately. Yield: 28 appetizer servings.

Spiced Rumaki

½ pound chicken livers
¼ cup soy sauce
2 tablespoons Chablis or other dry white wine
¼ teaspoon garlic powder
¼ teaspoon ground ginger
2 dashes of hot sauce
18 slices bacon, cut in half
1 (8-ounce) can sliced water chestnuts, drained

Cut chicken livers into 1-inch pieces. Combine soy sauce and next 4 ingredients in an 8-inch square baking dish; stir well. Add chicken livers; cover and marinate in refrigerator at least 3 hours.

Place half of bacon on a rack in a baking dish. Cover with paper towels and microwave at HIGH for 2½ to 3 minutes or until partially cooked; set bacon aside. Repeat procedure with remaining bacon.

Place a sliced water chestnut and a piece of chicken liver on each piece of bacon. Roll up, and secure with wooden picks. Line a 12-inch round glass platter with paper towels; arrange half of roll-ups around outer edge of platter. Cover with paper towels, and microwave at HIGH for 3½ to 4 minutes or until bacon is crisp and liver is done, rotating a half-turn after 2 minutes. Repeat procedure with remaining roll-ups. Yield: 1½ dozen appetizer servings.

Sweet And Saucy Meatballs

1 green onion, chopped
1 tablespoon butter or margarine
1 pound ground chuck
½ cup fine, dry breadcrumbs
1 egg, beaten
¼ teaspoon dry mustard
⅛ teaspoon pepper
1 (16-ounce) jar pineapple preserves
1 (12-ounce) bottle chili sauce
1 tablespoon minced green onions
1 tablespoon bourbon
½ teaspoon ground ginger

Combine chopped green onion and butter in a large bowl; microwave, uncovered, at HIGH for 2 minutes or until onion is tender. Stir in ground chuck, breadcrumbs, egg, mustard, and pepper; shape into ¾-inch meatballs. Arrange meatballs in a 12- x 8- x 2-inch baking dish; cover with wax paper and microwave at HIGH for 6 to 8 minutes or until no longer pink, stirring after 3 minutes. Set aside.

Combine preserves, chili sauce, 1 tablespoon minced green onions, bourbon, and ginger in a 1½-quart casserole, stirring until blended. Cover with heavy-duty plastic wrap and microwave at HIGH for 5½ to 6 minutes or until preserves melt, stirring after 3 minutes. Spoon sauce over meatballs; serve immediately. Yield: 2 dozen appetizer servings.

To freshen stale snacks, like pretzels, place them on paper towels and microwave at HIGH for 5 to 10 seconds. They will crispen upon standing. You may even use the same container, such as a wooden bowl, for heating and serving.

HAM APPETIZERS

1 medium onion, chopped
2 tablespoons butter or
  margarine
2 pounds ground cooked ham
1 cup fine, dry breadcrumbs
1 egg, beaten
2 tablespoons prepared
  mustard
¼ teaspoon pepper
¼ teaspoon dried whole
  marjoram
1 (12-ounce) bottle chili sauce
1 (10-ounce) jar apple jelly

Combine onion and butter in a large mixing bowl; microwave, uncovered, at HIGH for 2 minutes or until onion is tender. Stir in ham and next 5 ingredients; shape into 1-inch meatballs. Arrange about 2 dozen meatballs around outer edge of a 12-inch round glass platter; cover with paper towels. Microwave at HIGH for 5 to 6 minutes or until done, rotating a quarter-turn every 2 minutes; transfer meatballs to serving container. Repeat procedure with remaining meatballs.

Combine chili sauce and jelly in a 2-cup glass measure. Microwave, uncovered, at HIGH for 6 minutes or until jelly melts, stirring every 2 minutes. Spoon sauce over meatballs; serve immediately. Yield: 6½ dozen appetizer servings.

GRILLED CHEESE SANDWICHES

Butter or margarine
4 slices bread
4 (1-ounce) slices process
  American cheese

Spread butter on one side of each slice of bread. Place 2 slices of cheese between 2 bread slices, with buttered sides out.

Place a 10-inch browning skillet in microwave oven; preheat, uncovered, at HIGH for 5 to 6 minutes.

Place sandwiches in skillet. Reduce to MEDIUM HIGH (70% power); microwave, uncovered, for 30 seconds. Flatten sandwiches with a spatula; turn sandwiches over. Microwave, uncovered, at MEDIUM HIGH for 30 seconds or until cheese melts; serve sandwiches immediately. Yield: 2 servings.

Give Grilled Cheese Sandwiches a toasted appearance by microwaving in the browning skillet.

DILLED EGG SALAD SANDWICHES

6 eggs
¼ cup chopped celery
3 tablespoons mayonnaise
1 tablespoon chopped green
  onions
2 teaspoons capers, drained
2 teaspoons chopped fresh
  parsley
1 teaspoon prepared mustard
½ teaspoon salt
½ teaspoon dried whole
  dillweed
1 (14-ounce) loaf French bread,
  cut into 16 slices

Break eggs into a well greased 1-quart casserole. Pierce each yolk several times with a wooden pick or fork. Cover with heavy-duty plastic wrap and microwave at MEDIUM HIGH (70% power) for 5 to 8 minutes or until almost set. Let stand, covered, 2 minutes.

Coarsely chop eggs. Combine eggs and next 8 ingredients, mixing well. Spread 8 slices of bread with egg mixture; top each with another slice of bread before serving. Yield: 8 servings.

EGG AND CHEESE SALAD SANDWICHES

4 eggs
¾ cup (3 ounces) shredded
  Cheddar cheese
3 tablespoons chopped green
  onions
2 tablespoons mayonnaise
1 tablespoon plus 1½
  teaspoons sweet pickle relish
½ teaspoon prepared mustard
Dash of salt
Dash of pepper
1 tablespoon butter or
  margarine
2 English muffins, split and
  toasted

Break 1 egg into each of four 6-ounce custard cups. Pierce each yolk several times with a wooden pick or fork. Cover each cup with heavy-duty plastic wrap; arrange in a circle on a 12-inch round glass platter. Microwave at MEDIUM (50% power) for 3 to 4 minutes or until set, rotating a half-turn after 2 minutes. Let stand, covered, 2 minutes. Mash eggs with a fork until crumbled.

Combine eggs and next 7 ingredients; stir well. Spread butter evenly over muffin halves; top with egg mixture. Line a 12-inch round glass platter with paper towels. Arrange muffin halves on platter; microwave, uncovered, at MEDIUM HIGH (70% power) for 2 to 3 minutes or until cheese melts. Yield: 4 servings

GARDEN SALAD CHEESEWICHES

1 cup (4 ounces) shredded
  Monterey Jack cheese
1 large carrot, scraped and
  shredded (about ¾ cup)
1 medium tomato, chopped
1 small onion, thinly sliced
2 tablespoons mayonnaise
¼ teaspoon salt
¼ teaspoon dried whole thyme
4 slices whole wheat bread,
  toasted
⅓ cup fresh alfalfa sprouts

Combine first 7 ingredients, stirring well. Line a 12-inch round glass platter with paper towels; arrange 4 slices of bread on platter. Spread about ⅔ cup cheese mixture on each slice of bread. Microwave, uncovered, at HIGH for 3½ to 4 minutes or until cheese melts, rotating a half-turn after 2 minutes. Top with alfalfa sprouts. Serve immediately. Yield: 4 servings.

CRABMEAT LUNCHEON SANDWICHES

⅓ cup finely chopped celery
¼ cup mayonnaise
1 teaspoon lemon juice
2 dashes of hot sauce
1 cup fresh lump crabmeat,
  drained and flaked
2 tablespoons finely chopped
  green onions
2 English muffins, split and
  toasted
4 slices tomato
Salt and pepper to taste
½ cup (2 ounces) shredded
  Cheddar cheese

Combine celery, mayonnaise, lemon juice, and hot sauce; stir well. Set aside.

Combine crabmeat and onions in a small bowl; mix well. Microwave, uncovered, at HIGH for 3 to 4 minutes or until thoroughly heated. Drain well. Stir in celery mixture. Top each muffin half with a tomato slice, and sprinkle with salt and pepper. Spoon crab mixture onto tomato slices. Top with cheese. Line a 12-inch round glass platter with paper towels. Arrange muffin halves on platter; microwave, uncovered, at HIGH for 1 to 2 minutes or until cheese begins to melt. Yield: 4 servings.

Serve Crabmeat Luncheon Sandwiches for informal springtime gatherings.

HOT TUNA SANDWICHES

1 egg
1 (8-ounce) can crushed
   pineapple, undrained
1 (6½-ounce) can white tuna,
   drained and flaked
⅓ cup mayonnaise
¼ cup (1 ounce) shredded
   Cheddar cheese
¼ cup chopped pecans
2 tablespoons minced green
   onions
3 English muffins, split and
   toasted
Paprika
Parsley sprigs (optional)

Break egg into a 6-ounce custard cup. Pierce yolk several times with a wooden pick or fork. Cover cup with heavy-duty plastic wrap and microwave at MEDIUM (50% power) for 2½ to 3 minutes or until set. Let stand, covered, 1 minute. Mash egg with a fork until crumbled, and set aside.

Drain pineapple, reserving 2 tablespoons juice. Combine egg, pineapple, 2 tablespoons pineapple juice, tuna, mayonnaise, cheese, pecans, and onions, stirring well; spread over toasted muffins. Line a 12-inch round glass platter with paper towels. Arrange muffin halves on platter; microwave, uncovered, at HIGH for 2 to 2½ minutes or until thoroughly heated. Sprinkle with paprika; garnish with parsley sprigs, if desired. Yield: 6 servings.

CHICKEN PITA SANDWICHES

4 (3-ounce) skinned and boned
   chicken breast halves
½ cup water
3 eggs
¾ cup mayonnaise
½ cup minced celery
½ cup unpeeled, finely
   chopped apple
1 (4-ounce) jar diced pimiento,
   drained
¼ cup minced dill pickle
½ teaspoon salt
¼ teaspoon pepper
4 (6-inch) pita bread rounds,
   cut in half
Curly leaf lettuce

Place chicken and water in a 2-quart casserole. Cover with heavy-duty plastic wrap and microwave at HIGH for 13 to 15 minutes or until chicken is tender. Drain chicken; finely chop, and set aside.

Break 1 egg into each of three 6-ounce custard cups. Pierce each yolk several times with a wooden pick or fork. Cover each cup with heavy-duty plastic wrap. Reduce to MEDIUM (50% power), and microwave for 2½ to 3 minutes or until set, rearranging after 1 minute. Let stand, covered, 2 minutes. Mash eggs with a fork until crumbled.

Combine chicken, eggs, and next 7 ingredients; stir well. Cover and refrigerate at least 1 hour. Line cut bread rounds with lettuce; fill with chicken mixture, and serve immediately. Yield: 8 servings.

For more toasted flavor, taco shells can be heated in the microwave at HIGH for 30 seconds to 1 minute just before filling.

Pocket Sloppy Joes

1 pound ground beef
1 small onion chopped
¼ cup chopped celery
1 (15-ounce) can tomato sauce
  special
1 (15-ounce) can kidney beans,
  undrained
1 tablespoon plus 1½
  teaspoons chili powder
¼ teaspoon salt
⅛ teaspoon garlic powder
⅛ teaspoon pepper
4 (6-inch) pita bread rounds,
  cut in half
Curly leaf lettuce

Combine ground beef, onion, and celery in a large bowl. Microwave, uncovered, at HIGH for 6½ to 7½ minutes or until beef is no longer pink, stirring every 2 minutes. Drain well.

Stir in tomato sauce and next 5 ingredients. Cover with heavy-duty plastic wrap and microwave at HIGH for 3 to 4 minutes or until thoroughly heated.

Arrange cut bread rounds on a 12-inch round glass platter. Microwave, uncovered, at HIGH for 30 seconds to 1 minute or until thoroughly heated. Line cut bread rounds with lettuce; fill each with about ½ cup meat sauce, and serve immediately. Yield: 8 servings.

Chili Tortillas

6 (6-inch) flour tortillas
¾ pound ground beef
¼ cup chopped onion
1 (8-ounce) can tomato sauce
½ (1.4-ounce) package taco
  seasoning mix
¾ cup chopped tomato
1 cup (4 ounces) shredded
  Cheddar cheese
1 (3-ounce) jar pimiento-stuffed
  olives, drained and chopped
1 cup shredded lettuce
2 tablespoons chopped green
  chiles

Place 3 tortillas on a 12-inch round glass platter. Microwave, uncovered, at HIGH for 2 to 3 minutes or until crisp. Repeat procedure with remaining tortillas; set aside.

Combine ground beef and onion in a 1-quart casserole. Microwave, uncovered, at HIGH for 4 to 4½ minutes or until beef is no longer pink, stirring after 2 minutes. Drain well. Stir in tomato sauce and taco seasoning mix. Cover with heavy-duty plastic wrap and microwave at HIGH for 1 to 2 minutes or until beef mixture is thoroughly heated.

Spread beef mixture evenly over tortillas. Top with chopped tomato; sprinkle with cheese. Arrange 3 tortillas on a 12-inch round glass platter. Microwave, uncovered, at HIGH for 1 to 1½ minutes or until cheese melts. Repeat procedure with remaining tortillas. Top each with about 1 tablespoon chopped olives, lettuce, and 1 teaspoon green chiles. Yield: 6 servings.

To soften tortillas, place four tortillas at a time between paper towels and microwave at HIGH for 40 seconds to 1 minute or until softened.

Mexican Beef Tacos

1 pound ground beef
½ cup chopped onion
½ cup chopped green pepper
¾ cup chopped tomato
½ cup sliced pimiento-stuffed
  olives
¼ cup catsup
1 teaspoon chili powder
½ teaspoon salt
½ teaspoon pepper
½ teaspoon ground cinnamon
⅛ teaspoon garlic powder
12 taco shells
1½ cups shredded lettuce
1 medium tomato, chopped
1 cup (4 ounces) shredded
  Cheddar cheese
Commercial taco sauce

Combine ground beef, onion, and green pepper in a 1½-quart casserole. Cover with wax paper and microwave at HIGH for 4½ to 5½ minutes or until beef is no longer pink, stirring every 2 minutes. Drain well. Stir in ¾ cup chopped tomato and next 7 ingredients. Cover and microwave at HIGH for 1½ minutes or until thoroughly heated.

Arrange half the taco shells around outer edge of a 12-inch round glass platter. Microwave, uncovered, at HIGH for 1 minute or until thoroughly heated. Repeat procedure with remaining taco shells.

Spoon 2 to 3 tablespoons meat mixture into each shell. Top with lettuce, tomato, cheese, and taco sauce. Yield: 6 servings.

Pizza Burgers

1 pound ground beef
½ pound bulk pork sausage
1 cup commercial pizza sauce,
  divided
⅓ cup fine, dry breadcrumbs
¼ cup finely chopped green
  onions
½ teaspoon dried whole
  oregano
¼ teaspoon garlic salt
1 cup (4 ounces) shredded
  mozzarella cheese
8 kaiser rolls, toasted

Crumble beef and sausage into a large bowl; stir in ½ cup pizza sauce, and next 4 ingredients. Shape mixture into 8 patties, about ½-inch thick. Arrange half of patties on a rack in a baking dish. Spoon 1 tablespoon of remaining pizza sauce over each patty. Set remaining patties and sauce aside.

Cover patties with wax paper and microwave at HIGH for 9 to 11 minutes or until no longer pink, turning after 5 minutes. Sprinkle half of cheese over patties. Microwave, uncovered, at HIGH for 2 minutes. Repeat procedure with remaining patties, sauce, and cheese. Serve immediately on toasted rolls. Yield: 8 servings.

Liven up dinner by making Mexican Beef Tacos. Be sure to add your choice of toppings.

Barbecue Sandwiches

¼ cup finely chopped onion
1 clove garlic, minced
1 tablespoon butter or
  margarine
1 cup catsup
2 tablespoons brown sugar
2 tablespoons cider vinegar
2 tablespoons water
1 tablespoon Worcestershire
  sauce
1 teaspoon prepared mustard
1 pound cooked roast beef,
  thinly sliced
6 hamburger buns

Combine onion, garlic, and butter in a 2-quart casserole. Cover with heavy-duty plastic wrap and microwave at HIGH for 2 to 3 minutes or until onion is crisp-tender.

Stir in catsup, brown sugar, vinegar, water, Worcestershire sauce, and mustard. Reduce to MEDIUM HIGH (70% power); cover and microwave for 8 to 10 minutes or until thickened.

Add roast beef, stirring well. Cover and microwave at MEDIUM HIGH for 4 to 5 minutes or until thoroughly heated. Serve on hamburger buns. Yield: 6 servings.

Asparagus-Turkey Delights

½ pound fresh asparagus
  spears (8 to 16 spears)
¼ cup water
3 tablespoons commercial
  French salad dressing
1 tablespoon chopped green
  onions
⅛ teaspoon pepper
1 tablespoon butter or
  margarine
2 teaspoons mayonnaise
2 slices bread, toasted
4 (1-ounce) slices cooked
  turkey
¼ cup (1 ounce) shredded
  Swiss cheese

Place asparagus and water in a 1½-quart casserole. Cover with heavy-duty plastic wrap and microwave at HIGH for 4 to 5 minutes or until asparagus is crisp-tender. Let stand, covered, 1 minute; drain well. Combine salad dressing, onions, and pepper in a small bowl; stir well, and set aside.

Spread butter and mayonnaise on one side of each slice of toasted bread. Place bread slices, buttered side up, on a 12-inch round glass platter. Top each slice with 2 slices of turkey and half the asparagus spears; drizzle with salad dressing mixture. Sprinkle with cheese. Microwave, uncovered, at HIGH for 1 to 2 minutes or just until cheese begins to melt. Serve immediately. Yield: 2 servings.

Italian Turkey Sandwiches

1 pound raw ground turkey
¼ cup chopped green pepper
1 (8-ounce) can tomato sauce
½ cup chopped fresh
  mushrooms
1 (1.5-ounce) package spaghetti
  sauce mix
½ teaspoon dried whole
  oregano
4 whole wheat English
  muffins, split and toasted
1½ cups (6 ounces) shredded
  mozzarella cheese

Crumble turkey into a 2-quart casserole; add green pepper. Cover with heavy-duty plastic wrap and microwave at HIGH for 5 to 6 minutes or until turkey is no longer pink, stirring every 2 minutes. Drain well.

Combine tomato sauce and next 3 ingredients. Add to turkey, stirring well. Cover and microwave at HIGH for 2 to 3 minutes or until thoroughly heated.

Line a 12-inch round glass platter with paper towels. Arrange 4 muffin halves on platter; top with half of meat mixture. Reduce to MEDIUM HIGH (70% power); microwave, uncovered, for

ITALIAN TURKEY SANDWICHES
(continued)

2 minutes. Sprinkle with half of cheese; microwave, uncovered, at MEDIUM HIGH for 1½ to 2 minutes or until cheese melts. Repeat procedure with remaining muffin halves, meat mixture, and cheese. Yield: 8 servings.

HOT BROWN SANDWICHES

6 slices bacon
2 tablespoons butter or
  margarine
1½ tablespoons all-purpose
  flour
⅛ teaspoon salt
⅛ teaspoon pepper
½ cup diluted canned chicken
  broth
½ cup milk
½ pound sliced cooked turkey
6 slices bread, toasted
6 slices tomato
¼ cup (1 ounce) shredded
  Cheddar cheese

Place bacon on a rack in a baking dish. Cover with paper towels and microwave at HIGH for 5 to 7 minutes or until crisp. Crumble bacon, and set aside.

Place butter in a 4-cup glass measure. Microwave, uncovered, at HIGH for 45 seconds or until melted. Blend in flour, salt, and pepper. Gradually add chicken broth and milk, stirring well. Microwave, uncovered, at HIGH for 3 to 4 minutes or until thickened, stirring after 2 minutes. Stir in crumbled bacon; set aside.

Wrap turkey slices in heavy-duty plastic wrap. Microwave at HIGH for 1 to 1½ minutes or until thoroughly heated. Arrange turkey evenly over toasted bread; place on a 12-inch round glass platter. Pour sauce over each sandwich. Top each with 1 slice tomato, and sprinkle with cheese. Microwave, uncovered, at HIGH for 1½ to 2 minutes or until cheese melts. Serve immediately. Yield: 6 sandwiches.

HOT REUBEN SANDWICHES

¼ cup butter or margarine
8 slices rye or pumpernickel
  bread
3 tablespoons commercial
  Thousand Island salad
  dressing
1 (3-ounce) package thinly
  sliced corned beef
4 slices Swiss cheese
1 cup sauerkraut, drained

Spread butter on one side of each slice of bread; spread other side of bread with salad dressing. Arrange corned beef, Swiss cheese, and sauerkraut on top of 4 bread slices spread with salad dressing. Top with remaining bread slices, buttered side out.

Place a 10-inch browning skillet in microwave oven; preheat, uncovered, at HIGH for 5 minutes. Place 2 sandwiches in skillet; microwave, uncovered, at HIGH for 1 minute on each side or until browned and cheese begins to melt. Preheat browning skillet at HIGH for 2 additional minutes; place remaining sandwiches in skillet. Microwave, uncovered, at HIGH for 1 minute on each side or until browned. Serve immediately. Yield: 4 servings.

Deviled Ham Reubens

1½ cups (6 ounces) shredded
   Swiss cheese
1 cup canned sauerkraut,
   drained
¼ cup commercial Thousand
   Island salad dressing
1 tablespoon coarse-grained
   mustard
½ teaspoon dried whole
   dillweed
1 (4¼-ounce) can deviled ham
8 slices rye bread, toasted

Combine first 5 ingredients, stirring well; set aside. Spread ham evenly on one side of 4 slices of bread. Top each with about ½ cup cheese mixture; arrange on a 12-inch round glass platter. Microwave, uncovered, at MEDIUM HIGH (70% power) for 6 to 7 minutes or until cheese melts, rotating a half-turn after 3 minutes. Top with remaining bread. Yield: 4 servings.

Monte Cristo Sandwiches

2 tablespoons mayonnaise
2 teaspoons prepared mustard
8 slices white bread
4 (1-ounce) slices cooked
   turkey
4 (1-ounce) slices fully cooked
   ham
4 (1-ounce) slices Swiss cheese
3 eggs, slightly beaten
¼ cup commercial sour cream
2 tablespoons milk
1 cup fine, dry breadcrumbs
¼ cup butter or margarine,
   divided

Combine mayonnaise and mustard, mixing well; spread on one side of each bread slice. Place one slice each of turkey, ham, and cheese on top of 4 bread slices. Top with remaining bread. Cut each sandwich in half diagonally.

Combine eggs, sour cream, and milk, mixing well. Dip sandwiches in egg mixture, and coat with breadcrumbs.

Place a 10-inch browning skillet in microwave oven; preheat, uncovered, at HIGH for 5 to 6 minutes. Add 2 tablespoons butter to hot skillet, tilting to coat surface. Place 2 sandwiches in skillet; microwave, uncovered, at HIGH for 30 seconds to 1 minute on each side or until lightly browned. Flatten sandwiches slightly with a spatula. Preheat browning skillet at HIGH for 2 additional minutes; add remaining 2 tablespoons butter, tilting to coat. Place remaining sandwiches in skillet; microwave, uncovered, at HIGH for 30 seconds to 1 minute on each side or until lightly browned. Serve immediately. Yield: 4 servings.

Chili-Cheese Dogs

8 hot dog buns
Spicy brown mustard
1 (15-ounce) can chili with
   beans
8 frankfurters
1 cup (4 ounces) shredded
   process American cheese
Chopped onion (optional)
Shredded cabbage (optional)

Spread hot dog buns with mustard; set aside.

Place chili in a small bowl; cover with heavy-duty plastic wrap and microwave at HIGH for 3 to 4 minutes or until thoroughly heated, stirring after 2 minutes. Let stand, covered, while completing recipe.

Pierce each frankfurter several times with a fork, and place on a 12-inch round glass platter. Cover with paper towels and microwave at

CHILI-CHEESE DOGS
(continued)

HIGH for 2 to 3 minutes or until frankfurters are thoroughly heated.

Place frankfurters in buns; spoon on chili, and sprinkle with cheese. Arrange on platter and microwave, uncovered, at HIGH for 1 to 1½ minutes or until cheese begins to melt. Serve with chopped onion and shredded cabbage, if desired. Yield: 8 servings.

TANGY BARBECUED FRANK SANDWICHES

8 frankfurters
1 tablespoon all-purpose flour
2 tablespoons water
½ cup catsup
¼ cup finely chopped onion
2 tablespoons firmly packed
   brown sugar
2 tablespoons vinegar
1 tablespoon prepared mustard
1 tablespoon Worcestershire
   sauce
1 teaspoon paprika
2 teaspoons chili powder
½ teaspoon pepper
⅛ teaspoon garlic powder
8 hot dog buns

Pierce each frankfurter several times with a fork, and place in a 10- x 6- x 2-inch baking dish; set aside.

Combine flour and water in a small bowl, stirring until smooth; stir in catsup and next 9 ingredients, stirring well. Pour mixture over frankfurters; cover with heavy-duty plastic wrap and microwave at HIGH for 5 to 7 minutes or until frankfurters are thoroughly heated and sauce is thickened, stirring after 3 minutes. Place frankfurters in hot dog buns, and top with sauce. Yield: 8 servings.

SAUSAGE SANDWICHES

6 Italian sausage links
   (1 pound), cut in half
   lengthwise
2 small tomatoes, peeled and
   cut into wedges
1 small onion, sliced and
   separated into rings
1 medium-size green pepper,
   cut into strips
1 tablespoon water
¼ teaspoon salt
¼ teaspoon dried whole
   oregano
6 large French rolls, split and
   toasted
1½ cups (6 ounces) shredded
   mozzarella cheese

Place sausage in a 2-quart casserole. Cover with wax paper and microwave at HIGH for 5 to 6 minutes or until sausage is no longer pink, stirring after 3 minutes. Drain well. Add tomatoes, onion, green pepper, and water. Cover and microwave at HIGH for 2 to 3 minutes or until vegetables are crisp-tender. Stir in salt and oregano.

Spoon meat mixture on bottom half of each roll; sprinkle with cheese. Place in microwave oven on a layer of paper towels; cover each sandwich with roll top. Microwave, uncovered, at HIGH for 1 to 2 minutes or until cheese melts. Serve immediately. Yield: 6 servings.

HOT TOMATO COCKTAIL

2 (12-ounce) cans cocktail
  vegetable juice
1 (10½-ounce) can beef broth,
  undiluted
1 tablespoon lemon juice
1½ teaspoons Worcestershire
  sauce
½ teaspoon onion juice
¼ teaspoon pepper
⅛ teaspoon hot sauce
½ cup vodka
Lemon slices (optional)
Salad olives (optional)

Combine first 7 ingredients in a 3-quart casserole or bowl, stirring well. Cover with heavy-duty plastic wrap and microwave at HIGH for 10 to 12 minutes or until boiling, stirring every 4 minutes. Stir in vodka. Garnish each serving with a lemon slice and an olive, if desired. Serve immediately. Yield: 5¾ cups.

HOT MULLED CIDER

6 cups apple cider
2 tablespoons firmly packed
  brown sugar
16 whole cloves
8 lemon slices
6 (3-inch) sticks cinnamon
¾ cup rum

Combine cider and sugar in a 3-quart casserole or bowl. Place 2 cloves in rind of each lemon slice. Add lemon slices, cinnamon sticks, and rum to cider mixture. Cover with heavy-duty plastic wrap and microwave at HIGH for 10 to 12 minutes or until boiling; continue to microwave at HIGH for 1 minute. Strain mixture, discarding lemon slices and cinnamon sticks. Cover and microwave at HIGH for 2 minutes or until thoroughly heated. Serve immediately. Yield: 7 cups.

WINE AND CRANBERRY WARMER

2 cups cranberry juice cocktail
2 cups Burgundy or other dry
  red wine
1 cup orange juice
2 tablespoons lemon juice
2 tablespoons sugar
1 (3-inch) stick cinnamon
1 teaspoon grated orange rind
4 whole cloves

Combine all ingredients in a 2-quart casserole or bowl. Cover with heavy-duty plastic wrap and microwave at HIGH for 8 to 10 minutes or until boiling, stirring after 4 minutes. Strain, discarding cinnamon stick, rind, and cloves. Serve immediately. Yield: 5 cups.

Hot Tomato Cocktail gives any brunch a zesty beginning.

RICH AND CREAMY COCOA

2 tablespoons sugar
2 tablespoons cocoa
⅔ cup water
⅔ cup milk
⅔ cup evaporated milk
½ teaspoon vanilla extract

Combine sugar and cocoa in a 4-cup glass measure; add water, stirring well. Microwave, uncovered, at HIGH for 2 minutes or until boiling. Stir in milk and evaporated milk. Reduce to MEDIUM HIGH (70% power), and microwave 1½ to 2 minutes or just until thoroughly heated. Stir in vanilla, and serve cocoa immediately. Yield: 2 servings.

MEXICAN CHOCOLATE

3 cups milk
2 (3-inch) sticks cinnamon, broken into pieces
4 (1-ounce) squares semisweet chocolate, broken into pieces
¼ cup blanched almonds
1 tablespoon sugar
½ teaspoon vanilla extract
Whipped cream
Sliced almonds

Combine milk and cinnamon sticks in a 2-quart casserole or bowl. Microwave, uncovered, at HIGH for 5 to 6 minutes or just until thoroughly heated; discard cinnamon sticks.

Combine chocolate, ¼ cup almonds, sugar, and vanilla in container of an electric blender or food processor; process until finely chopped. Add half the hot milk mixture to chocolate; process until foamy. Add chocolate mixture to remaining milk, stirring well; microwave, uncovered, at HIGH for 3 to 4 minutes or until thoroughly heated. Top each serving with whipped cream and sliced almonds. Serve immediately. Yield: 4 servings.

CAFÉ ROYAL

½ cup whipping cream
1 tablespoon powdered sugar
3 cups water
2 (1-ounce) squares semisweet chocolate, coarsely chopped
2 tablespoons sugar
¾ teaspoon ground cinnamon
¼ teaspoon ground nutmeg
1 tablespoon instant coffee granules
2¼ cups milk
½ cup Kahlúa or other coffee-flavored liqueur
1 teaspoon vanilla extract
Ground cinnamon

Beat whipping cream until foamy. Add powdered sugar, beating until soft peaks form. Cover and chill in refrigerator.

Combine water and next 4 ingredients in a 3-quart casserole or bowl. Microwave, uncovered, at HIGH for 7 to 8 minutes or until boiling, stirring after 4 minutes. Add coffee granules, stirring until dissolved. Stir in milk. Cover with heavy-duty plastic wrap and microwave at HIGH for 2 to 4 minutes or just until thoroughly heated. Stir in Kahlúa and vanilla. Top each serving with whipped cream, and sprinkle with cinnamon. Serve immediately. Yield: 6 cups.

EASY MOCHA ESPRESSO

1½ cups instant nonfat dry
  milk powder
⅓ cup sugar
⅓ cup instant coffee granules
2 tablespoons plus 1½
  teaspoons cocoa
6 cups water
Sweetened whipped cream
Grated chocolate

Combine first 4 ingredients in a small bowl, stirring well; set aside. Place water in a 3-quart casserole or bowl. Microwave, uncovered, at HIGH for 8 to 10 minutes or until boiling. Stir in coffee mixture; microwave, uncovered, at HIGH for 2 to 3 minutes or until sugar is dissolved, stirring after 1 minute. Top each serving with a dollop of whipped cream and grated chocolate. Serve immediately. Yield: 6 servings.

COFFEE SUPREME

2 cups water
1 tablespoon brown sugar
1 (3-inch) stick cinnamon
1 tablespoon plus 1½
  teaspoons instant coffee
  granules

Combine water, brown sugar, and cinnamon stick in a 4-cup glass measure. Microwave, uncovered, at HIGH for 4½ to 5 minutes or until boiling. Add coffee; stir until dissolved. Remove and discard cinnamon stick; serve coffee immediately. Yield: 2 cups.

HOT SPICED TEA

2 cups water
1 tablespoon instant tea
4 whole cloves
1 (3-inch) stick cinnamon
½ teaspoon grated orange rind
2 teaspoons sugar

Combine water, tea, cloves, cinnamon stick, orange rind, and sugar in a 4-cup glass measure. Microwave, uncovered, at HIGH for 5 to 6 minutes or until boiling. Strain, discarding cloves, cinnamon stick, and rind. Serve tea immediately. Yield: 2 cups.

HONEY TEA

4 cups water
2 tablespoons black tea leaves
1 tablespoon whole cloves
½ cup orange juice
¼ cup plus 2 tablespoons
  honey
¼ cup lime or lemon juice

Place water in a 3-quart casserole or bowl. Microwave, uncovered, at HIGH for 10 to 12 minutes or until boiling. Combine tea leaves and cloves in a tea ball; place in boiling water. Cover with heavy-duty plastic wrap; let stand 5 minutes. Remove tea ball; stir in orange juice, honey, and lime juice. Microwave, uncovered, at HIGH for 1 to 2 minutes or until thoroughly heated. Serve immediately. Yield: 5 cups.

Breads, Grains, and Pasta

There are some drawbacks to making breads and cooking grains and pasta in the microwave oven. But with a few adjustments in recipes and expectations, you can achieve good results.

Yeast breads that are completely prepared in the microwave oven tend to be pale and tough. Quick breads may also look pale and rise unevenly. To compensate for the lack of a brown or crisp crust, we've often added a special topping, coated containers with crumbs, or used dark flour. Best results are obtained when browning in the conventional oven is combined with the microwave procedure.

On the plus side, you'll find breads cook extremely fast in the microwave oven. However, because of this, it is very easy to overcook breads. When microwaving breads, leave them uncovered to allow steam to escape. Breads should be slightly sticky on top when removed from the oven, because they will continue to cook while standing. After standing time is completed, it's important to cover cooked bread products with plastic wrap or place them in an airtight container. Otherwise, they dry out and become hard.

The microwave oven is an excellent tool for proofing yeast. You can find instructions for this procedure in our yeast bread recipes.

Grains and pasta require about the same amount of time to cook in the microwave as they do conventionally. You'll end up with good results, but be aware that you won't save much time.

Cinnamon-Orange Rolls (page 44) and Quick Cheese Grits (page 49) will turn an ordinary breakfast into a special occasion.

CINNAMON-NUT MUFFINS

A double layer of paper liners keeps the outer edges of Cinnamon-Nut Muffins from becoming too moist. Sprinkle a topping of cinnamon and sugar over the batter.

¾ cup all-purpose flour
1 teaspoon baking powder
⅛ teaspoon salt
½ cup finely chopped pecans
¼ cup firmly packed brown
   sugar
⅓ cup milk
3 tablespoons vegetable oil
1 egg yolk, beaten
1½ tablespoons sugar
1 teaspoon ground cinnamon

Combine flour, baking powder, salt, pecans, and brown sugar in a large bowl; make a well in center of mixture. Combine milk, oil, and egg yolk; add to dry ingredients, stirring just until moistened.

Line a microwave-safe muffin pan or six 6-ounce custard cups with a double layer of paper liners. Spoon batter into paper cups, filling half full. Combine 1½ tablespoons sugar and cinnamon; sprinkle evenly over each muffin. If using custard cups, arrange in a circle on a 12-inch round glass platter.

Microwave, uncovered, at HIGH for 2½ to 3½ minutes or until surface is only slightly wet, rotating a half-turn after 1 minute. Remove from pan and let cool on a wire rack. Serve immediately. Yield: ½ dozen.

BRAN MUFFINS

2 cups whole bran cereal
¾ cup milk
1 egg, beaten
¼ cup vegetable oil
¾ cup all-purpose flour
¼ cup plus 2 tablespoons sugar
2 teaspoons baking powder
¼ teaspoon salt
½ cup raisins

Combine cereal and milk in a large bowl, stirring well; let stand 15 minutes.

Stir egg and oil into cereal mixture. Combine flour and remaining ingredients; add to cereal mixture, stirring just until moistened.

Line a microwave-safe muffin pan or six 6-ounce custard cups with a double layer of paper liners. Spoon batter into paper cups, filling two-thirds full. If using custard cups, arrange in a circle on a 12-inch round glass platter. Microwave, uncovered, at MEDIUM (50% power) for 5 minutes or until surface is only slightly wet, rotating a half-turn every 2 minutes. Let stand 1 minute. Repeat procedure with remaining batter. Serve immediately. Yield: 1 dozen.

BROWN BREAD

½ cup all-purpose flour
½ cup cornmeal
½ cup whole wheat flour
¾ cup buttermilk
½ cup molasses
1 teaspoon baking soda
⅛ teaspoon salt
¾ cup raisins

Combine first 7 ingredients in a large bowl; beat at low speed of an electric mixer until blended. Stir in raisins.

Spoon half of batter into a lightly greased 2-cup glass measure. Cover with wax paper and microwave at MEDIUM (50% power) for 7 minutes or until surface is only slightly wet, rotating a half-turn after 3 minutes. Let stand, uncovered, 5 minutes. Unmold, and wrap in plastic wrap to prevent drying. Repeat procedure with remaining batter. Yield: 2 loaves.

Spread round slices of Brown Bread generously with butter. English Muffin Loaf (page 46) can be sliced and toasted conventionally, if desired.

ZUCCHINI-NUT BREAD

1½ cups all-purpose flour
1 teaspoon baking powder
1 teaspoon baking soda
½ teaspoon salt
2 teaspoons ground cinnamon
½ teaspoon nutmeg
3 eggs
¾ cup vegetable oil
1 cup sugar
¼ cup firmly packed brown
  sugar
2 teaspoons minced fresh
  ginger
1 teaspoon vanilla extract
3 cups shredded zucchini
1 cup chopped walnuts,
  divided
⅓ cup raisins
2 tablespoons all-purpose flour
Powdered sugar

Combine 1½ cups flour, baking powder, soda, salt, cinnamon, and nutmeg in a small bowl; set aside. Combine eggs, oil, sugars, ginger, and vanilla in a medium bowl; beat at medium speed of an electric mixer until blended. Stir in zucchini and ⅔ cup walnuts. Add flour mixture, stirring just until dry ingredients are moistened.

Lightly grease a microwave-safe 10-inch Bundt pan. Dredge remaining ⅓ cup walnuts and raisins in 2 tablespoons flour; sprinkle in prepared pan. Spoon batter into pan.

Place pan in microwave oven on an inverted pieplate. Microwave, uncovered, at HIGH for 13 to 15 minutes or just until bread begins to shrink away from sides of pan, rotating pan a quarter-turn every 3 minutes. Let stand 5 minutes. Sprinkle with powdered sugar. Serve immediately. Yield: one 10-inch loaf.

CINNAMON-ORANGE ROLLS

¼ cup sugar
3 tablespoons graham cracker
  crumbs
1½ teaspoons ground cinnamon
1½ teaspoons grated orange
  rind
3 tablespoons finely chopped
  pecans
2 cups all-purpose flour
1 tablespoon baking powder
¼ teaspoon salt
¼ cup butter or margarine
⅓ cup milk
⅓ cup orange juice
¼ cup butter or margarine
Orange Glaze

Combine sugar, cracker crumbs, cinnamon, orange rind, and pecans, stirring well; set aside.

Combine flour, baking powder, and salt in a large bowl; cut in ¼ cup butter with a pastry blender until mixture resembles coarse meal. Add milk and orange juice, and stir with a fork just until all dry ingredients are moistened. Turn dough out onto a lightly floured surface, and knead 10 times.

Place ¼ cup butter in a 1-cup glass measure; microwave, uncovered, at HIGH for 55 seconds or until melted. Set aside. Roll out dough to ¾-inch thickness; cut into eight 2¾-inch rounds. Dip each round in melted butter, then in sugar mixture. Place rounds, flat side down, around edge of a 1-quart microwave-safe ring mold, overlapping edges, if necessary. Sprinkle with any remaining sugar mixture, and drizzle with any remaining melted butter.

Microwave, uncovered, at HIGH for 4 to 4½ minutes or until top springs back when

CINNAMON-ORANGE ROLLS
(continued)

touched, rotating a half-turn after 2 minutes. Let stand 2 minutes; invert onto serving plate. Invert again, and drizzle with Orange Glaze while hot; serve immediately. Yield: 8 servings.

ORANGE GLAZE:

1 tablespoon butter or
  margarine
½ cup sifted powdered sugar
2 teaspoons orange juice
¼ teaspoon vanilla extract

Place butter in a 1-cup glass measure. Microwave, uncovered, at HIGH for 35 seconds or until melted. Combine butter and remaining ingredients in a small bowl; stir until smooth. Yield: about ¼ cup.

WHOLE WHEAT BREAD

4 cups whole wheat flour,
  divided
1 package dry yeast
1½ teaspoons salt
1 teaspoon caraway seeds
¾ cup milk
¾ cup water
3 tablespoons butter or
  margarine
2 tablespoons honey

Combine 2 cups flour, yeast, salt, and caraway seeds in a large mixing bowl; stir well. Combine milk, water, butter, and honey in a 2-cup glass measure. Microwave, uncovered, at HIGH for 2 to 2½ minutes or until butter is melted; stir well. Let mixture cool to 120° to 130°. Add to flour mixture. Beat at medium speed of an electric mixer 2 minutes or until blended. Stir in enough of remaining flour to make a stiff dough.

Turn dough out onto a lightly floured surface, and knead 8 to 10 times or until smooth and elastic. Place dough in a well-greased bowl, turning to grease top; cover with heavy-duty plastic wrap.

Pour 3 cups water into a 4-cup glass measure. Microwave, uncovered, at HIGH for 7 to 8 minutes or until boiling. Move glass measure to back of the microwave oven. Place dough in microwave oven with water. Reduce to MEDIUM LOW (30% power), and microwave for 2 minutes. Let rest 5 minutes. Repeat procedure 2 times or until dough is doubled in bulk.

Punch dough down; let rest 5 minutes. Shape dough into a loaf, and place in a lightly greased 9- x 5- x 3-inch microwave-safe loafpan. Cover with heavy-duty plastic wrap. Place dough in microwave oven with water and microwave at MEDIUM LOW for 2 minutes. Let rest 5 minutes. Repeat procedure once or until dough is doubled in bulk. Remove plastic wrap.

Place dough in conventional oven, and bake at 375° for 35 minutes or until loaf sounds hollow when tapped. Remove loaf from pan, and cool on a wire rack. Yield: 1 loaf.

For each rising, cover dough with heavy-duty plastic wrap. With hot water in the back of the oven, microwave at MEDIUM LOW (30% power) for 2 minutes; let rest 5 minutes.

Bake the bread in a conventional oven to get a crisp crust.

English Muffin Loaf

1 tablespoon plus 1 teaspoon
   yellow cornmeal, divided
¾ cup milk
½ cup water
1 package dry yeast
3 cups all-purpose flour,
   divided
1 tablespoon sugar
¾ teaspoon salt
¼ teaspoon baking soda

Lightly grease a microwave-safe 9- x 5- x 3-inch loafpan. Sprinkle bottom and sides of pan with 1 tablespoon cornmeal; set aside.

Combine milk and water in a medium bowl. Microwave, uncovered, at HIGH for 1 to 1½ minutes or until warm (105° to 115°). Stir yeast into warm mixture; let stand 3 minutes. Stir in 1 cup flour, sugar, salt, and soda; mix well. Gradually stir in remaining 2 cups flour to make a soft dough.

Place dough in prepared pan; sprinkle with remaining 1 teaspoon cornmeal. Cover with heavy-duty plastic wrap and place pan in a 12- x 8- x 2-inch baking dish. Pour 1 inch hot water into baking dish. Reduce to LOW (10% power), and microwave for 5 minutes; let stand 10 minutes. Repeat procedure once or until dough is doubled in bulk. Remove plastic wrap.

Place loafpan in microwave oven on an inverted pieplate. Cover with wax paper; microwave at HIGH for 6 to 7 minutes or until surface appears dry, rotating a half-turn after 3 minutes. Let stand, uncovered, 5 minutes. Slice and toast before serving, if desired. Yield: 1 loaf.

Curried Rice

¼ cup chopped green onions
2 tablespoons butter or
   margarine
1 cup uncooked long-grain rice
1½ teaspoons chicken-flavored
   bouillon granules
½ teaspoon curry powder
¼ teaspoon ground allspice
⅛ teaspoon white pepper
2 cups hot water
¼ cup sliced almonds
2 tablespoons currants

Combine onions and butter in a deep 2-quart casserole. Cover with heavy-duty plastic wrap and microwave at HIGH for 2 to 3 minutes or until onions are tender. Stir in rice and next 5 ingredients. Cover and microwave at HIGH for 5 to 6 minutes; stir well. Reduce to MEDIUM (50% power); cover and microwave for 14 to 15 minutes or until liquid is absorbed. Let stand, covered, 4 minutes.

Spread almonds in a pieplate; microwave, uncovered, at HIGH for 2 to 4 minutes or until lightly toasted, stirring after every minute. Sprinkle almonds and currants over rice; fluff with a fork. Yield: 4 servings.

You can substitute instant rice for long-grain rice in some casseroles or soups. It will be tender in the short time it takes to microwave the other ingredients in a casserole.

CONFETTI RICE

1½ cups uncooked long-grain
  rice
1 large carrot, scraped and
  diced
¼ cup chopped sweet red
  pepper
2 tablespoons golden
  Worcestershire sauce
½ teaspoon salt
¼ teaspoon garlic powder
2¾ cups hot water
½ cup frozen green peas

Combine first 6 ingredients in a 3-quart casserole. Stir in water. Cover with heavy-duty plastic wrap and microwave at HIGH for 5 minutes. Reduce to MEDIUM (50% power); cover and microwave for 16 to 17 minutes or until liquid is absorbed. Stir in peas. Cover and microwave at HIGH for 1 minute. Let stand, covered, 5 minutes; fluff with a fork. Yield: 8 to 10 servings.

Currants and microwave-toasted almonds add flavor and crunch to Curried Rice.

Rice Pilaf

1 medium tomato, peeled,
  seeded, and chopped
¾ cup uncooked instant rice
¼ cup chopped green onions
¼ cup chopped green pepper
1 tablespoon butter or
  margarine
½ teaspoon beef-flavored
  bouillon granules
¼ teaspoon salt
1 cup hot water

Combine first 7 ingredients in a deep 1-quart casserole. Stir in water. Cover with heavy-duty plastic wrap and microwave at HIGH for 6 to 7 minutes or until liquid is absorbed. Let stand, covered, 3 minutes. Serve immediately. Yield: 4 servings.

Chicken-Flavored Rice

1½ cups uncooked instant rice
¼ cup chopped green onions
2 tablespoons butter or
  margarine
2 teaspoons chicken-flavored
  bouillon granules
¼ teaspoon dried whole basil
⅛ teaspoon garlic powder
1½ cups hot water
1 (4-ounce) can mushroom
  stems and pieces, drained
1 tablespoon minced fresh
  parsley
1 tablespoon grated Parmesan
  cheese

Combine first 6 ingredients in a 2-quart casserole. Stir in water. Cover with heavy-duty plastic wrap and microwave at HIGH for 7 minutes. Stir in mushrooms. Cover and microwave at HIGH for 3 minutes or until liquid is absorbed. Let stand, covered, 4 minutes. Add parsley, and fluff rice with a fork; sprinkle with cheese. Serve immediately. Yield: 4 servings.

Almond Rice

2 cups uncooked instant rice
1 tablespoon minced fresh
  gingerroot
1 teaspoon butter or margarine
½ teaspoon salt
1⅔ cups hot water
¾ cup slivered almonds
¾ cup golden raisins
1 tablespoon chopped fresh
  chives
½ teaspoon ground cinnamon
¼ teaspoon ground nutmeg

Combine first 4 ingredients in a 2-quart casserole, stirring well. Stir in water. Cover with heavy-duty plastic wrap and microwave at HIGH for 6 to 7 minutes or until liquid is absorbed. Let stand, covered, 3 minutes.

Spread almonds in a pieplate; microwave, uncovered, at HIGH for 4 to 5 minutes or until lightly toasted, stirring after every minute. Add almonds, raisins, chives, cinnamon, and nutmeg to rice; fluff with a fork. Serve immediately. Yield: 6 servings.

Chicken bouillon, garlic, and green peas give Bulgur With Peas interesting flavor.

BULGUR WITH PEAS

2¼ cups water
1 cup uncooked bulgur wheat
½ cup chopped onion
2 tablespoons butter or
   margarine
2 teaspoons chicken-flavored
   bouillon granules
1 clove garlic, minced
½ teaspoon salt
1 cup frozen green peas

Place water in a 2-quart casserole. Cover with heavy-duty plastic wrap and microwave at HIGH for 2½ to 3 minutes or until boiling. Slowly pour in bulgur; add onion, butter, bouillon granules, garlic, and salt. Cover and microwave at HIGH for 12 minutes. Add peas; cover and microwave at HIGH for 5 to 7 minutes or until bulgur is tender and liquid is absorbed. Serve immediately. Yield: 6 servings.

QUICK CHEESE GRITS

2⅔ cups water
⅔ cup uncooked quick-cooking
   grits
¾ teaspoon salt
1 tablespoon butter or
   margarine
1 cup (4-ounces) shredded
   Cheddar cheese
1 tablespoon minced chives
⅛ teaspoon garlic powder

Combine water, grits, and salt in a deep 2-quart casserole. Microwave, uncovered, at HIGH for 9 to 10 minutes or until grits are done, stirring after 5 minutes. Add butter, cheese, chives, and garlic powder, stirring well. Microwave, uncovered, at HIGH for 1 minute or until butter and cheese melt; stir before serving. Yield: 4 servings.

Macaroni and Cheese

1 (8-ounce) package elbow
   macaroni
3 cups water
¼ teaspoon salt
¼ cup butter or margarine
¼ cup plus 2 tablespoons
   all-purpose flour
¼ teaspoon salt
2 cups milk
2 cups (8 ounces) shredded
   Cheddar cheese
1 (2-ounce) jar diced pimiento,
   drained
1 tablespoon butter or
   margarine
⅓ cup fine, dry breadcrumbs
½ teaspoon dried parsley
   flakes

Combine macaroni, water, and ¼ teaspoon salt in a deep 2-quart casserole. Cover with heavy-duty plastic wrap and microwave at HIGH for 10 to 12 minutes or until macaroni is tender, stirring after 5 minutes. Drain well, and set aside.

Place ¼ cup butter in a 4-cup glass measure; microwave, uncovered, at HIGH for 55 seconds or until melted. Blend in flour and ¼ teaspoon salt, stirring until smooth. Gradually stir in milk; microwave, uncovered, at HIGH for 5 to 6 minutes or until thickened, stirring after every minute. Add cheese, stirring until melted; stir in pimiento.

Add cheese sauce to macaroni, stirring well. Place macaroni mixture in a 1½-quart casserole; cover with heavy-duty plastic wrap. Reduce to MEDIUM HIGH (70% power), and microwave for 7 to 8 minutes or until thoroughly heated, stirring after 4 minutes.

Place 1 tablespoon butter in a 1-cup glass measure; microwave, uncovered, at HIGH for 35 seconds or until melted. Stir in breadcrumbs and parsley flakes; sprinkle over macaroni mixture. Let stand, uncovered, 1 minute. Serve immediately. Yield: 6 servings.

Parmesan Noodles

6 cups water
1 tablespoon olive oil
½ teaspoon salt
1 (8-ounce) package vermicelli,
   broken in half
1 (8-ounce) package cream
   cheese
¼ cup butter or margarine
½ cup water
3 tablespoons chopped fresh
   parsley
¾ cup grated Parmesan cheese
⅛ teaspoon garlic powder
Freshly ground black pepper

Combine 6 cups water, oil, and salt in a 3-quart casserole. Cover with heavy-duty plastic wrap and microwave at HIGH for 10 minutes or until boiling. Add vermicelli; cover and microwave at HIGH for 7 to 8 minutes or until tender, stirring after 4 minutes. Drain well.

Combine cream cheese and butter in a large bowl; beat at low speed of an electric mixer until smooth. Place ½ cup water in a 1-cup glass measure. Microwave, uncovered, at HIGH for 2 minutes or until boiling. Add boiling water and parsley to cream cheese mixture, beating until smooth. Combine cream cheese mixture and vermicelli in a large bowl; add Parmesan cheese, garlic powder, and pepper, tossing gently. Serve immediately. Yield: 6 servings.

Macaroni and Cheese, always a favorite, rounds out any menu.

Candies and Gifts

Candy making in the microwave oven is quick and simple and provides good results. You can microwave your classic, traditional favorites like fudge and peanut brittle, or try your hand with truffles and bourbon balls. Just be sure to pay special attention to the type and size of cookware used—heavy-duty glass containers are best because many candy mixtures cook at high temperatures that may crack stressed glass or melt plastic. We also recommend specific sizes of containers to help avoid spills from mixtures that bubble and boil.

You may find it difficult to decide which thermometer to use for making candy in the microwave. The oven temperature probe and the regular microwave thermometer probably don't register high enough temperatures for candy making, especially when cooking to the soft ball stage or beyond. There are two other choices: a traditional candy thermometer which must be used outside the oven and takes about 2 minutes to register accurately, and an instant-read or quick-recovery thermometer that is also used outside the oven but gives an immediate reading. Special microwave candy thermometers are also sold but are difficult to find.

Of course, you can always rely on the cold water technique for testing the doneness of candies. The candy mixture is at soft ball stage when a small amount dropped into cold water can be picked up, but flattens between your fingers. For hard crack stage, the mixture should separate into hard, brittle threads when dropped into cold water.

It's almost worth buying a microwave oven just to be able to melt chocolate and caramels so easily. The microwave eliminates the need to use the

Quick and Easy Fudge (page 56) is a treat everyone will enjoy.

traditional double-boiler procedure. Be sure to cut the chocolate into small pieces and stir well after microwaving to melt it completely.

We recommend keeping most microwaved jams or jellies in the refrigerator so that it will not be necessary to use a paraffin seal or to process them in a water bath or pressure canner. Paraffin cannot be melted in the microwave oven. If you want to give refrigerator jams or jellies as gifts sealed with paraffin, rather than a lid, the paraffin must be melted conventionally in a double boiler.

CHOCOLATE-MINT TRUFFLES

1 cup semisweet chocolate-mint
  morsels
3 tablespoons unsalted butter
½ cup sifted powdered sugar
2 tablespoons peppermint
  schnapps
1 egg yolk
2 (1.75-ounce) jars chocolate-
  flavored sprinkles

Place chocolate-mint morsels in a 1-quart casserole or bowl. Microwave, uncovered, at MEDIUM (50% power) for 3 to 3½ minutes or until melted, stirring after 2 minutes; stir until smooth. Add butter, stirring until smooth. Add powdered sugar and schnapps, stirring until blended.

Add egg yolk, beating at medium speed of an electric mixer until smooth. Cover mixture and let stand 8 hours in a cool, dry place (do not refrigerate).

Shape mixture into 1-inch balls; roll in chocolate sprinkles. Store in an airtight container. Yield: 2 dozen.

HAZELNUT TRUFFLES

8 (1-ounce) squares semisweet
  chocolate
3 tablespoons butter
¼ cup evaporated milk
2 tablespoons Triple Sec or
  other orange-flavored liqueur
24 whole hazelnuts
½ cup finely chopped
  hazelnuts

Break chocolate into pieces. Place chocolate and butter in a 4-cup glass measure. Microwave, uncovered, at MEDIUM (50% power) for 4 minutes or until melted, stirring after 2 minutes. Add milk and liqueur, stirring well; cover and refrigerate 45 minutes.

Shape about 1 teaspoon chocolate mixture into a ball around each whole hazelnut; roll in chopped hazelnuts. Place truffles on cookie sheet, and freeze at least 1 hour before serving. Yield: 2 dozen.

DOUBLE-COATED TRUFFLES

2 (12-ounce) packages
  semisweet chocolate morsels
⅔ cup whipping cream
½ teaspoon vanilla extract
2 cups ground pecans
1 pound vanilla-flavored
  almond bark

Combine chocolate morsels and whipping cream in a 2-quart casserole. Microwave, uncovered, at HIGH for 3 to 3½ minutes or until morsels are melted, stirring after 2 minutes. Stir well; let cool slightly. Add vanilla, stirring well. Beat mixture at low speed of an electric mixer until smooth. Cover and refrigerate 1 hour or until mixture is firm.

Shape mixture into ¾-inch balls; roll in ground pecans. Freeze 30 minutes.

Place almond bark in a 4-cup glass measure. Reduce to MEDIUM (50% power); microwave, uncovered, for 3½ to 4½ minutes or until melted, stirring after 2 minutes. Quickly dip balls into melted mixture, allowing excess to drain back into glass measure. Place on wax paper, and let stand 30 minutes or until set. Store in an airtight container in refrigerator. Yield: 5 dozen.

Double-Coated Truffles are rolled in pecans and dipped in melted almond bark.

CHOCOLATE-BOURBON BALLS

1¼ cups vanilla wafer crumbs
⅓ cup bourbon
1 cup semisweet chocolate
  morsels
3 tablespoons unsalted butter
½ cup finely chopped walnuts
1 cup sifted powdered sugar,
  divided

Combine crumbs and bourbon, stirring well; set aside. Place chocolate morsels and butter in a 1-quart casserole or bowl. Microwave, uncovered, at MEDIUM (50% power) for 3 to 3½ minutes or until melted, stirring after 2 minutes. Stir until smooth. Stir in walnuts and crumb mixture. Gradually stir in ⅓ cup powdered sugar. Shape mixture into 1-inch balls, and refrigerate at least 8 hours. Roll in remaining ⅔ cup powdered sugar. Store in an airtight container in refrigerator. Yield: about 4 dozen.

CRISPY PECAN-COCONUT CLUSTERS

1 cup pecan pieces
8 ounces vanilla-flavored
  almond bark
1 cup crisp rice cereal
¾ cup flaked coconut

Spread pecans in a pieplate. Microwave, uncovered, at HIGH for 4 to 5 minutes or until toasted, stirring after every minute. Set aside.

Place almond bark in a 2-quart casserole. Reduce to MEDIUM (50% power); microwave, uncovered, for 3 to 3½ minutes or until melted, stirring after 2 minutes. Let cool 2 minutes. Stir in pecans, cereal, and coconut. Drop mixture by rounded teaspoonfuls onto wax paper. Let cool completely. Yield: 4 dozen.

CHOCOLATE-CARAMEL CLUSTERS

Melt chocolate morsels for Chocolate-Caramel Clusters by microwaving until the morsels are melted; then stir until smooth.

1 (14-ounce) package caramels
1 tablespoon plus 1½
   teaspoons half-and-half
2 cups coarsely chopped pecans
1 (12-ounce) package semisweet
   chocolate morsels
1 tablespoon shortening

Unwrap caramels; place in a 2-quart casserole. Microwave, uncovered, at HIGH for 1 to 1½ minutes or until softened; stir gently. Add half-and-half. Microwave, uncovered, at HIGH for 1 to 1½ minutes or until caramels are melted; stir until smooth. Stir in pecans. Drop mixture by teaspoonfuls onto wax paper. Cover and chill thoroughly.

Place chocolate morsels and shortening in a 4-cup glass measure. Reduce to MEDIUM (50% power); microwave, uncovered, for 3½ to 4 minutes or until melted, stirring after 2 minutes. Stir until smooth. Quickly dip caramels into melted mixture, allowing excess chocolate to drain back into glass measure. Place clusters on lightly greased wax paper, and chill thoroughly. Store in an airtight container. Yield: 3½ dozen.

QUICK AND EASY FUDGE

1 (16-ounce) package powdered
   sugar, sifted
½ cup cocoa
¼ cup milk
1 tablespoon vanilla extract
¼ teaspoon salt
¼ teaspoon ground cinnamon
½ cup butter or margarine
1 cup chopped pecans

Line bottom of an 8-inch square baking pan with wax paper; set aside. Combine first 6 ingredients in a 2-quart casserole, stirring gently. Add butter; microwave, uncovered, at HIGH for 2 to 3 minutes or until thoroughly heated. Stir until smooth. Stir in pecans. Pour mixture into prepared pan. Refrigerate until firm; cut into squares. Yield: 16 squares.

CRISPY FUDGE BARS

⅓ cup butter or margarine
1 (10½-ounce) package
   miniature marshmallows
8 cups crisp rice cereal
1 (6-ounce) package semisweet
   chocolate morsels
1 cup peanut butter morsels
¼ cup butter or margarine
1 cup sifted powdered sugar
2 tablespoons milk
½ teaspoon vanilla extract

Place ⅓ cup butter in a large bowl; microwave, uncovered, at HIGH for 1 minute or until melted. Add marshmallows, stirring well. Microwave, uncovered, at HIGH for 1½ to 2 minutes or until melted, stirring after 1 minute. Stir until smooth. Gradually add cereal, stirring until blended. Using buttered hands, press half of cereal mixture into a greased 13- x 9- x 2-inch baking dish. Cover and refrigerate. Set remaining cereal mixture aside.

Combine chocolate morsels, peanut butter morsels, and ¼ cup butter in a small bowl. Microwave, uncovered, at HIGH for 1½ to 2½ minutes or until morsels begin to melt. Stir until smooth. Add sugar, milk, and vanilla; beat at medium speed of an electric mixer until blended. Spread mixture over chilled layer. Using buttered hands, press remaining cereal mixture over top. Cover and refrigerate at least 1 hour. Cut into bars. Yield: 2 dozen.

Chocolate-Peanut Butter Cups are easy to make. Begin by coating paper liners with melted chocolate, then refrigerate until firm.

CHOCOLATE-PEANUT BUTTER CUPS

⅓ cup butter or margarine
¼ cup crunchy peanut butter
2 tablespoons creamy peanut butter
¾ cup sifted powdered sugar
⅔ cup graham cracker crumbs
3 cups milk chocolate morsels
¼ cup plus 2 tablespoons shortening

Combine butter and peanut butters in a 2-cup glass measure or medium bowl. Microwave, uncovered, at MEDIUM (50% power) for 2 minutes or until butter melts, stirring after 1 minute. Stir in sugar and crumbs; set aside.

Combine chocolate morsels and shortening in a 2-quart casserole or medium bowl. Microwave, uncovered, at MEDIUM for 3 to 4 minutes or until melted, stirring after 2 minutes. Stir until smooth; place casserole or bowl in a dish of hot water.

Using a small, soft brush, thoroughly coat bottoms and sides of 24 miniature paper liners with melted chocolate mixture; refrigerate until firm. Press peanut butter mixture evenly into each cup. Coat top with remaining chocolate. Place in an airtight container; freeze until firm. Store in refrigerator. Yield: 2 dozen.

BOURBON PRALINES

2 cups sugar
2 cups pecan halves
½ cup plus 2 tablespoons buttermilk
2 tablespoons bourbon
2 tablespoons butter or margarine
Dash of salt
1 teaspoon baking soda

Combine sugar, pecan halves, buttermilk, bourbon, butter, and salt in a 5-quart casserole, stirring well. Microwave, uncovered, at HIGH for 12 minutes, stirring every 4 minutes. Stir in soda. Microwave, uncovered, at HIGH for 1 minute; beat with a wooden spoon just until mixture begins to thicken.

Working rapidly, drop mixture by rounded tablespoonfuls onto lightly greased wax paper; let stand until firm. Yield: 1½ dozen.

CARAMEL-MARSHMALLOW-PECAN LOGS

1 (16-ounce) package powdered
  sugar
1¾ cups marshmallow creme
1½ teaspoons vanilla extract
1 (14-ounce) package caramels
3 tablespoons water
2 cups chopped pecans

Combine first 3 ingredients in a large bowl, mixing well (mixture will be dry). Shape into three 8-inch logs or five 4-inch logs, pressing firmly. Cover and chill 3 hours.

Unwrap caramels; combine caramels and water in a 2-quart casserole. Microwave, uncovered, at HIGH for 1 to 1½ minutes or until softened; stir gently. Microwave, uncovered, at HIGH for 2 to 2½ minutes or until melted; stir until smooth. Working quickly with forks or tongs, roll each log in caramel mixture. Roll in pecans, pressing firmly to coat. Cover and refrigerate at least 8 hours. Yield: 3 long logs or 5 short logs.

FAVORITE DIVINITY

2 egg whites
2½ cups sugar
½ cup light corn syrup
½ cup water
¼ teaspoon salt
1½ teaspoons vanilla extract
1 cup chopped pecans

Beat egg whites (at room temperature) until stiff peaks form; set aside.

Combine sugar, syrup, water, and salt in a 3-quart casserole. Microwave, uncovered, at HIGH for 5 minutes; stir well. Microwave, uncovered, at HIGH for 12 to 14 minutes or until mixture reaches hard ball stage (260°) or until a small amount of mixture forms a hard but pliable ball when dropped into cold water. Slowly pour sugar mixture over egg whites, beating at high speed of an electric mixer.

Add vanilla, and continue beating 5 minutes or until mixture holds its shape. Stir in pecans. Quickly drop by heaping teaspoonfuls onto wax paper. Store in an airtight container. Yield: about 4 dozen.

When you want to give a delicious hostess gift, take along some Caramel-Marshmallow-Pecan Logs.

If you have a sweet tooth, you'll want lots of Pecan Toffee (front) and Peanut Brittle (back).

PECAN TOFFEE

1½ cups sugar
1 cup butter or margarine
¼ cup plus 2 tablespoons
  water
1 teaspoon vanilla extract
1 (12-ounce) package semisweet
  chocolate morsels
1 cup finely chopped pecans

Combine sugar, butter, and water in a deep 3-quart casserole. Microwave, uncovered, at HIGH for 17½ to 18 minutes or until mixture reaches hard crack stage (300°) or until a small amount of mixture separates into threads which are hard and brittle when dropped into cold water, stirring after 9 minutes. Stir in vanilla.

Quickly pour mixture into an ungreased 15- x 10- x 1-inch jellyroll pan. Sprinkle with chocolate morsels. Let stand 2 minutes. Spread chocolate evenly over toffee. Sprinkle with pecans. Cover and refrigerate until firm. Break into pieces. Store in an airtight container. Yield: about 2 pounds.

Peanut Brittle

1 cup sugar
1 cup firmly packed light
  brown sugar
½ cup light corn syrup
2 tablespoons water
2 cups roasted peanuts
2 tablespoons butter or
  margarine
2 teaspoons vanilla extract
2 teaspoons baking soda

Combine sugars, corn syrup, water, and peanuts in a deep 5-quart casserole, stirring well. Microwave, uncovered, at HIGH for 7 minutes or until mixture is light brown.

Add butter and vanilla, stirring well. Microwave, uncovered, at HIGH for 11 to 12 minutes or until mixture reaches hard crack stage (300°) or until a small amount of mixture separates into threads which are hard and brittle when dropped into cold water, stirring every 4 minutes. Stir in soda; pour mixture onto a greased cookie sheet, spreading thinly. Let cool; break into pieces. Yield: about 1½ pounds.

Caramel Apples

5 medium apples
1⅓ cups chopped peanuts
1 (14-ounce) package caramels
2 tablespoons milk

Wash and dry apples; remove stems. Insert wooden skewers into stem end of each apple. Set aside. Place peanuts in a pieplate. Microwave, uncovered, at HIGH for 6 minutes or until lightly toasted. Set aside.

Unwrap caramels; place caramels and milk in a 4-cup glass measure. Microwave, uncovered, at HIGH for 1 to 1½ minutes or until softened; stir gently. Microwave, uncovered, at HIGH for 2 to 2½ minutes or until melted; stir until mixture is smooth.

Dip apples in caramel mixture, covering entire surface; allow excess to drain back into glass measure. Roll lower half of each apple in peanuts. Place apples on lightly greased wax paper. Cover and chill at least 1 hour. Store in refrigerator. Yield: 5 apples.

Sweetly Spiced Walnuts

1 cup sugar
1 cup firmly packed brown
  sugar
½ cup water
2 teaspoons ground cinnamon
2 teaspoons ground nutmeg
1 teaspoon salt
5 cups walnut halves

Combine first 6 ingredients in a 3-quart casserole, stirring well. Cover with wax paper and microwave at HIGH for 4 minutes; stir well. Cover and microwave at HIGH for 3½ to 4½ minutes or until mixture reaches soft ball stage (234°) or until a small amount of mixture dropped into cold water forms a soft ball but flattens when removed from water. Add walnuts; stir until coated. Spread walnuts on wax paper, separating with a fork. Let stand until cool and dry. Store in an airtight container. Yield: 5 cups.

CHOCOLATE POPCORN BALLS

¼ cup sugar
¼ cup dark corn syrup
2 tablespoons cocoa
2 tablespoons butter or
   margarine
½ teaspoon vanilla extract
⅛ teaspoon salt
4 cups freshly popped popcorn
¾ cup pecan pieces

Combine first 6 ingredients in a 3-quart casserole. Microwave, uncovered, at HIGH for 2 to 2½ minutes or until boiling; stir until smooth. Stir in popcorn and pecans. Microwave, uncovered, at HIGH for 1 minute; stir gently. Spread mixture onto wax paper. Let cool 30 minutes. Shape mixture into six 2½-inch balls, pressing firmly. Wrap each ball in heavy-duty plastic wrap. Yield: 6 popcorn balls.

RED AND GREEN HOLIDAY JELLY

When making Red and Green Holiday Jelly, allow the cranberry jelly layer to set before spooning on the apple jelly layer.

2 cups cranberry juice
7 cups sugar, divided
2 (3-ounce) packages liquid
   pectin, divided
2 cups apple juice
4 drops green food coloring

Combine cranberry juice and 3½ cups sugar in a 2-quart glass measure. Microwave, uncovered, at HIGH for 10 to 11 minutes or until boiling, stirring after 5 minutes. Stir in 1 package of pectin. Microwave, uncovered, at HIGH for 4 to 5 minutes or until mixture boils hard for 1 full minute. Skim off foam with a spoon.

Pour into hot sterilized jars, filling each half full; set aside. Let cool until jelly is partially set.

Combine apple juice, food coloring, and remaining 3½ cups sugar in a 2-quart glass measure. Microwave, uncovered, at HIGH for 10 to 11 minutes or until boiling, stirring after 5 minutes. Stir in remaining package of pectin. Microwave, uncovered, at HIGH for 4 to 5 minutes or until mixture boils hard for 1 full minute. Skim off foam with a spoon.

Carefully spoon mixture into jars over first layer of jelly, leaving ¼-inch headspace. Cover with metal lids, and screw on bands. Let stand at room temperature until cool. Store in refrigerator. Yield: 10 half pints.

WINE JELLY

1 cup rosé or Burgundy wine
1 cup Chablis or other dry
   white wine
3½ cups sugar
1 (3-ounce) package liquid
   pectin

Combine wines and sugar in a 2-quart casserole. Microwave, uncovered, at HIGH for 10 to 11 minutes or until boiling. Stir in pectin. Microwave, uncovered, at HIGH for 3 to 4 minutes or until mixture boils hard for 1 full minute. Skim off foam with a spoon.

Pour into hot sterilized jars, leaving ¼-inch headspace. Cover with metal lids, and screw on bands. Let stand at room temperature until cool. Store in refrigerator. Yield: 4 half pints.

You'll want to keep some of these sweet spreads for yourself: (clockwise from bottom) Cranberry-Orange Relish (page 65), Peach Refrigerator Jam (page 64), Red and Green Holiday Jelly, and Wine Jelly.

STRAWBERRY REFRIGERATOR JAM

2 pints strawberries, washed
  and hulled
½ (1¾-ounce) package
  powdered pectin
½ teaspoon grated lemon rind
1 tablespoon lemon juice
2½ cups sugar

Mash strawberries in a 2-quart glass measure. Stir in pectin, lemon rind, and lemon juice; microwave, uncovered, at HIGH for 6 to 8 minutes or until mixture reaches a full rolling boil. Stir in sugar; microwave, uncovered, at HIGH for 5 to 6 minutes or until mixture boils hard for 1 full minute. Skim off foam with a spoon.

Pour into hot sterilized jars, leaving ¼-inch headspace. Cover with metal lids, and screw on bands. Let stand at room temperature until cool. Store in refrigerator up to 3 weeks. Yield: 4 half pints.

Peach Refrigerator Jam

4 cups fresh peaches, peeled, pitted, and mashed
4 cups sugar
2 tablespoons lemon juice
2 teaspoons ascorbic-citric powder
¼ teaspoon ground cinnamon
1 (3-ounce) package liquid pectin

Combine first 5 ingredients in a 5-quart casserole. Microwave, uncovered, at HIGH for 5 minutes; stir well. Microwave, uncovered, at HIGH for 15 to 17 minutes or until mixture reaches a full rolling boil. Stir in pectin; skim off foam with a spoon.

Pour into hot sterilized jars, leaving ¼-inch headspace. Cover with metal lids, and screw on bands. Let stand at room temperature until cool. Store in refrigerator up to 3 weeks. Yield: 7 half pints.

Stock up on Refrigerator Corn Relish and Brussels Sprouts Refrigerator Pickles (page 66). They can accompany any entrée.

CRANBERRY-ORANGE RELISH

4 cups fresh cranberries
2 oranges, peeled, seeded,
  and chopped
1 large apple, unpeeled,
  cored, and diced
1⅓ cups sugar
½ cup currants
½ cup chopped pecans
2 tablespoons Grand Marnier
  or other orange-flavored
  liqueur
2 tablespoons vinegar
¼ teaspoon ground ginger
¼ teaspoon ground cinnamon

Combine all ingredients in a 3-quart casserole; stir well. Cover with wax paper and microwave at HIGH for 14 to 15 minutes or until cranberry skins pop, stirring every 4 minutes.

Ladle relish into hot sterilized jars, leaving ¼-inch headspace. Cover with metal lids, and screw on bands. Let stand at room temperature until cool. Store in refrigerator up to 3 weeks. Yield: 5 half pints.

REFRIGERATOR CORN RELISH

10 ears fresh corn
1 small onion, chopped
1 cup sugar
2 tablespoons cornstarch
1 tablespoon mustard seeds
1 tablespoon celery seeds
¼ teaspoon ground turmeric
¾ cup cider vinegar
½ cup water
¾ cup finely chopped green or
  red pepper

Remove husks and silks from corn. Rinse corn, and pat dry. Cut corn from cobs (about 5 cups); set aside. Combine onion and next 7 ingredients in a 2½-quart casserole. Cover with heavy-duty plastic wrap and microwave at HIGH for 5 minutes. Stir in corn and green pepper; cover and microwave at HIGH for 11 to 12 minutes or until corn is crisp-tender, stirring every 4 minutes. Ladle into hot sterilized jars, leaving ¼-inch headspace. Cover with metal lids, and screw on bands. Let stand at room temperature until cool. Store in refrigerator up to 2 weeks. Yield: 5 half pints.

CUCUMBER REFRIGERATOR PICKLES

10 small cucumbers
2 medium onions, thinly sliced
¼ cup canning salt
1½ cups white vinegar
1 cup sugar
1 tablespoon mustard seeds
1 teaspoon celery seeds
½ teaspoon ground ginger
½ teaspoon whole peppercorns
⅛ teaspoon ground turmeric

Wash cucumbers; cut into ¼-inch-thick slices (about 5 to 5½ cups). Layer cucumbers, onion slices, and salt in a large bowl. Cover with ice; let stand 1½ to 2 hours. Rinse and drain well. Set aside.

Combine vinegar and remaining ingredients in a large bowl. Microwave, uncovered, at HIGH for 6 to 7 minutes or until boiling, stirring after 3 minutes. Add cucumbers and onions. Cover with heavy-duty plastic wrap and microwave at HIGH for 12 to 14 minutes or until boiling, stirring every 4 minutes. Ladle cucumber mixture into hot sterilized jars. Cover with metal lids, and screw on bands. Let stand at room temperature until cool. Store in refrigerator up to 2 weeks. Yield: 3 pints.

Brussels Sprouts Refrigerator Pickles

2 pounds small fresh brussels
  sprouts (about 8 cups)
¼ cup water
2 cups cider vinegar
¾ cup water
¾ cup sugar
2 tablespoons salt
2 cloves garlic, minced
2 small onions, thinly sliced
9 sprigs fresh dillweed

Wash brussels sprouts, and remove discolored leaves. Trim stems, and slash bottom of each sprout with a shallow X. Place sprouts and ¼ cup water in a 2-quart casserole. Cover with heavy-duty plastic wrap and microwave at HIGH for 8 to 9 minutes or until crisp-tender, stirring after 4 minutes. Let stand, covered, 3 minutes; drain.

Combine vinegar, ¾ cup water, sugar, salt, and garlic in a 4-cup glass measure, stirring well. Microwave, uncovered, at HIGH for 5 to 6 minutes or until boiling.

Pack sprouts and onion slices in hot sterilized jars. Add a sprig of dillweed to each jar. Pour hot vinegar mixture over sprouts, leaving ¼-inch headspace. Cover with metal lids, and screw on bands. Let stand at room temperature until cool. Store in refrigerator up to 2 weeks. Yield: 9 half pints.

Chive-Vinaigrette Dressing And Croutons

½ cup plus 2 tablespoons sugar
½ cup vinegar
3 tablespoons chopped fresh
  chives
1 teaspoon salt
1 teaspoon dry mustard
⅛ teaspoon freshly ground
  black pepper
1¼ cups vegetable oil
Croutons (recipe follows)

Combine sugar and vinegar in a 4-cup glass measure. Microwave, uncovered, at HIGH for 5 to 6 minutes or until sugar dissolves, stirring after 3 minutes. Let cool 1 minute. Pour into container of an electric blender; add chives, salt, mustard, and pepper. Cover and process 30 seconds. With motor running, add oil in a slow steady stream. Serve dressing with croutons over salad greens. Yield: 2¼ cups.

Croutons:

8 slices white bread, cut into
  ½-inch cubes
½ cup butter or margarine
½ teaspoon garlic powder
¼ cup grated Parmesan
  cheese
2 teaspoons minced fresh
  parsley

Place bread cubes in a 10-inch pieplate; set aside. Place butter and garlic powder in a 1-cup glass measure. Microwave, uncovered, at HIGH for 1 minute or until melted; stir well. Drizzle butter mixture over bread cubes; sprinkle with cheese and parsley, tossing gently. Microwave, uncovered, at HIGH for 5½ to 6 minutes or until crisp, stirring after 2 minutes. Yield: 2½ cups.

Do not attempt to can or process food in the microwave oven. You cannot be sure that all the food will reach and maintain the temperature needed for safe preservation.

Salad lovers will adore this unique gift of Chive-Vinaigrette Dressing and Croutons.

HOT HONEY MUSTARD

⅓ cup mustard seeds
⅓ cup water
1½ to 2 tablespoons dry
   mustard
¾ cup cider vinegar
1 small onion, chopped
3 tablespoons firmly packed
   brown sugar
2 cloves garlic, minced
1 teaspoon salt
½ teaspoon ground allspice
½ teaspoon ground cinnamon
3 tablespoons honey

Combine mustard seeds, water, and dry mustard in a small bowl. Let stand at room temperature at least 2 hours.

Combine vinegar and next 6 ingredients in a 2-cup glass measure. Microwave, uncovered, at HIGH for 6 to 7 minutes or until sugar dissolves. Strain mixture into container of an electric blender; discard onion. Add mustard mixture; cover and process 20 to 30 seconds or until partially smooth. Add honey; process 10 seconds or until blended.

Spoon mustard into hot sterilized jars. Cover with metal lids; screw on bands. Let cool. Refrigerate 3 days before serving. Store in refrigerator. Yield: 2 half pints.

Desserts

You can expect to have great success with most desserts in the microwave oven; puddings, custard mixtures, and fruit desserts are always excellent. But cake layers may not rise evenly, pastry shells for pies will not brown, and cookies are best made in smaller batches so that they can cook evenly. However, we believe that as long as you are aware of these differences you will be satisfied with the recipes we've included for these desserts.

Microwaved cake layers cook in one-fourth or one-third the time of conventionally cooked cakes. But because you must microwave each layer individually you may not actually save that much time.

Most of our cake recipes microwave at MEDIUM (50% power) to ensure a light, delicate texture. Elevating and rotating the layers during cooking helps them cook more evenly. The layers will probably look a little moist in the center even when done. But don't continue to cook them in an effort to totally eliminate any wet spots; this results in dried-out layers. Most microwaved cakes tend to have rough edges when removed from the pans; carefully spreading with frosting will conceal the uneven edges.

Microwaved cookies are chewy and moist, rather than crisp. To keep dropped or shaped cookies from spreading too thin, you must use a stiffer batter than would be used conventionally. Dropped or shaped cookies should also be microwaved in small batches of six to eight at a time on a round plate lined with wax paper. After microwaving, slide the wax paper onto the counter and let the cookies cool for two minutes; remove them from the wax paper to cool completely.

Who would have thought this gorgeous Lemon Meringue Pie (page 83) and Glazed Strawberry Pie (page 82) could be made in the microwave oven?

Because the corners of bar cookies cook faster than the center, you may need to shield the edges of the dish with aluminum foil. Be sure the foil is at least one inch from the oven walls. Shielding will prevent dry, hard corners (see *Shielding*, page 8).

Pies are always a favorite dessert, and they are easily made in the microwave oven. Although pastry shells cooked in the microwave oven do not brown, they are especially flaky. The light-colored crust doesn't bother most people; in fact, some like it better than an overbrowned traditional shell. However, spices may be added to the pastry for a browner-looking crust. Be sure to microwave or bake the pastry shells before they are filled, pricking with a fork, just as you would for a conventionally baked crust.

Double-crust pies are also possible in the microwave oven. To ensure doneness, the top pastry shell, the filling, and the bottom pastry shell are microwaved separately. Then the pie is assembled and microwaved again, if needed. Even with three steps, the pie is done in a fraction of the time required in a conventional oven. Remember, the pastry should appear opaque and dry when done. If only a few damp spots remain, continue microwaving for 30-second intervals.

Puddings and custards cook just as easily in the microwave oven as they do conventionally. In fact, they're actually easier to make in the microwave because they don't have to be stirred as often.

Some of our pudding and custard mixtures contain egg yolks for thickening, and this can be tricky. To prevent curdling, it's best to gradually add the beaten yolks to hot liquids, stirring constantly as they are added.

CHEWY BUTTERSCOTCH-PEANUT SQUARES

¼ cup plus 2 tablespoons
   butter or margarine
1 cup firmly packed brown
   sugar
2 tablespoons creamy peanut
   butter
¼ cup butterscotch morsels
½ cup chopped salted peanuts
2 eggs, beaten
1 cup all-purpose flour
½ teaspoon baking powder
¼ teaspoon salt
1 teaspoon vanilla extract
2 (1.65-ounce) chocolate bars,
   broken into pieces
¼ cup chopped salted peanuts

Place butter in a large bowl; microwave, uncovered, at HIGH for 1 minute or until melted. Add brown sugar, peanut butter, and butterscotch morsels, stirring well. Add ½ cup peanuts, eggs, flour, baking powder, salt, and vanilla, stirring well. Spoon batter into a lightly greased 8-inch square baking dish. Shield corners with triangles of aluminum foil, keeping foil smooth and close to dish. Place dish in microwave oven on an inverted pieplate. Reduce to MEDIUM (50% power), and microwave, uncovered, for 3 minutes; rotate a half-turn. Remove foil shields and microwave, uncovered, at HIGH for 3 to 5 minutes or until surface is almost dry and a wooden pick inserted in center comes out clean. Place dish on a sheet of aluminum foil. Sprinkle top immediately with chocolate pieces. Let stand 10 minutes; spread melted chocolate evenly over top, and sprinkle with ¼ cup peanuts. Cool; cut into squares. Store in an airtight container. Yield: 16 squares.

Here is a variety of cookies to snack on: Chocolate Chip Squares, Rich Chocolate-Mint Brownies (page 72), and Swedish Wedding Cookies (page 73).

Chocolate Chip Squares

½ cup butter or margarine
¾ cup firmly packed brown sugar
1 egg, beaten
1 tablespoon milk
1 teaspoon vanilla extract
1⅓ cups all-purpose flour
½ teaspoon baking powder
⅛ teaspoon salt
1 (6-ounce) package semisweet chocolate morsels, divided
½ cup chopped pecans

Place butter in a large bowl. Microwave, uncovered, at LOW (10% power) for 1 to 1½ minutes or until softened. Cream butter; gradually add sugar, beating at medium speed of an electric mixer until light and fluffy. Beat in egg, milk, and vanilla. Combine flour, baking powder, and salt. Add to creamed mixture, beating until blended. Stir in ½ cup chocolate morsels and pecans. Spoon mixture into a lightly greased 8-inch square baking dish. Sprinkle with remaining chocolate morsels. Shield corners with triangles of aluminum foil, keeping foil smooth and close to dish. Place dish in microwave oven on an inverted saucer. Microwave, uncovered, at MEDIUM HIGH (70% power) for 7 to 8 minutes or until surface is almost dry and a wooden pick inserted in center comes out clean, rotating a half-turn after 3½ minutes. Let cool; cut into 2-inch squares. Store in an airtight container. Yield: 16 squares.

Shield the corners of Chocolate Chip Squares with aluminum foil to prevent overcooking.

Rich Chocolate-Mint Brownies

½ cup butter or margarine
2 (1-ounce) squares
  unsweetened chocolate
1 cup sugar
2 eggs
¾ cup all-purpose flour
½ teaspoon baking powder
1 teaspoon vanilla extract
¼ cup butter or margarine,
  divided
1 cup sifted powdered sugar
2 tablespoons green crème de
  menthe
½ cup semisweet chocolate
  morsels

Place ½ cup butter and unsweetened chocolate in a medium bowl; microwave, uncovered, at HIGH for 2 to 2½ minutes or until melted. Stir mixture until smooth. Add 1 cup sugar, beating at medium speed of an electric mixer until light and fluffy. Add eggs, one at a time, beating well after each addition.

Combine flour and baking powder; add to chocolate mixture, beating well. Stir in vanilla. Pour batter into a greased and floured 8-inch square baking dish. Shield corners with triangles of aluminum foil, keeping foil smooth and close to dish. Reduce to MEDIUM HIGH (70% power); microwave, uncovered, for 6 to 8 minutes or until surface is almost dry and a wooden pick inserted in center comes out clean, rotating a quarter-turn every 2 minutes. Set aside to cool completely.

Place 2 tablespoons butter in a small bowl. Reduce to LOW (10% power); microwave, uncovered, for 20 seconds or until softened. Cream butter; gradually add powdered sugar and crème de menthe, mixing well. Spread evenly over chocolate layer; cover and refrigerate 1 hour.

Combine chocolate morsels and remaining 2 tablespoons butter in a 2-cup glass measure. Microwave, uncovered, at HIGH for 45 seconds or until softened. Stir mixture until melted; spread evenly over chilled filling. Cover and refrigerate 1 hour or until set. Cut into 2-inch squares. Store brownies in an airtight container. Yield: 16 squares.

Almond Fans

1 cup butter
½ teaspoon vanilla extract
½ teaspoon almond extract
¼ teaspoon salt
⅔ cup sugar
1½ cups all-purpose flour
1 egg white
Sliced almonds
Additional sugar

Place butter in a large bowl. Microwave, uncovered, at LOW (10% power) for 2 minutes or until softened. Cream butter, flavorings, and salt in a medium mixing bowl. Gradually add ⅔ cup sugar, beating at medium speed of an electric mixer until light and fluffy. Stir in flour just until blended.

Turn dough out onto a lightly floured surface, and knead 4 or 5 times. Shape dough into a 5-inch-long roll, and cut into 1-inch slices; place in refrigerator. Working with one slice at a time, pat to an 8-inch circle on a lightly floured surface. Cut each circle into 8 wedges.

Place wedges on a 12-inch round glass platter lined with parchment paper. Beat egg white until foamy. Lightly brush tops of wedges with egg white; sprinkle with almonds and additional sugar. Microwave, uncovered, at HIGH for 2½ to 3½ minutes or until surface is dry, rotating a half-turn after 1 minute. Repeat procedure for remaining slices. Store in an airtight container. Yield: 40 cookies.

NUTTY OATMEAL-CHOCOLATE CHIP COOKIES

1 cup all-purpose flour
1 teaspoon baking soda
¼ teaspoon salt
½ cup shortening
½ cup firmly packed brown sugar
1 egg
1 teaspoon vanilla extract
½ teaspoon ground cinnamon
1¼ cups quick-cooking oats, uncooked
½ cup semisweet chocolate morsels
¼ cup finely chopped pecans

Combine flour, soda, and salt; set aside. Cream shortening; gradually add sugar, beating at medium speed of an electric mixer. Add egg, vanilla, and cinnamon. Stir in flour mixture, oats, chocolate morsels, and pecans.

Drop 6 heaping teaspoonfuls of dough in a circle on a wax paper-lined 12-inch round glass platter. Microwave, uncovered, at MEDIUM (50% power) for 3½ to 4 minutes or until surface is dry, rotating a half-turn after every minute. Slide wax paper with cookies onto counter, and let cool 2 minutes. Remove cookies to wire racks to cool completely. Repeat procedure with remaining dough. Store in an airtight container. Yield: 3½ dozen.

To ensure even doneness, drop Nutty Oatmeal-Chocolate Chip Cookies in a circle on a platter lined with wax paper.

SWEDISH WEDDING COOKIES

¼ cup plus 3 tablespoons butter or margarine
1 cup all-purpose flour
⅛ teaspoon ground cinnamon
½ cup finely chopped pecans
¼ cup sifted powdered sugar
½ teaspoon vanilla extract
¼ teaspoon cream of tartar
¼ teaspoon baking soda
Additional powdered sugar

Place butter in a 1-cup glass measure. Microwave, uncovered, at LOW (10% power) for 30 seconds to 1 minute or until softened; set aside.

Combine flour and cinnamon in a large bowl. Add pecans, softened butter, ¼ cup powdered sugar, vanilla, cream of tartar, and soda; stir until blended (mixture will be stiff). Knead dough 3 or 4 times, if necessary, to blend.

Shape dough into ¾-inch balls. Arrange 9 balls in a circle on a wax paper-lined 12-inch round glass platter. Microwave, uncovered, at MEDIUM (50% power) for 4 to 5 minutes or until cookies are firm, rotating a quarter-turn after every minute. Slide wax paper with cookies onto counter, and let cool 2 minutes. Roll cookies in additional powdered sugar; cool completely on wire racks. Repeat procedure with remaining balls. Store cookies in an airtight container. Yield: 2 dozen.

White Chocolate Cupcakes

⅓ cup shortening
½ cup sugar
2 eggs
1 cup all-purpose flour
½ teaspoon baking soda
½ teaspoon salt
2 tablespoons cocoa
⅓ cup milk
½ teaspoon vanilla extract
White Chocolate Frosting

Cream shortening; gradually add sugar, beating at medium speed of an electric mixer until light and fluffy. Add eggs, one at a time, beating well after each addition. Combine flour, soda, salt, and cocoa; add to creamed mixture alternately with milk, beginning and ending with flour mixture. Mix well after each addition. Stir in vanilla.

Line a microwave-safe muffin pan or six 6-ounce custard cups with a double layer of paper liners. Spoon batter into cups, filling one-third full. If using custard cups, arrange in a circle on a 12-inch round glass platter. Microwave, uncovered, at HIGH for 2½ to 3 minutes or until surface is only slightly wet, rotating a half-turn after 1 minute. Remove from pan, and let cool on a wire rack; frost with White Chocolate Frosting. Repeat procedure with remaining batter and frosting. Store in an airtight container. Yield: 1 dozen.

White Chocolate Frosting:

1 (3-ounce) white chocolate bar
2 tablespoons butter or margarine
3 tablespoons milk
1½ cups sifted powdered sugar
½ teaspoon vanilla extract

Place white chocolate, butter, and milk in a medium bowl. Microwave, uncovered, at MEDIUM (50% power) for 3 minutes or until melted. Stir until smooth. Add powdered sugar and vanilla; beat at low speed of an electric mixer until smooth. Yield: enough for 1 dozen cupcakes.

German Chocolate Cake

3 (1-ounce) squares unsweetened chocolate
¾ cup butter or margarine
1½ cups sugar
3 eggs
1 teaspoon vanilla extract
1¾ cups all-purpose flour
1 teaspoon baking soda
½ teaspoon salt
¾ cup milk
Coconut-Pecan Frosting

Place chocolate in a 1-cup glass measure. Microwave, uncovered, at MEDIUM (50% power) for 2½ to 3 minutes or until softened. Stir until smooth and melted; set aside.

Place butter in a large bowl. Microwave, uncovered, at LOW (10% power) for 1½ to 2 minutes or until softened. Cream butter; gradually add sugar, beating at medium speed of an electric mixer until light and fluffy. Add eggs, one at a time, beating after each addition. Add chocolate and vanilla. Beat until blended. Combine flour, soda, and salt; add to creamed mixture alternately with milk, beginning and ending with flour mixture. Mix after each addition.

Grease bottom (not sides) of three 9-inch round microwave-safe cakepans, and line with a double layer of wax paper; spoon batter evenly into pans. Cut through batter with a knife to remove air bubbles.

Place 1 pan in microwave oven on an inverted pieplate or saucer. Microwave, uncovered, at MEDIUM for 7 minutes, rotating a half-turn every 2 minutes. Increase to HIGH power and microwave, uncovered, for 1½ to 2 minutes or until top is almost dry. Remove from oven, and place on a sheet of aluminum foil. Cool in pan 10 minutes; remove from pan, and cool on a wire rack 10 minutes. Wrap layer in heavy-duty plastic wrap. Repeat procedure with remaining cake layers.

Unwrap layers and spread Coconut-Pecan Frosting gently between layers and on top and sides of cake. Store in an airtight container. Yield: one 3-layer cake.

COCONUT-PECAN FROSTING:
1 cup butter or margarine
2 cups sugar
1⅔ cups evaporated milk
6 egg yolks
2 teaspoons vanilla extract
2 cups flaked coconut
2 cups chopped pecans

Place butter in a deep 2-quart casserole. Microwave, uncovered, at HIGH for 1½ to 2½ minutes or until melted. Add sugar, milk, and egg yolks; stir well. Reduce to MEDIUM (50% power) and microwave, uncovered, for 19 to 20 minutes or until thickened, stirring with a wire whisk every 4 minutes. Stir in vanilla, coconut, and pecans. Stir until frosting is cool and of spreading consistency. Yield: enough for one 3-layer cake.

Each layer of German Chocolate Cake is generously spread with Coconut-Pecan Frosting.

Peanut Butter Cake

Bake cake layers one at a time in a microwave-safe cakepan placed on an inverted pieplate or saucer.

½ cup butter or margarine
⅓ cup creamy peanut butter
¼ cup shortening
1½ cups firmly packed brown sugar
1 teaspoon vanilla extract
3 eggs
1¾ cups all-purpose flour
2 teaspoons baking powder
¼ teaspoon salt
¾ cup milk
Chocolate-Peanut Butter Frosting
¼ cup chopped peanuts

Cream butter, peanut butter, and shortening; gradually add sugar, beating at medium speed of an electric mixer until light and fluffy. Stir in vanilla. Add eggs, one at a time, beating well after each addition.

Combine flour, baking powder, and salt; add to creamed mixture alternately with milk, beginning and ending with flour mixture. Mix after each addition.

Grease bottom (not sides) of two 9-inch microwave-safe cakepans, and line with a double layer of wax paper; spoon batter evenly into pans. Cut through batter with a knife to remove air bubbles.

Place 1 pan in microwave oven on an inverted pieplate or saucer. Microwave, uncovered, at MEDIUM (50% power) for 6½ minutes, rotating a half-turn every 2 minutes. Increase to HIGH power and microwave, uncovered, for 2 to 3 minutes or until top is almost dry. Remove from oven, and place on a sheet of aluminum foil. Cool layer in pan 10 minutes; remove from pan, and cool on a wire rack 10 minutes. Wrap layer in heavy-duty plastic wrap. Repeat procedure with remaining layer.

Unwrap layers and spread Chocolate-Peanut Butter Frosting gently between layers and on top and sides of cake. Sprinkle peanuts over top. Store in an airtight container. Yield: one 2-layer cake.

CHOCOLATE-PEANUT BUTTER FROSTING:

2 (1-ounce) squares unsweetened chocolate
⅓ cup milk
¼ cup butter or margarine
¼ cup creamy peanut butter
3½ to 4 cups sifted powdered sugar
1 teaspoon vanilla extract

Combine chocolate, milk, butter, and peanut butter in a large bowl. Microwave, uncovered, at MEDIUM (50% power) for 3½ to 4 minutes or until chocolate and butter melt, stirring after 3 minutes. Stir in sugar and vanilla; let stand 10 minutes. Stir until frosting is of spreading consistency. Yield: enough for one 2-layer cake.

For a quick frosting, place chocolate mint patties over cake or cupcakes and microwave at HIGH—2 minutes for a cake or 15 to 20 seconds for a cupcake—then spread.

CARROT CAKE

2½ cups all-purpose flour
1¾ cups sugar
2 teaspoons baking powder
1 teaspoon baking soda
¼ teaspoon salt
1½ teaspoons ground cinnamon
4 eggs
½ cup vegetable oil
2 cups grated carrots
Cream Cheese Frosting

Combine first 6 ingredients in a large bowl, stirring well. Combine eggs and oil in a large bowl; beat at medium speed of an electric mixer until blended. Gradually add dry ingredients, beating just until moistened. Stir in carrots.

Grease bottom (not sides) of two 9-inch round microwave-safe cakepans, and line with a double layer of wax paper; spoon batter evenly into pans. Cut through batter with a knife to remove air bubbles.

Place 1 pan in microwave oven on an inverted pieplate or saucer. Microwave, uncovered, at MEDIUM (50% power) for 6 minutes, rotating a half-turn every 2 minutes. Increase to HIGH power and microwave, uncovered, for 4 to 6 minutes or until top is almost dry, rotating a half-turn every 2 minutes. Remove layer from oven, and place on a sheet of aluminum foil. Cool in pan 10 minutes; remove from pan, and cool on a wire rack 10 minutes. Repeat procedure with remaining cake layer.

Immediately spread Cream Cheese Frosting gently between layers and on top and sides of cake. Store in an airtight container. Yield: one 2-layer cake.

CREAM CHEESE FROSTING:

1 (8-ounce) package cream cheese
½ cup butter or margarine
1 (16-ounce) package powdered sugar, sifted
2 teaspoons vanilla extract
1 cup chopped pecans

Place cream cheese and butter in a 2-quart glass bowl. Microwave, uncovered, at LOW (10% power) for 4 minutes or until softened. Cream butter and cream cheese; gradually add sugar and vanilla, beating well at medium speed of an electric mixer. Stir in pecans. Yield: enough for one 2-layer cake.

To make shelling pecans or walnuts easier, microwave them before cracking. Combine 2 cups nuts and 1 cup water in a casserole. Microwave at HIGH for 1½ to 2 minutes or until heated.

Each step in the preparation of Glazed Strawberry-Peach Cheesecake takes place in the microwave oven.

GLAZED STRAWBERRY-PEACH CHEESECAKE

3 tablespoons butter or
  margarine
1 cup graham cracker crumbs
2 tablespoons sugar
2 (8-ounce) packages cream
  cheese
2 tablespoons butter or
  margarine
1 (8-ounce) carton commercial
  sour cream
⅔ cup sugar
2 eggs
1 tablespoon all-purpose flour
1 teaspoon grated lemon rind
1 teaspoon vanilla extract
1 (8½-ounce) can sliced
  peaches, drained
½ cup halved fresh
  strawberries
2 tablespoons red currant jelly

Place 3 tablespoons butter in a medium bowl. Microwave, uncovered, at HIGH for 50 seconds or until melted. Add cracker crumbs and 2 tablespoons sugar, stirring well. Press into bottom and up sides of a lightly greased 9-inch round baking dish. Microwave, uncovered, at HIGH for 1½ to 2 minutes or until firm, rotating a half-turn after 1 minute. Let cool; set aside.

Place cream cheese and 2 tablespoons butter in a 3-quart bowl; reduce to MEDIUM (50% power), and microwave, uncovered, for 2½ to 3 minutes or until cream cheese is softened and butter is melted. Add sour cream, ⅔ cup sugar, eggs, flour, lemon rind, and vanilla. Beat at medium speed of an electric mixer until blended. Cover with wax paper and microwave at HIGH for 6 to 7 minutes or until thickened, stirring with a wire whisk every 2 minutes. Pour cream cheese mixture into prepared crust.

Place dish in microwave oven on an inverted saucer. Microwave, uncovered, at MEDIUM for 8 to 9 minutes or until almost set in center, rotating a quarter-turn after 4 minutes. Cool to room temperature, and refrigerate until chilled.

Arrange peach slices and strawberry halves on chilled cheesecake. Place jelly in a 1-cup glass measure. Microwave, uncovered, at HIGH for 30 seconds to 1 minute or until melted. Brush jelly over fruit. Store in refrigerator. Yield: 8 servings.

BANANA-CARAMEL PIE

¼ cup plus 1 tablespoon butter
  or margarine
1⅓ cups graham cracker
  crumbs
½ cup plus 2 tablespoons
  firmly packed brown sugar,
  divided
2 tablespoons cornstarch
¼ teaspoon salt
1½ cups evaporated milk
1 egg yolk
2 tablespoons plus 1½
  teaspoons butter or
  margarine
2 teaspoons vanilla extract
2 medium bananas, peeled
  and sliced
½ cup whipping cream
¼ cup sifted powdered sugar
2 tablespoons toffee candy bits

Place ¼ cup plus 1 tablespoon butter in a 1-cup glass measure. Microwave, uncovered, at HIGH for 1 minute or until melted. Combine melted butter, graham cracker crumbs, and 2 tablespoons brown sugar; stir well. Press firmly into a lightly greased 9-inch pieplate. Microwave, uncovered, at HIGH for 2 minutes or until firm, rotating a half-turn after 1 minute. Let cool completely.

Combine remaining ½ cup brown sugar, cornstarch, and salt in a 1½-quart casserole. Gradually stir in milk. Microwave, uncovered, at HIGH for 4½ to 5 minutes or until thickened, stirring every 2 minutes.

Beat egg yolk until thick and lemon colored. Gradually stir about one-fourth of hot milk mixture into egg yolk. Add to remaining hot milk mixture, stirring constantly. Reduce to MEDIUM HIGH (70% power), and microwave, uncovered, for 1 to 1½ minutes or until thickened. Stir in 2 tablespoons plus 1½ teaspoons butter and vanilla, stirring until butter melts.

Arrange banana slices in bottom of cooled crust. Pour filling over bananas. Cover and refrigerate at least 5 hours or until set.

Beat whipping cream until foamy; gradually add powdered sugar, beating until soft peaks form. Spread whipped cream over pie. Sprinkle with candy bits. Serve immediately; store in refrigerator. Yield: one 9-inch pie.

Soften hardened brown sugar by placing it in a glass container; place 1 cup water in a glass measure alongside it. Microwave at HIGH for 30 seconds to 1 minute.

SINGLE-CRUST PASTRY SHELL

1 cup all-purpose flour
½ teaspoon salt
3 tablespoons shortening
3 tablespoons cold butter
2 tablespoons cold water
Vegetable cooking spray

Combine flour and salt; cut in shortening and butter with pastry blender until mixture resembles coarse meal. Sprinkle water, 1 tablespoon at a time, evenly over surface; stir with a fork until all ingredients are moistened. Shape into a ball; cover with plastic wrap, and freeze 5 minutes. Lightly spray a 9-inch pieplate with vegetable cooking spray; set aside.

Remove dough from freezer, and roll to ⅛-inch thickness on a lightly floured surface. Place pastry loosely in pieplate; trim off excess pastry. Fold edges under and flute.

Gently prick bottom and sides of pastry with a fork. Microwave, uncovered, at HIGH for 6½ to 7½ minutes or until pastry is opaque and bottom is dry, rotating a half-turn after 3 minutes. Yield: one 9-inch pastry shell.

DOUBLE-CRUST PASTRY SHELL

1½ cups all-purpose flour
½ teaspoon salt
4½ tablespoons shortening
4½ tablespoons cold butter
4 tablespoons cold water
Vegetable cooking spray

Combine flour and salt; cut in shortening and butter with pastry blender until mixture resembles coarse meal. Sprinkle water, 1 tablespoon at a time, evenly over surface; stir with a fork until all ingredients are moistened.

Set aside about ⅓ of dough for top pastry; wrap in plastic wrap, and freeze 5 minutes. Shape remaining dough into a ball; cover with plastic wrap, and freeze 5 minutes. Lightly spray a 9-inch pieplate with vegetable cooking spray; set aside.

Remove larger portion of pastry from freezer, and roll to ⅛-inch thickness on a lightly floured surface. Place loosely in pieplate; trim off excess pastry. Fold edges under and flute. Prick bottom and sides of pastry with a fork. Microwave, uncovered, at HIGH for 8 to 9 minutes or until pastry is opaque and bottom is dry, rotating a half-turn every 3 minutes. Set aside.

Remove smaller portion of pastry from freezer, and roll to ⅛-inch thickness on a lightly floured surface. Cut into decorative shapes or cut into strips, and weave into a lattice to fit top of pie. Arrange cutouts in a ring on lightly greased wax paper or weave lattice directly on wax paper. Place wax paper on bottom of an inverted pieplate; microwave, uncovered, at HIGH for 2 to 3 minutes or until pastry is dry,

Microwaved pastry shells do not brown, but they do have a very flaky texture. Choose a plain pastry shell (right), whole wheat pastry shell (bottom left), or spice pastry shell (top left).

DOUBLE-CRUST PASTRY SHELL
(continued)

rotating a half-turn after every minute. Peel pastry from paper, and place on pie filling. Yield: one 9-inch double-crust pastry shell.

SPICE CRUST:

Add 2 tablespoons sugar, ½ teaspoon ground cinnamon, and ¼ teaspoon ground nutmeg to flour and salt. Yield: one 9-inch double-crust pastry shell.

WHOLE WHEAT CRUST:

Substitute ¾ cup whole wheat flour for ¾ cup all-purpose flour. Yield: one 9-inch double-crust pastry shell.

Eggnog Fluff Pie

1½ cups commercial canned
   eggnog, divided
1 tablespoon cornstarch
4 eggs, separated
⅓ cup sugar
1 teaspoon vanilla extract
½ teaspoon rum extract
⅛ teaspoon salt
1 envelope unflavored gelatin
2 tablespoons milk
¼ cup whipping cream
Microwaved or baked 9-inch
   pastry shell
Whipped cream
Ground nutmeg

Combine ¼ cup eggnog and cornstarch in a medium bowl, stirring well. Add egg yolks, sugar, flavorings, and salt, stirring well.

Place remaining 1¼ cups eggnog in a large bowl. Microwave, uncovered, at HIGH for 2 minutes or until thoroughly heated. Gradually stir about one-fourth of hot eggnog into egg yolk mixture; add to remaining hot eggnog. Reduce to MEDIUM HIGH (70% power), and microwave, uncovered, for 3½ to 4½ minutes or until thickened, stirring every 1½ minutes with a wire whisk.

Combine gelatin and milk, stirring well; let stand 1 minute. Stir into thickened eggnog mixture. Cover and refrigerate until the consistency of unbeaten egg white.

Beat egg whites (at room temperature) at high speed of an electric mixer until stiff peaks form. Gently fold into chilled mixture. Beat ¼ cup whipping cream until soft peaks form. Gently fold into chilled mixture. Pour into pastry shell. Chill 2 hours or until set. Garnish with whipped cream, and sprinkle with nutmeg. Yield: one 9-inch pie.

Glazed Strawberry Pie

1 cup sugar
3½ tablespoons cornstarch
2 cups water
¼ cup strawberry-flavored
   gelatin
4 cups halved fresh
   strawberries
Microwaved or baked 9-inch
   pastry shell
Additional fresh strawberries
   (optional)
Fresh mint leaves (optional)
Whipped cream (optional)

Combine sugar and cornstarch in a large bowl; gradually stir in water. Microwave, uncovered, at HIGH for 7 to 9 minutes or until thickened and clear, stirring every 2 minutes. Stir in gelatin; set aside to cool slightly.

Arrange strawberries to cover bottom of pastry shell; cover with gelatin mixture. Refrigerate until thoroughly chilled. Garnish with additional strawberries and mint leaves, and serve with whipped cream, if desired. Yield: one 9-inch pie.

To thaw frozen whipped topping, microwave, uncovered, at MEDIUM LOW (30% power) until softened. A 4-ounce container takes from 30 to 40 seconds; an 8-ounce container takes 50 to 60 seconds.

Lemon Meringue Pie

1½ cups sugar
½ cup cornstarch
Dash of salt
1¾ cups water, divided
4 eggs, separated
1 tablespoon grated lemon rind
¼ cup lemon juice
Microwaved or baked 9-inch
  pastry shell
½ teaspoon cream of tartar
¼ cup plus 2 tablespoons sugar

Combine 1½ cups sugar, cornstarch, salt, and ¼ cup water in a 1½-quart bowl; stir well. Stir in remaining 1½ cups water. Microwave, uncovered, at HIGH for 8 minutes or until thickened and clear, stirring every 2 minutes.

Lightly beat egg yolks until thick and lemon colored. Gradually stir about one-fourth of hot mixture into yolks; add to remaining hot mixture. Microwave, uncovered, at HIGH for 1 minute. Stir in lemon rind and lemon juice. Cool slightly; pour into pastry shell.

Beat egg whites (at room temperature) and cream of tartar at high speed of an electric mixer 1 minute. Gradually add ¼ cup plus 2 tablespoons sugar, 1 tablespoon at a time, beating until stiff peaks form and sugar dissolves.

Spread meringue over hot filling, sealing to edge of pastry. Reduce to MEDIUM (50% power); microwave, uncovered, for 2 minutes or until meringue is set. Let stand at least 10 minutes before serving. Yield: one 9-inch pie.

Note: If a browned meringue is desired, microwave, uncovered, at MEDIUM for 1 minute (rather than 2 minutes); then place pie under conventional broiler for 30 seconds or until lightly browned.

Pumpkin Pie

1 cup canned pumpkin
½ cup firmly packed brown
  sugar
⅔ cup milk
⅔ cup whipping cream
3 eggs, separated
1 tablespoon all-purpose flour
⅛ teaspoon salt
1 teaspoon ground cinnamon
½ teaspoon ground ginger
Microwaved or baked 9-inch
  pastry shell
Whipped cream (optional)
Additional ground cinnamon
  (optional)

Combine pumpkin, sugar, milk, whipping cream, egg yolks, flour, salt, 1 teaspoon cinnamon, and ginger in a large mixing bowl. Beat at low speed of an electric mixer until blended.

Beat egg whites (at room temperature) at high speed of an electric mixer until stiff peaks form; fold into pumpkin mixture. Microwave, uncovered, at HIGH for 3 minutes, stirring gently after 1½ minutes. Reduce to MEDIUM (50% power), and microwave for 9 to 10 minutes or until thickened, stirring gently with a wire whisk every 3 minutes.

Pour pumpkin mixture into pastry shell. Microwave, uncovered, at MEDIUM for 19 to 20 minutes or until filling is set, rotating a quarter-turn every 5 minutes. Let cool. Garnish with whipped cream and cinnamon, if desired. Yield: one 9-inch pie.

PECAN PIE

2 tablespoons butter or
  margarine
¾ cup light corn syrup
⅓ cup firmly packed dark
  brown sugar
3 eggs, slightly beaten
2 tablespoons molasses
1 tablespoon all-purpose flour
½ teaspoon vanilla extract
1 cup chopped pecans
Microwaved or baked 9-inch
  pastry shell

Place butter in a large bowl; microwave, uncovered, at HIGH for 45 seconds or until melted. Add corn syrup and next 5 ingredients, stirring well. Stir in pecans. Microwave, uncovered, at HIGH for 3 minutes or until sugar dissolves, stirring after 2 minutes. Pour into pastry shell. Reduce to MEDIUM (50% power), and microwave, uncovered, for 8½ to 10 minutes or until filling is set, rotating a half-turn every 4 minutes. Let cool before slicing. Yield: one 9-inch pie.

CRANBERRY-APPLE PIE

3 cups peeled, cored, and
   sliced cooking apples
2 cups fresh cranberries
⅔ cup sugar
¼ cup plus 2 tablespoons
   apple juice, divided
¼ teaspoon ground cinnamon
1 tablespoon cornstarch
Microwaved or baked 9-inch
   pastry shell
¾ cup chopped pecans

Combine apples, cranberries, sugar, ¼ cup apple juice, and cinnamon in a 2-quart casserole, stirring well. Cover with heavy-duty plastic wrap and microwave at HIGH for 7 to 8 minutes or until cranberry skins pop, stirring after 4 minutes. Combine remaining 2 tablespoons apple juice and cornstarch, stirring well. Add to apple mixture, stirring well. Microwave, uncovered, at HIGH for 4½ to 5 minutes or until thickened, stirring after 2 minutes. Pour into pastry shell.

Spread pecans in a pieplate. Microwave, uncovered, at HIGH for 4 to 5 minutes or until lightly toasted, stirring after every minute. Sprinkle evenly over pie. Microwave, uncovered, at HIGH for 2 minutes or until heated. Serve immediately. Yield: one 9-inch pie.

Make cutouts from top pastry. Arrange in a ring on wax paper, and microwave until dry.

SWEET APPLE PIE

6 cups peeled, cored, and
   thinly sliced cooking apples
⅔ cup sugar
¼ cup all-purpose flour
Dash of salt
½ teaspoon ground cinnamon
½ teaspoon ground nutmeg
2 tablespoons butter or
   margarine
Microwaved or baked
   double-crust 9-inch pastry
   shell

Combine apples and sugar in a 3-quart casserole; toss gently. Combine flour, salt, cinnamon, and nutmeg. Spoon over apple mixture. Dot with butter. Cover with heavy-duty plastic wrap and microwave at HIGH for 11 to 13 minutes or until apples are tender, stirring every 4 minutes. Spoon into pastry shell. Cover with top pastry. Microwave, uncovered, at HIGH for 1½ to 2 minutes or until heated. Serve immediately. Yield: one 9-inch pie.

CHERRY PIE

¾ cup sugar
2 tablespoons cornstarch
2 (16-ounce) cans red tart pitted
   cherries, undrained
3 to 4 drops red food coloring
½ teaspoon ground cinnamon
¼ teaspoon ground nutmeg
¼ teaspoon almond extract
Microwaved or baked
   double-crust 9-inch pastry
   shell

Combine sugar and cornstarch in a 1½-quart bowl, stirring well. Drain cherries, reserving ¾ cup juice; set cherries aside. Stir cherry juice into sugar mixture, and add food coloring. Microwave, uncovered, at HIGH for 5 to 6 minutes or until mixture is thickened, stirring after every minute. Stir in cherries, cinnamon, nutmeg, and almond extract.

Spoon into pastry shell. Cover with top pastry. Microwave, uncovered, at HIGH for 2 to 3 minutes or until thoroughly heated. Cool completely before serving. Yield: one 9-inch pie.

Transfer microwaved pastry cutouts to top of pie.

APPLE CRUNCH

6 cups peeled, cored, and
  thinly sliced cooking apples
⅔ cup firmly packed brown
  sugar, divided
1 tablespoon lemon juice
½ cup all-purpose flour
⅓ cup butter or margarine
⅔ cup regular oats, uncooked
½ cup chopped pecans
Vanilla ice cream

Combine apples, ⅓ cup brown sugar, and lemon juice; toss gently. Place in an 8-inch square baking dish; set aside.

Combine remaining ⅓ cup brown sugar and flour in a medium bowl. Cut in butter with a pastry blender until mixture resembles coarse meal. Stir in oats and pecans. Spoon mixture over apples. Microwave, uncovered, at HIGH for 12 to 13 minutes or until apples are tender, rotating a half-turn after 6 minutes. Spoon into individual dessert dishes, and top with ice cream. Yield: 6 to 8 servings.

CHERRY CRUNCH

⅓ cup butter or margarine
¾ cup quick-cooking oats,
  uncooked
½ cup firmly packed brown
  sugar
¾ cup all-purpose flour
½ teaspoon ground cinnamon
1 (21-ounce) can cherry pie
  filling
½ teaspoon almond extract
Vanilla ice cream

Place butter in a small bowl. Microwave, uncovered, at HIGH for 1 minute or until melted. Stir in oats and brown sugar. Microwave, uncovered, at HIGH for 2 minutes. Stir in flour and cinnamon.

Place pie filling in a 1-quart casserole. Stir in almond extract. Sprinkle crumb mixture over filling. Microwave, uncovered, at HIGH for 5 minutes or until thoroughly heated. Spoon into individual dessert dishes, and top with ice cream. Yield: 4 to 6 servings.

EASY APPLE-PECAN COBBLER

¼ cup chopped pecans
1 (21-ounce) can apple pie
  filling
½ cup biscuit mix
1 tablespoon brown sugar
3 tablespoons buttermilk
1 tablespoon sugar
¼ teaspoon ground cinnamon
Dash of nutmeg
Vanilla ice cream (optional)

Spread pecans in a pieplate. Microwave, uncovered, at HIGH for 2 to 4 minutes or until lightly toasted, stirring after every minute. Combine pie filling and pecans in a 1½-quart casserole. Microwave, uncovered, at HIGH for 3 to 5 minutes or until hot and bubbly, stirring after 2 minutes. Set aside.

Combine biscuit mix and brown sugar in a bowl. Add buttermilk, stirring well. Drop biscuit dough in 6 tablespoonfuls onto filling mixture. Combine sugar, cinnamon, and nutmeg; sprinkle over dough. Microwave, uncovered, at HIGH for 4½ to 5½ minutes or until dough is set, rotating a half-turn after 2 minutes. Spoon into individual dessert dishes, and top with ice cream, if desired. Yield: 4 to 6 servings.

Cinnamon Apples

3 tablespoons butter or
   margarine
2 tablespoons honey
1 tablespoon brandy
1 tablespoon orange juice
¼ teaspoon ground cinnamon
3 medium-size cooking apples,
   unpeeled, cored, and cut into
   ½-inch-thick rings

Place butter in a 12- x 8- x 2-inch baking dish. Microwave, uncovered, at HIGH for 50 seconds or until melted. Stir in honey, brandy, orange juice, and cinnamon.

Place apple rings in butter mixture, turning to coat well. Cover with heavy-duty plastic wrap and microwave at HIGH for 4 to 5 minutes or until apples are tender, rearranging apples after 2 minutes. Serve warm. Yield: 6 servings.

Bananas Foster

Place liqueur and rum in a glass measure, and microwave until hot. Ignite with a long match, and pour over Bananas Foster.

4 medium bananas
¼ cup butter or margarine
¼ cup firmly packed brown
   sugar
3 tablespoons pineapple
   preserves
½ teaspoon ground cinnamon
¼ cup banana-flavored liqueur
¼ cup light rum
Vanilla ice cream

Peel bananas, and slice in half lengthwise, then slice in half crosswise. Set aside.

Place butter in a shallow 2-quart casserole. Microwave, uncovered, at HIGH for 55 seconds or until melted. Stir in sugar, preserves, and cinnamon. Microwave, uncovered, at HIGH for 30 to 45 seconds or just until hot; stir well. Gently stir in bananas. Microwave, uncovered, at HIGH for 1½ to 2 minutes or until bananas are hot; stir gently.

Place liqueur and light rum in a 1-cup glass measure; microwave, uncovered, at HIGH for 1 minute or until hot. Ignite rum with a long match, and pour over bananas. After flames die down, serve immediately over ice cream. Yield: 8 servings.

Ruby Peach Melba

¼ cup slivered almonds
1 (10-ounce) package frozen
   raspberries
¼ cup sugar
¼ cup strawberry preserves
1 tablespoon lemon juice
1 tablespoon plus 1½
   teaspoons Cointreau or other
   orange-flavored liqueur
1 tablespoon cornstarch
1 (16-ounce) can peach halves,
   drained
Vanilla or peach ice cream

Spread almonds in a pieplate. Microwave, uncovered, at HIGH for 2 to 4 minutes or until lightly toasted, stirring after every minute; set almonds aside.

Place raspberries in a medium bowl; reduce to MEDIUM (50% power), and microwave, uncovered, for 5 to 6 minutes or until thawed. Press raspberries through a food mill or sieve; discard seeds. Add sugar, preserves, and lemon juice to raspberry puree; microwave, uncovered, at MEDIUM for 3 to 4 minutes or until preserves melt, stirring every 2 minutes.

Combine Cointreau and cornstarch; stir well. Add to raspberry mixture. Increase to HIGH

RUBY PEACH MELBA

(continued)

power; microwave, uncovered, for 3 to 4 minutes or until thickened. Cover and refrigerate.

Place peach halves, cut side up, in individual dessert dishes; top each with a scoop of ice cream and raspberry sauce. Sprinkle with almonds. Yield: 6 servings.

ZESTY WINE-POACHED ORANGES

4 large oranges
½ cup sugar
1⅓ cups sparkling white wine
    or champagne
3 tablespoons Grand Marnier
    or other orange-flavored
    liqueur
Orange rind curls (optional)

Remove fine strips of rind from 2 oranges with a zester; set zest aside. Peel all oranges, and cut into ½-inch-thick slices; arrange in a 12- x 8- x 2-inch baking dish.

Combine sugar and wine in a 4-cup glass measure. Microwave, uncovered, at HIGH for 8 to 9 minutes or until mixture has boiled 3 minutes. Stir in orange zest and Grand Marnier. Pour mixture over oranges; refrigerate at least 2 hours. Garnish each serving with an orange rind curl, if desired. Yield: 4 to 6 servings.

Zesty Wine-Poached Oranges is a simple but pretty fruit dessert.

PINEAPPLE PEARS

⅔ cup pineapple preserves
¼ cup orange juice
¼ cup Cointreau or other
  orange-flavored liqueur
2 (16-ounce) cans pear halves,
  drained
Orange rind strips (optional)

Combine pineapple preserves, orange juice, and Cointreau in an 8-inch square baking dish, stirring well. Arrange pears, cut side down, in dish. Cover with heavy-duty plastic wrap and microwave at HIGH for 6 to 8 minutes or until pears are hot. Let stand, covered, 2 minutes, basting with pineapple mixture after 1 minute.

Spoon pears into dessert dishes; spoon pineapple mixture over top, and garnish with orange rind strips, if desired. Yield: 6 servings.

RASPBERRY-POACHED PEARS

1 (10-ounce) package frozen
  raspberries
2 tablespoons Chambord or
  other raspberry-flavored
  liqueur
2 tablespoons Burgundy or
  other dry red wine
4 medium-size ripe pears
  (about 1½ pounds)
Fresh mint sprigs (optional)

Place raspberries in a medium bowl; microwave, uncovered, at MEDIUM (50% power) for 5 to 6 minutes or until thawed. Combine raspberries, liqueur, and wine in container of an electric blender; cover and process until smooth. Strain mixture through a food mill or sieve; discard seeds. Pour mixture into a deep 3-quart casserole. Set aside.

Carefully peel pears, removing core from bottom and leaving stems intact. Slice about ¼-inch from base of each pear so that it will sit flat.

Place pears, upright, in corners of casserole. Cover with heavy-duty plastic wrap and microwave at HIGH for 5 to 6 minutes or until pears are tender, rotating a quarter-turn every 2 minutes. Let stand, covered, 2 minutes.

Baste pears generously with raspberry puree; cover and refrigerate until thoroughly chilled. Transfer pears to a serving dish; spoon puree over pears, and garnish with mint sprigs, if desired. Yield: 4 servings.

To soften peach skins for easier peeling, place a small amount of water in the bottom of a bowl and add peaches; cover with heavy-duty plastic wrap and microwave at HIGH for 1 to 2 minutes or until steaming.

CUSTARD VANILLA ICE CREAM

2¼ cups sugar
¼ cup plus 2 tablespoons
   all-purpose flour
½ teaspoon salt
5 cups milk
5 eggs, beaten
1 quart whipping cream
1½ tablespoons vanilla extract

Combine sugar, flour, and salt in a large bowl; set aside. Place milk in a medium bowl; microwave, uncovered, at HIGH for 8 to 9 minutes or just until hot but not boiling. Gradually stir milk into sugar mixture. Microwave, uncovered, at HIGH for 10 to 11 minutes or until thickened, stirring every 4 minutes.

Gradually stir about one-fourth of hot milk mixture into beaten eggs; add to remaining hot milk mixture, stirring constantly. Microwave, uncovered, at HIGH for 1 minute. Let cool to room temperature; refrigerate 2 hours.

Combine whipping cream and vanilla in a large bowl; add chilled custard, stirring with a wire whisk to combine. Pour mixture into freezer can of a 1-gallon hand-turned or electric freezer. Freeze according to manufacturer's instructions. Let ripen at least 1½ to 2 hours. Yield: 2½ quarts.

CUSTARD PEACH ICE CREAM

4 cups mashed peaches
¾ cup sugar
3 eggs
1½ cups sugar
2 tablespoons all-purpose flour
½ teaspoon salt
1 quart milk
1 cup whipping cream
1 tablespoon vanilla extract

Combine peaches and ¾ cup sugar; stir well, and set aside.

Beat eggs at medium speed of an electric mixer until foamy. Combine 1½ cups sugar, flour, and salt; stir well. Gradually add sugar mixture to eggs, beating until thick and lemon colored. Set aside.

Place milk in a 4-cup glass measure; microwave, uncovered, at HIGH for 8 minutes or just until hot but not boiling. Gradually stir milk into egg mixture in a slow steady stream, stirring constantly. Cover with heavy-duty plastic wrap; reduce to MEDIUM (50% power), and microwave for 11 to 12 minutes or until mixture thickens and coats a metal spoon, stirring every 4 minutes. Set bowl in cold water; stir gently until custard is cool. Stir in whipping cream and vanilla. Add peach mixture, stirring well.

Pour mixture into freezer can of a 1-gallon hand-turned or electric freezer. Freeze according to manufacturer's instructions. Let ripen at least 1 hour. Yield: about 2½ quarts.

Individual Custards

1½ cups milk
½ cup sugar
3 eggs, beaten
1 teaspoon vanilla extract
Nutmeg

Combine milk and sugar in a 2-cup glass measure. Microwave, uncovered, at HIGH for 4 minutes or just until hot but not boiling. Gradually stir hot milk mixture into beaten eggs in a slow steady stream, stirring constantly; stir in vanilla. Pour mixture into four 6-ounce custard cups; set cups in a 9-inch square baking dish.

Place 1½ cups water in a 2-cup glass measure; microwave, uncovered, at HIGH for 4 minutes or until boiling. Pour water into baking dish around custard cups. Place baking dish in microwave oven; microwave, uncovered, at HIGH for 3 minutes. Rotate each cup a half-turn. Microwave, uncovered, at HIGH for 6 to 7 minutes or until edges of custards are set but centers still quiver, checking for doneness every 30 seconds and removing each custard when done. Let stand 15 minutes. Sprinkle with nutmeg; refrigerate until chilled. Yield: 4 servings.

Vanilla Crème Custard

¼ cup plus 1 tablespoon sugar, divided
2 tablespoons cornstarch
2 cups milk
2 egg yolks, beaten
1 teaspoon vanilla extract
Candied violets (optional)
Fresh mint leaves (optional)

Combine 3 tablespoons sugar and cornstarch in a 2-quart casserole; gradually add milk, stirring with a wire whisk. Microwave, uncovered, at HIGH for 6½ to 9 minutes or until mixture becomes thickened and bubbly, stirring every 3 minutes.

Gradually add remaining 2 tablespoons sugar to egg yolks, beating well. Gradually stir one-fourth of hot milk mixture into yolk mixture; add to remaining hot milk mixture, stirring constantly. Microwave, uncovered, at HIGH for 2 to 2½ minutes or until thickened, stirring after every minute. Add vanilla; stir with a wire whisk for 3 minutes. Spoon custard into stemmed glasses. Refrigerate until set. Garnish with candied violets and mint leaves, if desired. Yield: 4 servings.

Serve elegant Vanilla Crème Custard in stemmed glasses; garnish with mint leaves and candied violets.

One taste of our Pots de Crème and you will agree that it is the ultimate in rich chocolate desserts.

CHOCOLATE-ALMOND PUDDING

2 cups milk
⅓ cup sugar
3 tablespoons cocoa
2 tablespoons cornstarch
⅛ teaspoon salt
2 egg yolks, beaten
½ teaspoon vanilla extract
¼ teaspoon almond extract
¼ cup sliced almonds
½ cup whipping cream
2 tablespoons powdered sugar

Place milk in a 1½-quart casserole. Microwave, uncovered, at HIGH for 3 to 3½ minutes or just until hot but not boiling. Combine ⅓ cup sugar, cocoa, cornstarch, and salt; stir into hot milk. Gradually stir about one-fourth of hot milk mixture into egg yolks; add to remaining hot milk mixture, stirring constantly. Microwave, uncovered, at HIGH for 3½ minutes or until thickened, stirring after 1½ minutes. Stir in flavorings. Spoon into serving dishes; refrigerate until chilled.

CHOCOLATE-ALMOND PUDDING

(continued)

Spread almonds in a 9-inch pieplate. Microwave, uncovered, at HIGH for 2 to 4 minutes or until lightly toasted, stirring after every minute.

Beat whipping cream until foamy; gradually add powdered sugar, beating until soft peaks form. Spoon over pudding; sprinkle with almonds. Yield: 4 servings.

POTS DE CRÈME

2 (4-ounce) packages sweet
  baking chocolate
1 tablespoon powdered sugar
1 cup whipping cream
4 egg yolks, beaten
1 tablespoon Grand Marnier or
  other orange-flavored liqueur
Whipped cream (optional)
Chocolate leaves (optional)

Place chocolate in a 4-cup glass measure. Microwave, uncovered, at HIGH for 2½ to 3½ minutes or until softened, stirring after 1 minute. Stir until smooth and melted. Stir in sugar. Gradually add 1 cup whipping cream, stirring until smooth. Microwave, uncovered, at HIGH for 2 to 2½ minutes or just until hot but not boiling, stirring after 1 minute.

Gradually stir about one-fourth of chocolate mixture into egg yolks; add to remaining chocolate mixture, stirring constantly. Stir in liqueur. Spoon into small cordial glasses or demitasse cups. Cover and refrigerate 1 to 2 hours or until set. Garnish with whipped cream and chocolate leaves, if desired. Yield: 6 servings.

LEMON TAPIOCA CREAM

2 cups milk
⅓ cup sugar
3 tablespoons quick-cooking
  tapioca
⅛ teaspoon salt
2 eggs, separated
1 tablespoon sugar
2 teaspoons grated lemon rind
2 tablespoons lemon juice
Lemon slices (optional)

Combine milk, ⅓ cup sugar, tapioca, salt, and egg yolks in a 2-quart bowl; beat at low speed of an electric mixer until blended. Microwave, uncovered, at HIGH for 7 to 8 minutes or until thickened, stirring every 3 minutes. Let cool to room temperature.

Beat egg whites (at room temperature) at high speed of an electric mixer until foamy. Gradually add 1 tablespoon sugar, beating until stiff peaks form. Gently fold in lemon rind and juice. Fold egg white mixture into cooled pudding mixture; spoon into dessert dishes. Refrigerate until set. Garnish with lemon slices, if desired. Yield: 4 servings.

Kahlúa Mousse

6 (1-ounce) squares semisweet
  chocolate
¼ cup water
½ teaspoon instant coffee
  powder
2 eggs
½ cup sugar
3 tablespoons Kahlúa or other
  coffee-flavored liqueur
1 cup whipping cream,
  whipped
Additional whipped cream
  (optional)
Fresh mint leaves (optional)
Mandarin orange slices
  (optional)

Combine chocolate, water, and coffee powder in a small bowl; microwave, uncovered, at MEDIUM (50% power) for 2 to 3 minutes or until chocolate is softened, stirring after 2 minutes. Stir until smooth and melted. Set chocolate mixture aside, and let cool.

Beat eggs in a medium bowl at medium speed of an electric mixer until thick and lemon colored. Add sugar and Kahlúa, beating well. Gradually add melted chocolate mixture in a slow steady stream, beating until blended. Cool completely. Fold in whipped cream. Spoon into small cordial glasses or custard cups. Cover and refrigerate at least 2 hours. Garnish with additional whipped cream, mint leaves, and orange slices, if desired. Yield: 6 servings.

Crème De Menthe Soufflé

2 envelopes unflavored gelatin
1 cup cold water
1½ cups hot water
4 eggs, separated
¾ cup sugar
1 (8-ounce) package cream
  cheese
¼ cup green crème de menthe
¼ cup sugar
1 cup whipping cream,
  whipped
Fresh mint leaves (optional)

Cut a piece of aluminum foil or wax paper long enough to fit around a 1½-quart soufflé dish, allowing a 1-inch overlap; fold lengthwise into thirds. Lightly oil one side; wrap around outside of dish, oiled side against dish, allowing it to extend 3 inches above rim to form a collar. Secure with freezer tape; set aside.

Combine gelatin and 1 cup cold water; stir well, and set aside. Place 1½ cups hot water in a 3-quart casserole; microwave, uncovered, at HIGH for 6 minutes or until boiling. Add gelatin mixture, stirring until dissolved.

Beat egg yolks until thick and lemon colored; gradually add ¾ cup sugar, beating well. Gradually stir about one-fourth of hot gelatin mixture into yolks; add to remaining hot gelatin mixture, stirring constantly. Microwave, uncovered, at HIGH for 4 minutes or until thickened, stirring after 2 minutes. Set aside. Place cream cheese in a large bowl; microwave, uncovered, at HIGH for 45 seconds to 1 minute or until softened. Beat cream cheese at low speed of an electric mixer until smooth; gradually add yolk mixture, beating well. Stir in crème de menthe; refrigerate until slightly thickened.

The custard-like base of Crème de Menthe Soufflé is held firm by the addition of gelatin, beaten egg whites, and whipped cream.

CRÈME DE MENTHE SOUFFLÉ
(continued)

Beat egg whites (at room temperature) at high speed of an electric mixer until foamy; gradually add ¼ cup sugar, 1 tablespoon at a time, beating until stiff peaks form. Gently fold whipped cream and beaten egg whites into chilled cream cheese mixture. Spoon into prepared dish, and refrigerate until firm. Remove collar from dish; garnish soufflé with mint leaves, if desired. Yield: 8 servings.

BAVARIAN CREAM

½ cup plus 2 tablespoons
   sugar, divided
3 tablespoons cornstarch
2 envelopes unflavored gelatin
¼ teaspoon salt
2¾ cups milk
2 eggs, separated
2 tablespoons crème de cacao
1 cup whipping cream,
   whipped
Fresh raspberries (optional)
Fresh mint leaves (optional)

Combine ½ cup sugar, cornstarch, gelatin, and salt in a large bowl; stir well. Gradually add milk, stirring well. Microwave, uncovered, at HIGH for 8 to 10 minutes or until thickened, stirring every 3 minutes.

Beat egg yolks. Gradually stir about one-fourth of hot milk mixture into yolks; add to remaining hot milk mixture, stirring constantly. Reduce to MEDIUM HIGH (70% power); microwave, uncovered, for 2 to 3 minutes or until slightly thickened, stirring after every minute. Cool in refrigerator until mixture mounds slightly (about 1 hour). Stir in crème de cacao.

Beat egg whites (at room temperature) at high speed of an electric mixer until soft peaks form. Gradually add 2 tablespoons remaining sugar, 1 tablespoon at a time, beating until stiff peaks form. Fold egg whites and whipped cream into gelatin mixture. Spoon into a lightly oiled 6-cup mold. Refrigerate until set. Unmold onto serving platter, and garnish with raspberries and mint leaves, if desired. Yield: 6 cups.

CHARLOTTE RUSSE

1 envelope unflavored gelatin
¼ cup milk
2 eggs
¾ cup sugar
1 cup milk
1 cup orange juice
⅛ teaspoon salt
¼ cup cream sherry
1 teaspoon vanilla extract
2 cups whipping cream,
   whipped
About 7 ladyfingers, split
   lengthwise
2 tablespoons slivered almonds

Soften gelatin in ¼ cup milk; set aside. Beat eggs at low speed of an electric mixer until thick and lemon colored; gradually add sugar, beating well. Stir in 1 cup milk, orange juice, and salt. Microwave, uncovered, at HIGH for 5 to 6 minutes or until slightly thickened, stirring every 2 minutes. Stir in gelatin mixture; refrigerate until slightly thickened.

Add sherry and vanilla to thickened mixture, stirring gently; fold in whipped cream. Line sides of a 2-quart bowl with ladyfingers. Pour in filling; refrigerate at least 8 hours.

Spread almonds in a pieplate; microwave, uncovered, at HIGH for 2 to 3 minutes or until lightly toasted, stirring after every minute. Sprinkle almonds over chilled mixture. Yield: 8 to 10 servings.

Stately Bavarian Cream stands tall at even the most formal of occasions.

Eggs and Cheese

Eggs should always be treated with a gentle hand, and this is especially true when cooking in the microwave oven. You can make scrambled, poached, fried, or hard-cooked eggs in your microwave, but keep the following special techniques in mind.

When scrambling eggs, be sure to mix the yolks and whites thoroughly, maybe even adding a little milk or liquid to keep them moist. Before frying or poaching eggs, prick the yolks several times with a wooden pick or fork so that they won't explode. For fried eggs, use a special microwave browning dish, being sure to prick the yolks.

Hard-cooked eggs as we usually think of them are absolutely forbidden in the microwave oven. If left in the shell the egg can explode, sometimes with disastrous results. However, you can break the egg into a custard cup, pierce the yolk, and microwave until firm enough to chop for salads or sauces.

Omelets are made with satisfactory results in the microwave, but hot soufflés are generally too tricky. We had good results with our quiche recipes. You can prepare them using our microwaved quiche pastry shell or your own conventionally baked pastry shell. For a microwaved quiche, the pastry shell is microwaved first so that it will stay crisper and drier. Elevating the quiche while microwaving and allowing it to stand after cooking will produce the best results.

Cheese is another item that must be treated with care in the microwave oven. If cooked too long at too high of power, cheese will become tough and stringy. But it will melt perfectly if added to the dish at the last minute or added and heated only briefly. If cheese is a major ingredient in a casserole, the casserole will probably be best cooked at MEDIUM (50% power).

For a change of pace, enjoy Sunny Eggs With Asparagus and Crabmeat (page 111) with morning coffee and juice.

Start your day off right with Cream Cheese Scrambled Eggs.

CREAM CHEESE SCRAMBLED EGGS

6 eggs
¼ cup milk
¼ cup club soda
1 (3-ounce) package cream
** cheese, cubed**
¼ teaspoon salt
⅛ teaspoon pepper
2 tablespoons butter or
** margarine**
3 tablespoons chopped green
** onions**

Combine eggs, milk, club soda, cream cheese, salt, and pepper in container of an electric blender; cover and process until foamy (7 to 10 seconds). Set aside.

Place butter in a 1½-quart casserole; microwave, uncovered, at HIGH for 45 seconds or until melted. Add egg mixture; sprinkle with onions, and stir well. Cover with heavy-duty plastic wrap and microwave at HIGH for 2½ minutes. Break up set portions with a fork, and push towards center of dish. Cover and microwave at HIGH for 3 to 4½ minutes or until eggs are almost set, stirring after every minute. Let stand, covered, 2 minutes. Serve immediately. Yield: 4 servings.

BACON AND EGG SCRAMBLE

4 slices bacon, diced
¼ cup sliced green onions
4 eggs
2 tablespoons club soda
¼ teaspoon garlic salt
⅛ teaspoon pepper
⅛ teaspoon dry mustard

Place bacon in a 1-quart casserole. Microwave, uncovered, at HIGH for 2 minutes; add onions, stirring well. Microwave, uncovered, at HIGH for 3 minutes or until bacon is almost done and onion is tender. Drain off drippings.

Combine eggs, club soda, salt, pepper, and mustard in a small bowl; beat slightly. Add egg mixture to bacon mixture; stir well. Cover with heavy-duty plastic wrap and microwave at HIGH for 1 minute. Break up set portions of egg with a fork, and push toward center of dish. Cover and microwave at HIGH for 2 minutes or until eggs are almost set, stirring after 1 minute. Let stand, covered, 1 minute. Serve immediately. Yield: 2 servings.

CHEDDARY EGGS AND CHILES

4 slices bacon
¼ cup chopped green onions
2 teaspoons butter or margarine
1 (4-ounce) can chopped green
  chiles, drained
4 eggs
2 tablespoons milk
2 tablespoons diced pimiento
¼ teaspoon celery salt
Dash of pepper
½ cup (2 ounces) shredded
  Cheddar cheese

Place bacon on a rack in a baking dish. Cover with paper towels and microwave at HIGH for 3½ to 4½ minutes or until crisp. Crumble bacon, and set aside.

Combine onions and butter in a 9-inch pieplate. Microwave, uncovered, at HIGH for 30 seconds to 1 minute or until onions are tender. Stir in green chiles.

Combine eggs, milk, pimiento, salt, and pepper in a medium bowl; beat slightly. Pour into pieplate. Add bacon, stirring well. Cover with heavy-duty plastic wrap and microwave at HIGH for 3 minutes, stirring after 1½ minutes. Sprinkle with cheese. Reduce to MEDIUM HIGH (70% power); cover and microwave for 1 minute or until cheese melts. Let stand, covered, 1 minute. Serve immediately. Yield: 4 servings.

SCRAMBLED EGG PITAS

6 eggs
⅓ cup milk
¼ teaspoon garlic salt
¼ teaspoon pepper
¼ cup (1 ounce) shredded
  American cheese
1 small tomato, seeded and
  chopped
2 (8-inch) pita bread rounds,
  cut in half
Curly leaf lettuce
¼ cup commercial picante
  sauce
¼ cup fresh alfalfa sprouts

Combine eggs, milk, salt, and pepper in a 1-quart casserole, stirring well. Cover with heavy-duty plastic wrap and microwave at HIGH for 4 to 4½ minutes or until eggs are set, stirring every 2 minutes. Sprinkle with cheese. Cover and microwave at HIGH for 30 seconds or until cheese is melted. Stir in tomato.

Line cut bread rounds with lettuce leaves; fill with egg mixture. Top each with picante sauce and alfalfa sprouts. Serve immediately. Yield: 4 servings.

EGG AND SAUSAGE TORTILLAS

½ pound bulk pork sausage
½ cup chopped green onions
2 tablespoons butter or margarine
4 eggs
2 tablespoons whipping cream
½ teaspoon salt
¼ teaspoon pepper
½ cup (2 ounces) shredded sharp Cheddar cheese
8 (6-inch) flour tortillas
Shredded lettuce
Commercial taco sauce
Commercial sour cream

Combine sausage and green onions in a 1½-quart casserole. Cover with wax paper and microwave at HIGH for 3½ to 4 minutes or until sausage is no longer pink, stirring after 2 minutes. Drain well, and set aside.

Place butter in a 9-inch pieplate. Microwave, uncovered, at HIGH for 45 seconds or until melted. Combine eggs, cream, salt, and pepper; stir well. Pour into pieplate. Cover with heavy-duty plastic wrap and microwave at HIGH for 2½ to 3 minutes or until eggs are set, stirring after 1½ minutes. Add egg mixture and cheese to sausage mixture. Cover with heavy-duty plastic wrap and microwave at HIGH for 1 minute or until cheese begins to melt.

Place 4 tortillas between damp paper towels. Microwave at HIGH for 40 seconds to 1 minute or until thoroughly heated. Repeat procedure with remaining tortillas. Spoon egg mixture into tortillas, and roll up jellyroll fashion. Place tortillas, seam side down, on a 12-inch round glass platter. Microwave, uncovered, at HIGH for 1 minute or until thoroughly heated. Serve tortillas immediately with lettuce, taco sauce, and sour cream. Yield: 8 servings.

Ensure a puffy omelet by gently folding egg yolks into stiffly beaten egg whites.

PUFFED CHEESE OMELET

4 eggs, separated
3 tablespoons milk
¼ teaspoon salt
¼ teaspoon baking powder
¼ teaspoon paprika
⅛ teaspoon pepper
1 tablespoon butter or margarine
¼ cup (1 ounce) shredded Swiss or Cheddar cheese

Beat egg whites (at room temperature) at high speed of an electric mixer until stiff but not dry. Combine egg yolks, milk, salt, baking powder, paprika, and pepper; beat well. Gently fold egg yolk mixture into egg whites.

Place butter in a 9-inch pieplate. Microwave, uncovered, at HIGH for 35 seconds or until melted. Pour egg mixture into pieplate. Place pieplate in microwave oven on an inverted saucer. Reduce to MEDIUM (50% power); microwave, uncovered, for 3 to 4 minutes or until center is partially set, rotating a quarter-turn after 2 minutes. Gently lift edges of omelet with a spatula so uncooked portion spreads to outside of pieplate. Microwave, uncovered, at HIGH for 2 to 3 minutes or until center is set.

Sprinkle cheese over half of omelet. Loosen omelet with spatula, and fold in half. Gently slide omelet onto a serving plate. Serve immediately. Yield: 4 servings.

Delight early risers with a puffy Vegetable Omelet. It's filled with green pepper, onion, pimiento, and cheese.

VEGETABLE OMELET

¼ cup chopped green pepper
¼ cup chopped onion
1 tablespoon sliced pimiento
1 tablespoon butter or
  margarine
⅛ teaspoon dried whole basil
3 eggs, separated
⅛ teaspoon cream of tartar
1 tablespoon commercial sour
  cream
1 tablespoon mayonnaise
Dash of white pepper
2 teaspoons butter or margarine
¼ cup (1 ounce) shredded
  Monterey Jack cheese
Sprigs of fresh basil (optional)
Orange slices (optional)

Combine first 5 ingredients in a 1-quart casserole; cover with heavy-duty plastic wrap and microwave at HIGH for 3 to 3½ minutes or until vegetables are crisp-tender. Set aside.

Beat egg whites (at room temperature) and cream of tartar at medium speed of an electric mixer until stiff but not dry. Combine yolks, sour cream, mayonnaise, and pepper; beat well. Gently fold egg yolk mixture into whites.

Place 2 teaspoons butter in a 9-inch pieplate. Microwave, uncovered, at HIGH for 35 seconds or until melted. Pour egg mixture into pieplate. Place pieplate in microwave oven on an inverted saucer. Microwave, uncovered, at HIGH for 2½ to 3 minutes or just until center is set. Spread vegetable mixture over half of omelet; sprinkle with cheese. Loosen omelet with a spatula, and fold in half. Gently slide omelet onto a serving plate; garnish with basil and orange slices, if desired. Serve immediately. Yield: 2 servings.

Loosen one side of omelet with a spatula, and fold over filling.

Fluffy Sausage Omelet

¼ pound bulk pork sausage
2 tablespoons chopped green
 onions
¼ cup commercial sour cream
1 tablespoon minced fresh
 parsley
3 eggs, separated
⅛ teaspoon cream of tartar
2 tablespoons mayonnaise
⅛ teaspoon white pepper
1 tablespoon butter or
 margarine
¼ cup strawberry or peach
 preserves

Combine sausage and onions in a 1-quart casserole. Cover with wax paper and microwave at HIGH for 3½ to 4 minutes or until sausage is no longer pink; drain off drippings. Stir in sour cream and parsley; set aside.

Beat egg whites (at room temperature) and cream of tartar at high speed of an electric mixer until stiff but not dry; set aside. Combine egg yolks, mayonnaise, and pepper; beat well. Gently fold egg yolk mixture into egg whites.

Place butter in a 9-inch pieplate. Microwave, uncovered, at HIGH for 35 seconds or until melted. Pour egg mixture into pieplate. Place pieplate in microwave oven on an inverted saucer. Microwave, uncovered, at HIGH for 2½ to 3 minutes or just until center is set, rotating a half-turn after 1½ minutes.

Spread sausage mixture over half of omelet. Loosen omelet with a spatula, and fold in half. Gently slide omelet onto a serving plate; set aside. Place preserves in a 1-cup glass measure; microwave, uncovered, at HIGH for 45 seconds or until melted. Drizzle over omelet; serve immediately. Yield: 2 servings.

Open-Faced Pizza Omelet

2 teaspoons butter or margarine
4 eggs, separated
¼ teaspoon cream of tartar
⅛ teaspoon white pepper
¼ cup tomato sauce
2 tablespoons finely chopped
 green onions
⅛ teaspoon dried whole
 oregano
⅛ teaspoon dried whole thyme
4 ripe olives, sliced
¼ cup (1 ounce) shredded
 mozzarella cheese
12 thin slices pepperoni

Place butter in a 9-inch pieplate; microwave, uncovered, at HIGH for 35 seconds or until melted; set aside.

Beat egg whites (at room temperature) and cream of tartar at high speed of an electric mixer until stiff but not dry. Combine yolks and pepper; beat well. Gently fold egg yolk mixture into whites. Pour mixture into prepared pieplate. Microwave, uncovered, at HIGH for 2 to 3 minutes or until center is partially set, rotating a quarter-turn after 1½ minutes.

Spoon tomato sauce over center of omelet; sprinkle with onions, oregano, thyme, olives, and cheese. Arrange pepperoni slices around outer edge. Microwave, uncovered, at HIGH for 1 minute or just until center is set and cheese begins to melt. Cut into wedges; serve immediately. Yield: 6 servings.

CREAMED EGGS IN PATTY SHELLS

4 eggs
2 tablespoons butter or
   margarine
1 tablespoon all-purpose flour
⅛ teaspoon pepper
1 cup milk
1 (2½-ounce) jar dried beef,
   rinsed, drained, and chopped
½ cup (2 ounces) shredded
   Cheddar cheese
¼ cup chopped pimiento,
   drained
2 tablespoons chopped fresh
   parsley
4 baked patty shells
Chopped fresh chives

Gently break 1 egg into each of four 6-ounce custard cups. Pierce each yolk several times with a wooden pick or fork. Cover each cup with heavy-duty plastic wrap; arrange cups in a circle in microwave oven. Microwave at MEDIUM (50% power) for 5 to 7 minutes or until partially set. Let stand, covered, 2 minutes. Chop eggs, and set aside.

Place butter in a 4-cup glass measure. Microwave, uncovered, at HIGH for 45 seconds or until melted. Stir in flour and pepper. Gradually stir in milk. Microwave, uncovered, at HIGH for 3½ to 4 minutes or until thickened, stirring after 2 minutes. Stir in chopped eggs, beef, cheese, pimiento, and parsley. Reduce to MEDIUM, and microwave, uncovered, for 1 minute or until thoroughly heated. Spoon mixture into patty shells. Sprinkle with chives. Serve immediately. Yield: 4 servings

To hard-cook eggs, break each egg into a custard cup, and pierce each yolk. Cover and microwave until firm enough to chop.

EGG SPREAD ON BAGELS

3 eggs
1 (8-ounce) package cream
   cheese
2 tablespoons mayonnaise
1 tablespoon milk
2 teaspoons chopped fresh
   chives
¼ teaspoon salt
⅛ teaspoon pepper
3 bagels, split and toasted
Paprika (optional)

Gently break 1 egg into each of three 6-ounce custard cups. Pierce each yolk several times with a wooden pick or fork. Cover each cup with heavy-duty plastic wrap; arrange eggs in a triangle in microwave oven. Microwave at MEDIUM (50% power) for 4 to 5 minutes or until partially set. Let stand, covered, 2 minutes. Chop eggs, and set aside.

Place cream cheese in a small bowl. Microwave, uncovered, at HIGH for 45 seconds to 1 minute or until softened. Add chopped eggs, mayonnaise, milk, chives, salt, and pepper, stirring well. Spread on toasted bagels. Sprinkle with paprika, if desired. Serve immediately. Yield: 3 to 6 servings.

When poaching an egg, add vinegar to the water to help prevent the egg white from spreading. You will end up with a more compact, prettier egg.

Brunch Eggs Over Corn Muffins

4 eggs
½ cup all-purpose flour
½ cup yellow cornmeal
1 tablespoon sugar
2 teaspoons baking powder
½ teaspoon salt
⅓ cup milk
¼ cup vegetable oil
1 egg, slightly beaten
2 tablespoons butter or
   margarine
1 tablespoon plus 2 teaspoons
   all-purpose flour
1⅓ cups milk
¼ cup mayonnaise
⅛ teaspoon salt
⅛ teaspoon pepper
2 green onions, chopped
½ cup (2 ounces) finely
   shredded Cheddar cheese

Gently break 1 egg into each of four 6-ounce custard cups. Pierce each yolk several times with a wooden pick or fork. Cover each cup with heavy-duty plastic wrap; arrange eggs in a circle in microwave oven. Microwave at MEDIUM (50% power) for 3 to 4 minutes, or until partially set. Let stand, covered, 2 minutes. Chop eggs, and set aside.

Combine ½ cup flour, cornmeal, sugar, baking powder, and ½ teaspoon salt in a large bowl; make a well in center of mixture. Combine ⅓ cup milk, vegetable oil, and beaten egg; add to dry ingredients, stirring just until moistened. Line eight 6-ounce custard cups with a double layer of paper liners. Spoon batter into paper liners. Place 4 cups in a circle in microwave oven. Microwave, uncovered, at HIGH for 1½ to 2 minutes or until surface is only slightly wet, rearranging cups after 1 minute. Remove muffins from cups, and let stand on a wire rack for 2 minutes. Repeat procedure with remaining batter; set aside.

Place butter in a 4-cup glass measure and microwave, uncovered, at HIGH for 45 seconds or until melted. Stir in 1 tablespoon plus 2 teaspoons flour. Gradually add 1⅓ cups milk, stirring well. Microwave, uncovered, at HIGH for 4 to 5 minutes or until thickened, stirring every 2 minutes. Stir in mayonnaise, ⅛ teaspoon salt, pepper, and eggs; set aside.

Remove muffins from paper liners, and slice in half horizontally. Spoon egg mixture over muffins. Sprinkle with onions and cheese. Serve immediately. Yield: 8 servings.

Breakfast Cheese Sandwiches

8 slices bacon
4 eggs
4 slices bread, toasted
4 (1-ounce) slices process
   American cheese
4 slices tomato
Hot Cheese Sauce

Place bacon on a rack in a baking dish. Cover with paper towels and microwave at HIGH for 6 to 8 minutes or until crisp. Crumble bacon, and set aside.

Gently break 1 egg into each of four 6-ounce custard cups. Pierce each yolk several times with a wooden pick or fork. Cover each cup with heavy-duty plastic wrap; arrange cups in a circle in microwave oven. Reduce to MEDIUM (50% power); microwave for 3 minutes or until partially set. Let stand, covered, 2 minutes.

Sprinkle slices of toast with bacon; top each with a slice of cheese and tomato. Remove eggs from custard cups; place 1 egg on each slice of tomato. Top with Hot Cheese Sauce; serve immediately. Yield: 2 to 4 servings.

HOT CHEESE SAUCE:

2 tablespoons finely chopped sweet red or green pepper
1 tablespoon butter or margarine
1 tablespoon all-purpose flour
⅛ teaspoon salt
½ cup milk
Dash of hot sauce
½ cup (2 ounces) shredded sharp Cheddar cheese

Place red pepper and butter in a 2-cup glass measure; microwave, uncovered, at HIGH for 1 to 2 minutes or until pepper is crisp-tender. Stir in flour and salt. Gradually add milk and hot sauce, stirring well; microwave, uncovered, at HIGH for 3 to 4 minutes or until thickened, stirring after every minute. Add cheese; stir until melted. Yield: about ¾ cup.

EASY EGGS BENEDICT

½ cup water, divided
1 teaspoon vinegar, divided
4 eggs
4 thin slices Canadian bacon
2 English muffins, split and toasted
Blender Hollandaise Sauce
Paprika

Place 2 tablespoons water in each of four 6-ounce custard cups; add ¼ teaspoon vinegar to each. Arrange cups in a circle in microwave oven or on a 12-inch round glass platter. Microwave, uncovered, at HIGH for 2 to 3 minutes or until water is boiling. Gently break 1 egg into each cup; pierce yolks several times with a wooden pick or fork. Cover cups with heavy-duty plastic wrap. Reduce to MEDIUM HIGH (70% power), and microwave for 2 to 3 minutes or until almost all of white is opaque, rearranging cups or rotating platter a half-turn after 1 minute. Let stand, covered, 2 minutes.

Arrange bacon on a plate; cover with wax paper and microwave at HIGH for 1 to 1½ minutes or until thoroughly heated. Place 1 slice bacon on each muffin half. Remove eggs from custard cups with a slotted spoon; place 1 egg on each bacon slice. Top with Blender Hollandaise Sauce, and sprinkle with paprika. Serve immediately. Yield: 2 to 4 servings.

To poach eggs, break each egg into a custard cup filled with 2 tablespoons water and ¼ teaspoon vinegar. Pierce egg yolks; cover and microwave until egg whites are opaque.

BLENDER HOLLANDAISE SAUCE:

½ cup butter or margarine
3 egg yolks
1 tablespoon plus 1½ teaspoons lemon juice
¼ teaspoon salt
Dash of white pepper

Place butter in a 2-cup glass measure; microwave, uncovered, at HIGH for 1 minute or until melted (do not allow butter to boil).

Combine yolks and remaining ingredients in container of an electric blender; process until thick and lemon colored. With blender running, add hot butter in a slow steady stream; process until thickened. Yield: about ¾ cup.

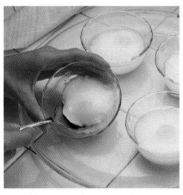

Remove poached eggs with a slotted spoon.

FLORENTINE EGGS

4 slices bacon
1 (10-ounce) package frozen
   chopped spinach
¼ cup finely chopped onion
2 tablespoons butter or
   margarine
1 clove garlic, crushed
⅓ cup commercial sour cream
1 (2-ounce) jar sliced pimiento,
   drained
1 teaspoon grated lemon rind
¼ teaspoon pepper
Dash of hot sauce
4 eggs
¼ cup (1 ounce) finely
   shredded sharp Cheddar
   cheese

Place bacon on a rack in a baking dish; cover with paper towels. Microwave at HIGH for 3½ to 4½ minutes or until bacon is crisp; drain. Crumble bacon, and set aside. Remove wrapper from spinach package; place package in a baking dish. Microwave at HIGH for 3 to 5 minutes or until thawed. Drain spinach, pressing between layers of paper towels to remove excess moisture; set aside.

Combine onion, butter, and garlic in a 2-cup glass measure. Cover with heavy-duty plastic wrap and microwave at HIGH for 3 to 4 minutes or until onion is tender. Combine onion mixture, spinach, sour cream, pimiento, lemon rind, pepper, and hot sauce, stirring well. Spoon mixture evenly into four 6-ounce custard cups. Arrange cups in a circle in microwave oven. Microwave, uncovered, at HIGH for 3½ to 4 minutes or until thoroughly heated.

Gently break 1 egg into each cup; pierce each yolk several times with a wooden pick or fork. Cover each cup with heavy-duty plastic wrap;

arrange cups in a circle in microwave oven. Microwave at HIGH for 2 minutes, rearranging cups after 1 minute. Let stand, covered, 1 minute. Sprinkle eggs with bacon and cheese. Serve immediately. Yield: 4 servings.

SUNNY EGGS WITH ASPARAGUS AND CRABMEAT

1 pound fresh asparagus spears
(16 to 32 spears)
⅓ cup water
½ pound fresh lump crabmeat,
drained and flaked
2 tablespoons chopped green
onions
1 tablespoon plus 1½
teaspoons butter or
margarine
¼ teaspoon salt
¼ teaspoon white pepper
½ cup water, divided
1 teaspoon vinegar, divided
4 eggs
½ cup butter or margarine
2 tablespoons chopped fresh
tarragon or 2 teaspoons dried
whole tarragon
2 tablespoons Chablis or other
dry white wine
1 tablespoon lemon juice
¼ teaspoon salt
4 egg yolks, beaten
Chopped fresh mint (optional)
Fresh mint sprigs (optional)
Strawberries (optional)

Snap off tough ends of asparagus. Remove scales from stalks with a knife or vegetable peeler, if desired. Arrange spears in a 10- x 6- x 2-inch baking dish with stem ends towards outside. Add ⅓ cup water. Cover with heavy-duty plastic wrap and microwave at HIGH for 4 to 6 minutes or until crisp-tender. Let stand, covered, 5 minutes. Drain and keep warm.

Place crabmeat, green onions, and 1 tablespoon plus 1½ teaspoons butter in a 1-quart casserole. Cover with heavy-duty plastic wrap and microwave at HIGH for 1½ to 2½ minutes or until butter melts and crabmeat is thoroughly heated, stirring after 1 minute. Stir in ¼ teaspoon salt and white pepper; set aside.

Place 2 tablespoons water in each of four 6-ounce custard cups; add ¼ teaspoon vinegar to each. Arrange cups in a circle in microwave oven or on a 12-inch round glass platter. Microwave, uncovered, at HIGH for 2 to 3 minutes or until water is boiling. Gently break 1 egg into each cup; pierce yolks several times with a wooden pick or fork. Cover cups with heavy-duty plastic wrap. Reduce to MEDIUM HIGH (70% power), and microwave for 2 to 3 minutes or until almost all of white is opaque, rearranging cups or rotating platter a half-turn after 1 minute. Let stand, covered, 2 minutes.

Place ½ cup butter in a 1-quart casserole. Microwave, uncovered, at HIGH for 1 minute or until melted. Stir in tarragon, wine, lemon juice, and ¼ teaspoon salt. Let cool to room temperature. Add 4 beaten egg yolks, stirring well. Reduce to MEDIUM (50% power), and microwave, uncovered, for 1½ minutes or until thickened, stirring every 30 seconds.

Divide asparagus evenly among 4 serving plates. Spoon crabmeat mixture evenly over each serving. Remove eggs from custard cups with a slotted spoon; place over crabmeat. Top with sauce mixture. Garnish with mint and strawberries, if desired. Serve immediately. Yield: 4 servings.

QUICHE PASTRY

Gently prick bottom and sides of quiche pastry shell with a fork.

Microwave the quiche pastry shell until it looks opaque and the bottom of the shell is dry.

1 cup all-purpose flour
½ teaspoon salt
¼ cup shortening
2 tablespoons cold butter
2 tablespoons plus 1 teaspoon cold water
Vegetable cooking spray

Combine flour and salt; cut in shortening and butter with a pastry blender until mixture resembles coarse meal. Sprinkle water, 1 tablespoon at a time, evenly over surface; stir with a fork until all ingredients are moistened. Shape into a ball. Cover with heavy-duty plastic wrap, and freeze 10 minutes. Lightly spray a 9-inch quiche dish or pieplate with vegetable cooking spray; set aside.

Remove pastry from freezer, and roll to ⅛-inch thickness on a lightly floured surface. Place pastry loosely in quiche dish, leaving a ½-inch overhang. Fold edges under, and press firmly to seal; flute if using a pieplate.

Gently prick bottom and sides of pastry with a fork. Microwave, uncovered, at HIGH for 6½ to 7½ minutes or until pastry is opaque and bottom is dry, rotating a half-turn after 3 minutes. Yield: one 9-inch quiche pastry.

SAUSAGE-CHILE QUICHE

½ pound bulk pork sausage
½ cup chopped green pepper
½ cup chopped green onions
1 (4-ounce) can chopped green chiles, drained
¼ teaspoon dried whole thyme
2 dashes of hot sauce
1 cup (4 ounces) shredded Cheddar cheese
Microwaved or baked 9-inch quiche pastry
3 eggs, beaten
1½ cups half-and-half
¼ teaspoon salt
⅛ teaspoon pepper
Paprika

Crumble sausage into a 1½-quart casserole; add green pepper and onions. Cover with wax paper and microwave at HIGH for 4 minutes or until sausage is no longer pink, stirring after 2 minutes. Drain sausage mixture. Stir in chiles, thyme, and hot sauce.

Sprinkle cheese evenly into pastry. Top with sausage mixture. Combine eggs, half-and-half, salt, and pepper; stir well. Pour into pastry; sprinkle with paprika. Place in microwave oven on an inverted saucer. Reduce to MEDIUM HIGH (70% power); microwave, uncovered, for 24 to 28 minutes or until set, rotating a half-turn every 6 minutes. Let stand 10 minutes before serving. Yield: one 9-inch quiche.

To separate slices of cold bacon, heat the entire package for just a few seconds on HIGH.

Ham Quiche

¼ cup chopped green pepper
¼ cup chopped pimiento, drained
1 cup diced cooked ham
Microwaved or baked 9-inch quiche pastry
3 eggs, beaten
1½ cups half-and-half
1 cup (4 ounces) shredded Swiss cheese
½ teaspoon salt
⅛ teaspoon pepper

Place chopped green pepper in a 1-cup glass measure. Microwave, uncovered, at HIGH for 1 minute or until crisp-tender. Stir in pimiento. Sprinkle ham evenly into pastry; top with green pepper mixture.

Combine eggs and remaining ingredients; stir well. Pour into pastry. Place in microwave oven on an inverted saucer. Reduce to MEDIUM HIGH (70% power); microwave, uncovered, for 24 to 28 minutes or until set, rotating a half-turn every 6 minutes. Let stand 10 minutes before serving. Yield: one 9-inch quiche.

Crab Quiche

½ pound fresh lump crabmeat, drained and flaked
1 cup (4 ounces) shredded Swiss cheese
⅓ cup chopped green onions
4 eggs, slightly beaten
1½ cups half-and-half
½ teaspoon salt
½ teaspoon grated lemon rind
¼ teaspoon dry mustard
Dash of pepper
Microwaved or baked 9-inch quiche pastry

Combine all ingredients, except pastry, in a large bowl, stirring well; pour into pastry.

Place quiche in microwave oven on an inverted saucer. Microwave, uncovered, at MEDIUM HIGH (70% power) for 28 to 32 minutes or until set, rotating a quarter-turn every 7 minutes. Let stand 5 minutes before serving. Yield: one 9-inch quiche.

Leek Tart

6 slices bacon
¾ cup finely chopped leeks
2 tablespoons diced pimiento
1 cup (4 ounces) shredded Swiss cheese
Microwaved or baked 9-inch quiche pastry
3 eggs, beaten
¾ cup half-and-half
½ teaspoon salt
¼ teaspoon pepper

Place bacon on a rack in a baking dish. Cover with paper towels and microwave at HIGH for 5 to 7 minutes or until bacon is crisp. Crumble bacon, and set aside. Place leeks in a 2-cup glass measure; microwave at HIGH for 3 to 4 minutes or until tender. Drain. Sprinkle bacon, leeks, pimiento, and cheese into pastry; set aside.

Combine eggs, half-and-half, salt, and pepper, stirring well. Pour mixture into pastry. Place tart in microwave oven on an inverted saucer. Reduce to MEDIUM HIGH (70% power); microwave, uncovered, for 11 to 12 minutes or until set, rotating a half-turn every 3 minutes. Let tart stand 10 minutes before serving. Yield: one 9-inch tart.

TORTILLA-CHEESE PIE

6 (6-inch) flour tortillas
½ cup chopped sweet red
  pepper
½ cup chopped green onions
½ cup chopped tomato
1 (4-ounce) can chopped green
  chiles, drained
½ cup (2 ounces) shredded
  Monterey Jack cheese
½ cup (2 ounces) shredded
  Cheddar cheese
¼ cup sliced pimiento-stuffed
  olives
3 eggs, beaten
¾ cup half-and-half
½ teaspoon chili powder
Shredded lettuce
Commercial sour cream
Commercial taco sauce

Line bottom and sides of a 9-inch pieplate or quiche dish with tortillas. Sprinkle with red pepper and next 6 ingredients; set aside.

Combine eggs, half-and-half, and chili powder in a 2-quart casserole. Microwave, uncovered, at MEDIUM (50% power) for 4½ to 5 minutes or until partially set, stirring every 2 minutes. Pour egg mixture into prepared pieplate. Place pie in microwave oven on an inverted saucer. Increase to MEDIUM HIGH (70% power); microwave, uncovered, for 12 to 14 minutes or until set, rotating a half-turn every 4 minutes. Let stand 15 minutes before serving. Serve with lettuce, sour cream, and taco sauce. Yield: one 9-inch pie.

SOUR CREAM-CHEESE ENCHILADAS

2 (10¾-ounce) cans cream of
  mushroom soup, undiluted
1 (8-ounce) carton commercial
  sour cream
1 (4-ounce) can chopped green
  chiles, undrained
½ teaspoon garlic powder
¼ teaspoon pepper
8 (6-inch) corn tortillas
2 cups (8 ounces) shredded
  sharp Cheddar cheese,
  divided
1 cup chopped green onions,
  divided

Combine soup, sour cream, chiles, garlic powder, and pepper in a 2-quart casserole, stirring well. Cover casserole with heavy-duty plastic wrap and microwave at HIGH for 3 to 4 minutes or until mixture is thoroughly heated, stirring after 2 minutes.

Place 4 tortillas between damp paper towels. Microwave at HIGH for 40 seconds to 1 minute or until thoroughly heated. Repeat procedure with remaining tortillas. Immediately spoon 2 tablespoons soup mixture into center of each tortilla, and sprinkle with 1 tablespoon each of cheese and onions; roll up jellyroll fashion. Place tortillas, seam side down, in a lightly greased 12- x 8- x 2-inch baking dish. Spoon remaining soup mixture over top. Sprinkle with remaining cheese and onions. Cover with heavy-duty plastic wrap and microwave at HIGH for 1 to 2 minutes or until cheese melts. Let stand, covered, 5 to 10 minutes. Serve immediately. Yield: 4 servings.

Chiles, cheese, olives, and onions fill Tortilla-Cheese Pie with Mexican flavor.

Fish and Shellfish

Fish and shellfish are excellent choices for microwaving. Due to its high moisture content, fish cooks quickly, retains its fresh flavor, and can usually be microwaved on HIGH power.

Because fish cooks so quickly, care must be taken to prevent overcooking. If overcooked, fish will be dry and tough. Try to arrange thicker portions towards the outside of the container. Fish is done when it is opaque and flakes easily when tested with a fork. Always cook fish for the minimum time suggested. If it does not test done, continue cooking briefly.

You can also thaw frozen fish in the microwave oven. Place the fish on a rack so that the bottom will not start to cook in the liquid that drains off. Cover one pound of frozen fillets with heavy-duty plastic wrap and microwave at MEDIUM LOW (30% power) for 6 to 8 minutes. Then let stand 10 minutes. Rather than allowing the fish to stand, you could place the still icy fish under cold running water to complete defrosting.

When microwaving shrimp, be sure to stir often and arrange it in a circle around the outer edge of the dish to allow the shrimp to cook more evenly. A tight covering of heavy-duty plastic wrap will also help ensure even cooking. Shrimp is done when it turns pink.

Lobster tails work wonderfully in the microwave oven, but whole, live lobsters are best cooked conventionally. Scallops need to be watched carefully to tell when they're done. Remove scallops when they become opaque and are no longer transparent. Standing time will gently and gradually complete the cooking process.

Party Paella (page 134) is brimming with rice, chunks of chicken, shrimp, and clams. Add a salad and beverage and you're ready for a party.

Clams, mussels, and oysters are also microwave compatible. It's easy to steam open clam and mussel shells by following our basic procedures. Arrange a dozen unopened clam or mussel shells in a casserole; cover with heavy-duty plastic wrap and microwave at HIGH for 4 to 6 minutes. Once the shells open, it takes only seconds to complete the cooking.

We also tried opening oyster shells in the microwave, but were not pleased with the results. However, you may find the steaming process does make it a little easier to pry open the shells. Try arranging six small to medium oysters in a circle in a pieplate; cover with heavy-duty plastic wrap and microwave at HIGH for 45 to 50 seconds. To get the very best, most reliable results with our oyster recipes, we suggest purchasing oysters on the half shell or opening the shells without using the microwave steaming procedure.

CATFISH SOUTHERN STYLE

⅓ cup corn flake crumbs
1 tablespoon yellow cornmeal
1 teaspoon dried parsley flakes
½ teaspoon paprika
¼ teaspoon salt
2 (4-ounce) catfish fillets
2 tablespoons milk

Combine first 5 ingredients in a shallow container. Dip fillets in milk; dredge in crumb mixture. Arrange fillets in a lightly greased 10- x 6- x 2-inch baking dish with thickest portions towards outside of dish. Microwave, uncovered, at HIGH for 4 to 6 minutes or until fish flakes easily when tested with a fork, turning fillets over after 2½ minutes. Serve immediately. Yield: 2 servings.

To make Nouvelle Flounder Papillote, arrange ingredients on one side of a parchment heart.

NOUVELLE FLOUNDER PAPILLOTE

2 tablespoons olive oil, divided
1 cup cherry tomatoes, cut into wedges
⅓ cup chopped green onions
2 tablespoons lemon juice
1 teaspoon dried whole oregano
½ pound fresh snow pea pods, trimmed
4 (4-ounce) flounder fillets
¼ teaspoon salt
⅛ teaspoon pepper

Cut four 18- x 12-inch pieces of parchment paper; cut each into a large heart shape. Fold each parchment heart in half; open out flat. Lightly brush one side of parchment hearts with 1 tablespoon olive oil.

Combine remaining 1 tablespoon olive oil, tomatoes, green onions, lemon juice, and oregano in a small bowl; set aside.

Arrange snow peas in a fan design near crease on one side of each parchment heart. Place one fillet over each arrangement of snow peas. Sprinkle with salt and pepper. Spoon vegetable mixture evenly over fillets.

Bring opposite sides of parchment hearts together; fold edges over twice to seal securely. Fold pointed ends underneath. Arrange pouches on a 12-inch round glass platter. Microwave at HIGH for 7 minutes or until pouches are puffed. Cut an opening in pouches before serving. Serve immediately. Yield: 4 servings.

Fold heart over, and seal edges. The pouch will hold in moisture and flavor.

SPINACH-FLOUNDER DELIGHT

2 tablespoons butter or
   margarine
1 pound fresh spinach, coarsely
   chopped
½ cup sliced green onions,
   divided
4 (4-ounce) flounder fillets
¼ teaspoon salt
¼ teaspoon pepper
3 tablespoons barbecue sauce
1 tablespoon plus 1 teaspoon
   lemon juice
½ cup sliced fresh mushrooms
Paprika

Grease a 10- x 6- x 2-inch baking dish with butter; set aside. Place spinach in baking dish; sprinkle with ¼ cup green onions. Arrange fillets over onions with thickest portions towards outside of dish; sprinkle with salt and pepper.

Combine barbecue sauce and lemon juice, stirring well. Spoon sauce over fish; top with mushrooms and remaining ¼ cup green onions. Sprinkle with paprika. Cover with heavy-duty plastic wrap and microwave at HIGH for 9 minutes or until fish flakes easily when tested with a fork, rotating a half-turn after 4 minutes. Serve immediately. Yield: 4 servings.

CRUMB-TOPPED GROUPER

1 (1-pound) grouper fillet
¼ cup mayonnaise
½ teaspoon prepared mustard
¼ teaspoon dried whole
   tarragon
2 tablespoons corn flake
   crumbs

Cut fillet into four equal portions. Arrange fish in a circular pattern in a 9-inch pieplate with thickest portions towards outside of dish.

Combine mayonnaise, mustard, and tarragon in a small bowl; spread evenly over fish. Sprinkle fish evenly with corn flake crumbs, pressing lightly to adhere to top and sides. Microwave, uncovered, at HIGH for 7 minutes or until fish flakes easily when tested with a fork, rotating a quarter-turn after 3½ minutes. Serve immediately. Yield: 4 servings.

GROUPER AMANDINE

¼ cup butter or margarine
¼ cup sliced almonds
1½ teaspoons lemon juice
1 teaspoon dry vermouth
1 (1-pound) grouper fillet
¼ teaspoon salt
½ teaspoon minced fresh
   dillweed
Lemon slices
Fresh parsley sprigs

Place butter, almonds, lemon juice, and vermouth in a 12- x 8- x 2-inch baking dish. Microwave, uncovered, at HIGH for 10 to 11 minutes or until almonds are golden, stirring every 3 minutes. Remove almonds with a slotted spoon, reserving butter mixture in baking dish. Set almonds aside.

Cut fillet into four equal portions, and coat in butter mixture; arrange in dish with thickest portions towards outside of dish. Sprinkle with salt and dillweed. Cover with heavy-duty plastic wrap and microwave at HIGH for 6 to 8 minutes or until fish flakes easily when tested with a fork. Spoon almonds over fish. Garnish with lemon slices and parsley sprigs. Serve immediately. Yield: 4 servings.

Offer Grouper With Confetti Vegetables when you want a colorful entrée. The vegetable, olive, and cheese topping is the perfect complement for the fish.

GROUPER WITH CONFETTI VEGETABLES

1 (1-pound) grouper fillet
¼ cup lemon juice
1 small onion, chopped
1 small green pepper, chopped
1½ tablespoons butter or
   margarine
1 small tomato, seeded and
   chopped
¼ teaspoon salt
⅛ teaspoon pepper
¼ cup sliced ripe olives
1 cup (4 ounces) shredded
   mozzarella cheese

Arrange fish with thickest portions towards outside of dish.

Cut fillet into four equal portions. Place fish in a shallow container; add lemon juice. Cover and refrigerate 2 hours.

Place onion, green pepper, and butter in a 9-inch pieplate. Microwave, uncovered, at HIGH for 2 to 3 minutes or until vegetables are crisp-tender. Add tomato; microwave, uncovered, at HIGH for 1 minute. Drain and set aside.

Remove fish from lemon juice, and arrange in a 9-inch baking dish with thickest portions towards outside of dish. Sprinkle with salt and pepper. Cover with wax paper and microwave at HIGH for 6 to 7 minutes or until fish flakes easily when tested with a fork. Drain off any excess liquid. Spoon vegetable mixture over fish; sprinkle with olives and cheese. Reduce to MEDIUM HIGH (70% power); cover and microwave for 2 minutes or just until cheese melts. Serve immediately. Yield: 4 servings.

TANGY LEMON GROUPER

1 (1-pound) grouper fillet
¼ cup butter or margarine
1 tablespoon lemon juice
¼ teaspoon salt
⅛ teaspoon pepper
¾ cup seasoned, dry
   breadcrumbs
½ cup commercial sour cream
2 tablespoons lemon juice
1 tablespoon butter or
   margarine
⅛ teaspoon ground turmeric
Paprika

Cut fillet into four equal portions. Set aside. Place ¼ cup butter in a medium bowl. Microwave, uncovered, at HIGH for 55 seconds or until melted. Stir in 1 tablespoon lemon juice, salt, and pepper. Dredge fish in butter mixture; coat in breadcrumbs. Arrange fish in a 12- x 8- x 2-inch baking dish with thickest portions towards outside of dish. Cover with wax paper and microwave at HIGH for 5 to 6 minutes or until fish flakes easily when tested with a fork. Remove fish to a serving platter.

Combine sour cream and 2 tablespoons lemon juice in a 1-cup glass measure. Microwave, uncovered, at HIGH for 1 to 1½ minutes or just until thoroughly heated. Add 1 tablespoon butter and turmeric, stirring until butter melts; spoon over fish. Sprinkle with paprika, and serve immediately. Yield: 4 servings.

GROUPER WITH HERBED BUTTER SAUCE

¼ cup butter or margarine
2 tablespoons minced fresh
   parsley
2 teaspoons lemon juice
¼ teaspoon dried whole basil
¼ teaspoon dried whole
   marjoram
¼ teaspoon celery seeds
⅛ teaspoon dried whole
   oregano
1 (1-pound) grouper fillet
1 tablespoon grated Parmesan
   cheese

Combine butter, parsley, lemon juice, basil, marjoram, celery seeds, and oregano in a 9-inch square baking dish. Microwave, uncovered, at HIGH for 55 seconds or until butter melts.

Cut fillet into four equal portions. Coat fish in butter mixture. Arrange fish in baking dish with thickest portions towards outside of dish. Cover with heavy-duty plastic wrap and microwave at HIGH for 6 minutes or until fish flakes easily when tested with a fork, brushing with butter mixture after 3 minutes. Remove fish to serving plate; sprinkle with cheese. Serve immediately. Yield: 4 servings.

Haddock Italian Style

1¼ cups sliced fresh
   mushrooms
1 medium tomato, seeded and
   chopped
¼ cup sliced green olives
¼ cup chopped onion
¼ cup chopped green pepper
2 tablespoons chopped fresh
   parsley
1 tablespoon lemon juice
1 tablespoon olive oil
1 clove garlic, minced
½ teaspoon dried whole
   oregano
¼ teaspoon pepper
4 (4-ounce) haddock fillets,
   skinned
2 tablespoons grated Parmesan
   cheese

Combine first 11 ingredients in a 12- x 8- x 2-inch baking dish, stirring well. Cover with heavy-duty plastic wrap and microwave at HIGH for 4 to 6 minutes or until vegetables are tender, stirring after 3 minutes. Push vegetable mixture to side of dish.

Arrange fillets in baking dish with thickest portions towards outside of dish. Spoon vegetable mixture over fillets. Cover and microwave at HIGH for 5 to 6 minutes or until fish flakes easily when tested with a fork. Sprinkle with cheese; microwave, uncovered, at HIGH for 1 minute. Serve immediately. Yield: 4 servings.

Halibut With Creamy Crab Sauce

5 green onions, chopped
1 medium carrot, scraped and
   sliced
1 stalk celery, sliced
1 small lemon, thinly sliced
¼ cup Chablis or other dry
   white wine
2 tablespoons chopped fresh
   parsley
2 tablespoons water
4 whole peppercorns
1 bay leaf
4 (4-ounce) halibut steaks
   (1-inch thick)
3 tablespoons chopped green
   onions
1 tablespoon plus 1½
   teaspoons butter or
   margarine
2 tablespoons dry vermouth
1 tablespoon all-purpose flour
⅛ teaspoon salt
⅛ teaspoon white pepper
⅓ cup whipping cream
4 ounces fresh lump crabmeat,
   drained and flaked
1 (2-ounce) jar diced pimiento,
   drained

Combine first 9 ingredients in a 10- x 6- x 2-inch baking dish. Cover with heavy-duty plastic wrap and microwave at HIGH for 4 minutes or until vegetables are crisp-tender. Arrange halibut steaks over vegetable mixture with thickest portions towards outside of dish. Cover and microwave at HIGH for 4½ to 5½ minutes or until fish flakes easily when tested with a fork. Remove fish to serving plates. Strain vegetable mixture, reserving ¼ cup fish stock; discard vegetable mixture.

Place 3 tablespoons green onions and butter in a 4-cup glass measure. Microwave, uncovered, at HIGH for 1 minute. Stir in vermouth, flour, salt, and pepper. Microwave, uncovered, at HIGH for 1 minute. Gradually add whipping cream and reserved fish stock. Microwave, uncovered, at HIGH for 4 to 5 minutes or until thickened, stirring after 2½ minutes. Stir in crabmeat and pimiento. Reduce to MEDIUM (50% power), and microwave, uncovered, for 1 to 2 minutes or until thoroughly heated. Spoon sauce over halibut, and serve immediately. Yield: 4 servings.

ORANGE ROUGHY WITH MEXICAN SAUCE

2 tablespoons water
2 tablespoons Chablis or other dry white wine
1 small lemon, sliced
1 bay leaf
1 tablespoon minced fresh parsley
⅛ teaspoon salt
4 (4-ounce) orange roughy fillets (¾-inch thick)
1 cup chopped onion
1 clove garlic, minced
⅓ cup chopped tomato
1 tablespoon vegetable oil
1 tablespoon chopped jalapeño pepper
¼ teaspoon dried whole oregano
¼ teaspoon ground cumin
⅛ teaspoon salt
⅓ cup water
½ teaspoon cornstarch
½ (8-ounce) can tomato sauce
1 tablespoon vinegar

Combine 2 tablespoons water, wine, lemon, bay leaf, parsley, and ⅛ teaspoon salt in a 12- x 8- x 2-inch baking dish, stirring well. Cover with heavy-duty plastic wrap and microwave at HIGH for 3 to 4 minutes or until thoroughly heated. Add fillets, arranging with thickest portions towards outside of dish. Cover and microwave at HIGH for 3 to 4 minutes or until fish flakes easily when tested with a fork. Remove fish to serving plates, discarding liquid.

Combine onion and garlic in a 1-quart casserole. Cover with heavy-duty plastic wrap and microwave at HIGH for 2 to 3 minutes or until onion is tender. Add tomato, oil, jalapeño pepper, oregano, cumin, and ⅛ teaspoon salt; cover and microwave at HIGH for 1 minute. Set aside. Combine ⅓ cup water and cornstarch in a 1-cup glass measure, stirring until blended. Add tomato sauce and vinegar; stir well. Add to onion mixture; microwave, uncovered, at HIGH for 4 to 5 minutes or until thickened, stirring after every minute. Spoon sauce over fish; serve immediately. Yield: 4 servings.

POACHED SALMON WITH WATERCRESS SAUCE

2 tablespoons butter or margarine
¼ teaspoon ground nutmeg
6 (1-inch-thick) salmon steaks (about 2½ to 3 pounds)
½ cup dry white wine
½ cup whipping cream
1 bunch watercress (about ¼ pound), coarsely chopped
1 tablespoon lemon juice
1 tablespoon Dijon mustard
¼ teaspoon salt
⅛ teaspoon pepper
⅛ teaspoon ground nutmeg
Additional watercress sprigs (optional)

Place butter and ¼ teaspoon nutmeg in a 13- x 9- x 2-inch baking dish. Microwave, uncovered, at HIGH for 45 seconds or until butter melts. Coat salmon steaks in butter mixture; arrange in dish with thickest portions towards outside of dish. Pour wine over salmon. Cover with heavy-duty plastic wrap and microwave at HIGH for 4 minutes.

Turn salmon over; cover and microwave at HIGH for 2 to 4 minutes or until fish flakes easily when tested with a fork. Remove salmon to a serving platter with a slotted spoon, reserving liquid.

Add whipping cream and watercress to liquid in baking dish; cover and microwave at HIGH for 4 minutes. Position knife blade in food processor bowl; add watercress mixture, lemon juice, mustard, salt, pepper, and ⅛ teaspoon nutmeg. Process until smooth. Spoon sauce over salmon; garnish with watercress sprigs, if desired. Serve warm or cold. Yield: 6 servings.

Salmon Loaf With Cucumber Sauce

2 (15½-ounce) cans red or pink
    salmon, drained and flaked
1 cup fine, dry breadcrumbs
1 cup milk
½ cup diced green onions
¼ cup chopped celery
2 eggs, beaten
2 tablespoons lemon juice
2 tablespoons sweet pickle
    relish
2 teaspoons prepared mustard
½ teaspoon dried whole
    dillweed
⅛ teaspoon hot sauce
¾ cup commercial sour cream
½ cup unpeeled, diced
    cucumber
¼ cup mayonnaise
1 tablespoon minced green
    onions
1 teaspoon minced fresh
    parsley
¼ teaspoon dried whole
    dillweed
⅛ teaspoon salt

Combine first 11 ingredients in a large bowl; stir well. Press mixture into a 9-inch round baking dish. Place dish in microwave oven on an inverted saucer. Cover with wax paper and microwave at MEDIUM HIGH (70% power) for 8 minutes, rotating a half-turn after 4 minutes. Reduce to MEDIUM (50% power); cover and microwave for 8 to 10 minutes or until center is set. Let stand, covered, 5 minutes.

Combine sour cream, cucumber, mayonnaise, 1 tablespoon green onions, parsley, ¼ teaspoon dillweed, and salt in a small bowl; stir well. Cut loaf into wedges, and serve immediately with sauce. Yield: 8 servings.

Red Snapper Creole

1 cup coarsely chopped green
    pepper
¾ cup coarsely chopped onion
½ cup sliced celery
2 tablespoons butter or
    margarine
1 clove garlic, minced
1 (16-ounce) can whole
    tomatoes, drained and
    coarsely chopped
3 tablespoons tomato paste
1 teaspoon sugar
1 bay leaf
1 clove garlic, minced
½ teaspoon paprika
¼ teaspoon red pepper
6 (4-ounce) red snapper fillets

Combine first 5 ingredients in a 4-cup glass measure, stirring well. Cover with heavy-duty plastic wrap and microwave at HIGH for 6 to 8 minutes or until vegetables are tender. Stir in tomatoes, tomato paste, sugar, and bay leaf. Cover and microwave at HIGH for 2 to 4 minutes or until slightly thickened. Remove and discard bay leaf. Set sauce aside.

Combine 1 clove minced garlic, paprika, and red pepper; rub over fillets. Arrange fillets in a circular pattern on a 12-inch round glass platter with thickest portions towards outside of dish. Cover with heavy-duty plastic wrap and microwave at HIGH for 4 minutes, rotating a half-turn after 2 minutes. Drain off liquid.

Spoon sauce over fish. Cover and microwave at HIGH for 2 to 3 minutes or until fish flakes easily when tested with a fork. Let stand, covered, 2 minutes. Drain off any excess liquid, if necessary, before serving. Yield: 6 servings.

Give Sunshine Trout a crisp brown appearance by dredging the fillets in corn flake crumbs.

SUNSHINE TROUT

½ cup orange juice
¼ teaspoon salt
¼ teaspoon lemon-pepper seasoning
4 (5- to 6-ounce) trout fillets, skinned
⅔ cup corn flake crumbs
2 tablespoons butter or margarine
½ cup orange juice
¼ cup Chablis or other dry white wine
¼ cup water
1½ tablespoons sugar
1 tablespoon grated orange rind
1 tablespoon cornstarch
1 tablespoon white wine vinegar
Orange slices (optional)

Combine ½ cup orange juice, salt, and lemon-pepper seasoning. Dip fillets in juice mixture, and dredge in corn flake crumbs. Arrange fillets in a lightly greased 12- x 8- x 2-inch baking dish with thickest portions towards outside of dish; set aside.

Place butter in a 1-cup glass measure; microwave, uncovered, at HIGH for 45 seconds or until melted. Drizzle over fish; microwave, uncovered, at HIGH for 7 to 8 minutes or until fish flakes easily when tested with a fork, rotating a half-turn after 4 minutes. Remove fish to serving platter.

Combine ½ cup orange juice and next 6 ingredients in a 4-cup glass measure. Microwave, uncovered, at HIGH for 4 to 5 minutes or until thickened, stirring after 3 minutes. Serve immediately with fish. Garnish with orange slices, if desired. Yield: 4 servings.

SPINACH SOLE WITH RED PEPPER SAUCE

1 (10-ounce) package frozen
   chopped spinach
1 egg, beaten
1 cup herbed croutons, crushed
¼ cup grated Parmesan cheese
¼ cup commercial sour cream
¼ teaspoon onion powder
6 (4-ounce) sole or flounder
   fillets
1 small sweet red pepper,
   chopped
2 teaspoons butter or margarine
2 medium tomatoes, peeled,
   seeded, and chopped
½ teaspoon dried whole
   marjoram
⅛ teaspoon salt
⅛ teaspoon pepper
Fresh spinach leaves (optional)

Remove wrapper from spinach package; place package in a medium baking dish. Microwave at HIGH for 3 to 5 minutes or until thawed. Drain spinach well, pressing between layers of paper towels. Combine spinach and next 5 ingredients in a medium bowl, stirring well. Spoon spinach mixture evenly over each fillet. Roll up lengthwise; secure with wooden picks.

Place rolls, seam side down, in a 12- x 8- x 2-inch baking dish. Cover with heavy-duty plastic wrap and microwave at HIGH for 6 to 8 minutes or until fish flakes easily when tested with a fork, rotating a half-turn after 4 minutes. Remove rolls to serving plates.

Place red pepper and butter in a 4-cup glass measure. Microwave, uncovered, at HIGH for 2 minutes. Stir in tomatoes. Microwave, uncovered, at HIGH for 2 minutes. Transfer mixture to container of an electric blender or food processor. Cover and process until smooth. Return mixture to 4-cup glass measure. Stir in marjoram, salt, and pepper. Microwave, uncovered, at HIGH for 4 minutes or until thickened, stirring after 2 minutes. Spoon sauce over fish. Garnish with fresh spinach leaves, if desired. Serve immediately. Yield: 6 servings.

SOLE WITH CUCUMBER SAUCE

1 cup fresh lump crabmeat, drained and flaked
1 (2-ounce) jar sliced pimiento, drained
¼ cup chopped green onions
1 egg, beaten
2 tablespoons fine, dry breadcrumbs
2 tablespoons finely chopped pecans or almonds
1 teaspoon grated lemon rind
6 (4-ounce) sole or flounder fillets
2 tablespoons butter or margarine
½ cup peeled, seeded, and chopped cucumber
½ cup mayonnaise
⅓ cup commercial sour cream
2 tablespoons milk
1 tablespoon chopped green onions
1 teaspoon grated lemon rind
½ teaspoon chopped fresh parsley
¼ teaspoon salt
¼ teaspoon dried whole dillweed
Paprika (optional)
Chopped fresh parsley (optional)

Combine first 7 ingredients, mixing well. Spoon mixture evenly over each fillet. Roll up lengthwise; secure with wooden picks. Place rolls, seam side down, in an 8-inch square baking dish.

Place butter in a 1-cup glass measure. Microwave, uncovered, at HIGH for 45 seconds or until melted; brush over rolls. Cover rolls with heavy-duty plastic wrap and microwave at HIGH for 6 to 8 minutes or until fish flakes easily when tested with a fork, rotating a quarter-turn every 2 minutes. Let stand, covered, 2 minutes; remove rolls to serving platter.

Pat cucumber with paper towels to remove excess moisture. Combine cucumber, mayonnaise, sour cream, and milk; stir in 1 tablespoon green onions, 1 teaspoon lemon rind, ½ teaspoon parsley, salt, and dillweed. Spoon over fish, and sprinkle with paprika and parsley, if desired. Serve immediately. Yield: 6 servings.

SHRIMP IN SHERRY-CREAM SAUCE

¼ cup chopped green onions
¼ cup butter or margarine
1 pound unpeeled medium-size fresh shrimp, peeled and deveined
1 (4-ounce) can sliced mushrooms, drained
¼ cup all-purpose flour
¼ teaspoon salt
Dash of red pepper
½ cup half-and-half
¼ cup dry sherry
Hot cooked rice
Minced fresh parsley

Combine onions and butter in a 2-quart casserole. Microwave, uncovered, at HIGH for 55 seconds or until butter melts. Arrange shrimp around outer edges of casserole. Place mushrooms in center of shrimp; sprinkle with flour, salt, and pepper. Gradually add half-and-half and sherry to flour and mushroom mixture, stirring until smooth. Cover with heavy-duty plastic wrap and microwave at HIGH for 5 to 6 minutes or until mixture is thickened and shrimp are pink, stirring after 3 minutes. Spoon over rice; sprinkle with parsley. Serve immediately. Yield: 4 servings.

Shrimp And Pasta Toss

8 ounces uncooked linguine
¼ cup olive oil
6 green onions, cut into ½-inch
  pieces
4 cloves garlic, minced
2 pounds unpeeled
  medium-size fresh shrimp,
  peeled and deveined
¼ cup red wine vinegar
2 tablespoons lemon juice
¼ cup chopped fresh parsley
1½ teaspoons dried whole basil
1 teaspoon dried whole
  oregano
¾ teaspoon salt
¾ teaspoon pepper
½ pound fresh snow pea pods
4 small tomatoes, peeled and
  chopped
¼ cup grated Parmesan cheese

Cook linguine according to package directions, omitting salt; drain well. Set aside, and keep warm.

Combine olive oil, green onions, and garlic in a 3-quart casserole. Cover with heavy-duty plastic wrap and microwave at HIGH for 3 to 3½ minutes or until onions are crisp-tender. Add shrimp, stirring to coat. Arrange shrimp around outer edges of dish. Cover and microwave at HIGH for 5 to 6 minutes or until shrimp are pink, rearranging shrimp every 2 minutes.

Combine vinegar, lemon juice, parsley, basil, oregano, salt, and pepper in a small mixing bowl, stirring well. Stir vinegar mixture into shrimp mixture. Add snow peas, tossing gently. Cover and microwave at HIGH for 1 minute or just until thoroughly heated.

Add tomatoes and linguine to shrimp mixture; toss well. Sprinkle with cheese, and serve immediately. Yield: 6 servings.

Garlic-Buttered Shrimp

2 pounds unpeeled large fresh
  shrimp
½ cup butter or margarine
½ cup olive oil
¼ cup minced fresh parsley
1 tablespoon plus 1½
  teaspoons lemon juice
1 green onion, minced
3 cloves garlic, minced
¼ teaspoon coarsely ground
  black pepper
8 ounces uncooked linguine

Peel and devein shrimp, leaving tails intact (tails may be removed, if desired). Set aside.

Place butter in a 13- x 9- x 2-inch baking dish. Microwave, uncovered, at HIGH for 1 minute or until melted. Stir in olive oil and next 5 ingredients; arrange shrimp around outer edges of dish. Cover with heavy-duty plastic wrap, and marinate in refrigerator at least 1 hour. Remove from refrigerator and microwave, covered, at HIGH for 7 to 7½ minutes or until shrimp are pink, rearranging shrimp every 2 minutes.

Cook linguine according to package directions. Drain; place on a serving platter. Top with shrimp mixture. Serve immediately. Yield: 6 servings.

For a grand entrée, serve spicy Garlic-Buttered Shrimp over linguine.

EASY CURRIED SHRIMP

⅓ cup flaked coconut
2 tablespoons butter or
 margarine
½ cup chopped green onions
⅓ cup chopped sweet red
 pepper
1 clove garlic, minced
1½ pounds unpeeled
 medium-size fresh shrimp,
 peeled and deveined
1 (8-ounce) carton commercial
 sour cream
1 teaspoon curry powder
½ teaspoon ground cinnamon
¼ teaspoon salt
Pepper to taste
Hot cooked rice
¼ cup raisins

Spread coconut evenly in a 9-inch pieplate. Microwave, uncovered, at HIGH for 2 to 2½ minutes or until lightly toasted, stirring after every minute (coconut will darken as it cools). Set aside.

Place butter in a 2-quart casserole; microwave, uncovered, at HIGH for 45 seconds or until melted. Add onions, red pepper, and garlic. Arrange shrimp around outer edges of casserole. Cover with heavy-duty plastic wrap and microwave at HIGH for 3 to 5 minutes or until shrimp are pink, rearranging shrimp every 2 minutes. Drain. Stir in sour cream, curry, cinnamon, salt, and pepper. Reduce to MEDIUM (50% power); cover and microwave for 2 to 3 minutes or until thoroughly heated, stirring after every minute. Spoon shrimp mixture over rice; sprinkle with coconut and raisins. Serve immediately. Yield: 4 to 6 servings.

SWEET-AND-SOUR SHRIMP

1 (15¼-ounce) can pineapple
 tidbits, undrained
2 tablespoons vegetable oil
2 medium carrots, scraped
 and sliced
1 medium-size red pepper,
 cut into strips
1 clove garlic, minced
1½ pounds unpeeled
 medium-size fresh shrimp,
 peeled and deveined
½ cup undiluted canned
 chicken broth
¼ cup brown sugar
¼ cup red wine vinegar
1 tablespoon soy sauce
2 tablespoons water
1½ tablespoons cornstarch
Hot cooked rice

Drain pineapple, reserving juice; set pineapple and juice aside. Combine oil, carrots, pepper, and garlic in a 12- x 8- x 2-inch baking dish. Cover with heavy-duty plastic wrap and microwave at HIGH for 3 minutes or until vegetables are crisp-tender. Arrange shrimp around outer edges of dish. Cover and microwave at HIGH for 3 to 5 minutes or until shrimp are pink, rearranging shrimp after 2 minutes. Set aside.

Combine reserved pineapple juice, chicken broth, sugar, vinegar, and soy sauce in a small bowl. Combine water and cornstarch, stirring well; stir into juice mixture. Cover and microwave at HIGH for 4 to 5 minutes or until thickened, stirring after 3 minutes. Gently stir sauce into shrimp mixture; add reserved pineapple. Spoon over rice, and serve immediately. Yield: 4 to 6 servings.

Lemon Shrimp In Dill Sauce

½ cup butter or margarine
¼ cup chopped green onions
2 cloves garlic, crushed
2 pounds unpeeled large fresh shrimp, peeled and deveined
1 tablespoon white wine
1 teaspoon lemon juice
½ teaspoon salt
⅛ teaspoon pepper
1 tablespoon chopped fresh parsley
1½ teaspoons chopped fresh dillweed or ½ teaspoon dried whole dillweed
3 French rolls, split and toasted

Combine butter, green onions, and garlic in a 13- x 9- x 2-inch baking dish. Cover with heavy-duty plastic wrap and microwave at HIGH for 2 to 4 minutes or until onions are tender.

Add shrimp, wine, lemon juice, salt, and pepper, stirring to coat. Arrange shrimp around outer edges of dish. Cover and microwave at HIGH for 5 to 6 minutes or until shrimp are pink, rearranging shrimp every 2 minutes. Stir in parsley and dillweed. Let stand, covered, 1 minute. Spoon hot shrimp mixture over toasted rolls, and serve immediately. Yield: 6 servings.

Coastal Shrimp Salad

2 pounds unpeeled large fresh shrimp, peeled and deveined
3 tablespoons Chablis or other dry white wine
1 (8-ounce) bottle commercial Italian salad dressing
⅔ cup sliced ripe olives
⅔ cup chopped green pepper
⅓ cup chopped celery
¼ cup chopped sweet pickles
3 tablespoons olive oil
1 tablespoon minced fresh parsley
1 tablespoon minced green onions
2 teaspoons lemon juice
Curly leaf lettuce
2 medium tomatoes, cut into wedges

Arange shrimp around outer edges of a 13- x 9- x 2-inch baking dish; add wine. Cover with heavy-duty plastic wrap and microwave at HIGH for 5 to 6 minutes or until shrimp are pink, rearranging shrimp after 3 minutes. Drain; place shrimp in refrigerator until thoroughly chilled.

Combine Italian dressing and next 8 ingredients in a large bowl, stirring well. Stir in shrimp. Cover and marinate in refrigerator at least 8 hours, stirring occasionally. Spoon salad onto a lettuce-lined serving platter. Garnish with tomato wedges. Yield: 6 servings.

Fresh lemon juice is easily obtained by halving or quartering a lemon then microwaving the sections at HIGH for 25 to 30 seconds. Squeeze out the juice.

Offer Crab Imperials for an appetizer or light lunch. They're pretty garnished with lemon slices and pimiento strips.

CRAB IMPERIALS

3 tablespoons butter or
  margarine
2 tablespoons finely chopped
  onion
1 tablespoon finely chopped
  green pepper
1 tablespoon sliced pimiento
1 teaspoon dry mustard
⅛ teaspoon dried whole thyme
3 tablespoons all-purpose flour
1 cup milk
1 teaspoon golden
  Worcestershire sauce
¼ teaspoon salt
1 pound fresh lump crabmeat,
  drained and flaked
3 tablespoons mayonnaise
Lemon slices (optional)
Pimiento strips (optional)

Combine butter, onion, and green pepper in a 1½-quart casserole. Microwave, uncovered, at HIGH for 2 minutes or until vegetables are crisp-tender. Stir in 1 tablespoon sliced pimiento, mustard, and thyme. Add flour, stirring until smooth. Gradually add milk, stirring well. Microwave, uncovered, at HIGH for 3 to 4 minutes or until thickened and bubbly, stirring every 2 minutes. Stir in golden Worcestershire sauce and salt. Add crabmeat and mayonnaise, stirring well.

Spoon mixture evenly into 6 baking shells or custard cups. Arrange 3 shells or cups on a 12-inch round glass platter. Cover with wax paper and microwave at HIGH for 3 minutes or until thoroughly heated. Repeat procedure with remaining shells or cups. Garnish with lemon slices and pimiento strips, if desired. Serve immediately. Yield: 6 servings.

Clams Oreganata

1 dozen fresh cherrystone
  clams
½ cup water
¼ cup fine, dry breadcrumbs
2 tablespoons olive oil
1 tablespoon chopped fresh
  parsley
1 tablespoon lemon juice
2 teaspoons grated Parmesan
  cheese
1 teaspoon anchovy paste
1 large clove garlic, minced
½ teaspoon dried whole
  oregano
⅛ teaspoon pepper

Scrub clams thoroughly, discarding any shells that are cracked or open.

Place ½ cup water in a 2-quart casserole. Microwave, uncovered, at HIGH for 2 to 3½ minutes or until boiling. Arrange clams in casserole; cover tightly with heavy-duty plastic wrap and microwave at HIGH for 4 to 6 minutes or just until clam shells begin to open (remove shells from casserole as they begin to open).

Pry open shells with an oyster knife; discard top shells, and cut clams loose from bottom shells. Drain bottom shells on paper towels. Mince clams, and set aside.

Combine breadcrumbs, oil, parsley, lemon juice, cheese, anchovy paste, garlic, oregano, and pepper; stir in clams. Spoon 1½ tablespoons breadcrumb mixture onto each bottom shell. Arrange shells around outer edge of a 12-inch round glass platter. Reduce to MEDIUM (50% power); cover with wax paper and microwave for 3 to 4 minutes or until thoroughly heated. Serve immediately. Yield: 1 dozen.

Open fresh clam shells by arranging the clams in a casserole and covering with plastic wrap. Microwave just until the shells begin to open.

Sailor's Clams

1 dozen fresh cherrystone
  clams
½ cup water
2 tablespoons olive oil
1 tablespoon finely chopped
  parsley
2 teaspoons lemon juice
¼ teaspoon paprika
⅛ teaspoon garlic powder
⅛ teaspoon pepper
¼ cup finely chopped cooked
  ham
¼ cup seasoned, dry
  breadcrumbs

Scrub clams thoroughly, discarding any shells that are cracked or open.

Place ½ cup water in a 2-quart casserole. Microwave, uncovered, at HIGH for 2 to 3½ minutes or until boiling. Arrange clams in casserole; cover tightly with heavy-duty plastic wrap and microwave at HIGH for 4 to 6 minutes or just until clam shells begin to open (remove shells from casserole as they begin to open).

Pry open shells with an oyster knife; discard top shells, and cut clams loose from bottom shells. Drain bottom shells on paper towels. Mince clams, and set aside.

Combine oil and next 5 ingredients in a small bowl. Microwave, uncovered, at HIGH for 1 minute or until thoroughly heated. Stir in ham, breadcrumbs, and minced clams. Spoon 1½ tablespoons breadcrumb mixture onto each bottom shell. Arrange shells around outer edge of a 12-inch round glass platter. Reduce to MEDIUM (50% power); cover with wax paper and microwave for 3 to 4 minutes or until thoroughly heated. Serve immediately. Yield: 1 dozen.

Party Paella

2 (10¾-ounce) cans chicken
  broth, undiluted
1 bunch green onions, chopped
1 medium-size green pepper,
  chopped
½ cup sliced ripe olives
¼ cup finely chopped fresh
  parsley
¼ teaspoon ground saffron
2 cloves garlic, minced
2½ cups uncooked instant rice
2 medium tomatoes, peeled
  and chopped
1 tablespoon dried whole
  oregano
2 teaspoons ground cumin
1 teaspoon chili powder
4 (8-ounce) chicken breast
  halves, skinned, boned, and
  cut into 8 pieces
1 dozen unpeeled jumbo fresh
  shrimp, peeled and deveined
14 to 16 fresh littleneck clams
Fresh parsley sprigs (optional)

Combine first 7 ingredients in a large bowl. Microwave, uncovered, at HIGH for 10 to 12 minutes or until boiling. Stir in rice; let stand 5 minutes. Stir in tomatoes; set aside.

Combine oregano, cumin, and chili powder, mixing well. Sprinkle over chicken. Arrange chicken in a 3½-quart shallow baking dish with thickest portions towards outside of dish. Cover with heavy-duty plastic wrap and microwave at HIGH for 12 to 15 minutes or until tender, rotating a half-turn every 5 minutes.

Spoon rice mixture over chicken. Arrange shrimp on top of rice; arrange clams around outer edges of dish with hinge ends in rice. Cover and microwave at HIGH for 5 to 7 minutes or until clam shells begin to open. Let stand, covered, 5 minutes. Garnish with parsley sprigs, if desired. Serve immediately. Yield: 8 servings.

Oriental Scallops

4 green onions, cut into 1-inch
  pieces
2 teaspoons butter or margarine
1 pound fresh bay scallops,
  drained
1 teaspoon grated orange rind
1 tablespoon grated fresh
  gingerroot
1 tablespoon teriyaki sauce
⅛ teaspoon pepper
2 tablespoons water
2 teaspoons cornstarch
½ pound fresh snow pea pods
Sweet red or yellow pepper
  rings (optional)
Green onion fan (optional)

Place onions and butter in a 2-quart casserole. Microwave, uncovered, at HIGH for 1 to 2 minutes or until onions are crisp-tender. Stir in scallops, orange rind, gingerroot, teriyaki sauce, and pepper. Cover with heavy-duty plastic wrap and microwave at HIGH for 2 to 3 minutes or until scallops are opaque, stirring after 1 minute. Remove scallops and onions with a slotted spoon, reserving liquid.

Combine water and cornstarch in a small bowl, stirring well; add to liquid in casserole. Microwave, uncovered, at HIGH for 2 to 4 minutes or until thickened. Stir in scallop mixture.

Wash snow peas; trim ends, and remove strings. Place snow peas in a 2-quart casserole; cover with heavy-duty plastic wrap and microwave at HIGH for 2 to 2½ minutes or until crisp-tender. Arrange snow peas on a serving platter; top with scallop mixture. Garnish with pepper rings and an onion fan, if desired. Serve immediately. Yield: 4 servings.

Oriental Scallops makes a dramatic presentation. Add a garnish of pepper rings and a green onion fan.

CREAMED SCALLOPS

2 tablespoons butter or
  margarine
2 tablespoons minced celery
2 tablespoons minced green
  onions
¼ teaspoon dried whole
  rosemary, crushed
2 tablespoons all-purpose flour
1 cup half-and-half
¼ cup milk
1 cup sliced fresh mushrooms
¼ teaspoon salt
⅛ teaspoon red pepper
1 pound fresh bay scallops,
  drained
1 (2-ounce) jar diced pimiento,
  drained
6 frozen patty shells, baked

Combine butter, celery, onions, and rosemary in a 1½-quart casserole. Cover with heavy-duty plastic wrap and microwave at HIGH for 3 to 4 minutes or until onions are tender. Add flour, stirring until smooth. Gradually add half-and-half and milk, stirring well. Stir in mushrooms, salt, and pepper. Microwave, uncovered, at HIGH for 4 to 6 minutes or until thickened, stirring every 2 minutes. Stir in scallops. Reduce to MEDIUM HIGH (70% power), and microwave, uncovered, for 4 to 6 minutes or until scallops are opaque, stirring after 3 minutes. Stir in diced pimiento. Spoon filling into patty shells, and serve immediately. Yield: 6 servings.

CASINO OYSTERS

4 slices bacon
¼ cup finely chopped onion
¼ cup chopped pecans
⅓ cup seasoned, dry
  breadcrumbs
1 tablespoon Chablis or other
  dry white wine
1 tablespoon butter or
  margarine
½ teaspoon lemon juice
1 dozen oysters on the half
  shell, drained

Place bacon on a rack in a baking dish. Cover with paper towels and microwave at HIGH for 3½ to 4½ minutes or until bacon is crisp. Crumble bacon, and set aside, reserving 1 tablespoon of drippings.

Combine 1 tablespoon bacon drippings and onion in a small bowl. Microwave, uncovered, at HIGH for 2 minutes or until onion is tender. Stir in pecans, breadcrumbs, wine, and crumbled bacon; set aside.

Place butter in a 1-cup glass measure. Microwave, uncovered, at HIGH for 35 seconds or until melted. Stir in lemon juice. Dip oysters in butter mixture, and place in half shells. Pierce each oyster with a fork; top with crumb mixture. Arrange shells around outer edge of a 12-inch round glass platter. Reduce to MEDIUM (50% power); cover with wax paper and microwave for 4 to 5 minutes or until thoroughly heated, rotating a half-turn after 2 minutes. Serve oysters immediately. Yield: 1 dozen.

To clarify butter, place it in a glass measure and microwave at HIGH until bubbly. The clear layer is the clarified butter; carefully pour it into a serving container.

LEMON-BUTTERED LOBSTER TAILS

4 (6-ounce) frozen lobster tails
¼ cup butter or margarine
2 tablespoons lemon juice
Paprika
Lemon slices (optional)
Parsley sprigs (optional)

Place frozen lobster in a 12- x 8- x 2-inch baking dish. Cover with heavy-duty plastic wrap and microwave at MEDIUM LOW (30% power) for 6 minutes. Let stand 10 minutes.

Split lobster lengthwise with kitchen shears, cutting through hard upper shell and meat to, but not through, bottom shell. Grasp lobster and spread open; return to baking dish with thickest portions towards outside of dish.

Place butter and lemon juice in a 1-cup glass measure. Microwave, uncovered, at HIGH for 1 minute or until bubbly. Brush lobster with butter mixture, and sprinkle with paprika. Cover and microwave at HIGH for 5 to 6 minutes or until lobster meat is tender, rotating a half-turn after 3 minutes. Let stand, covered, 5 minutes. Garnish with lemon slices and parsley, if desired. Serve immediately. Yield: 4 servings.

Meats

Microwaved meats can be tender and juicy and save preparation and cleanup time. The key to success is matching the correct microwave technique with the correct cut of meat.

Chuck pot roasts or rump roasts cook nicely in the microwave oven as do small cuts of pork and lamb, sausage, ground beef, and bacon. Very large cuts of meat are generally better when cooked conventionally.

Uniformly shaped meat cooks the most evenly. Protruding areas of irregularly shaped roasts and steaks will cook too fast. You can help prevent overcooking of these spots by covering or shielding with aluminum foil (see *Shielding*, page 8).

Fat areas attract microwaves and may cause meat near the fat to overcook. Therefore, it's a good idea to trim off any excess fat. On the other hand, bones shield microwaves so that the meat near them may cook very slowly. In this case, you may want to remove the bones or avoid purchasing that cut of meat.

It's also critical to use the correct power level when microwaving meats. HIGH power works well with ground beef, bacon, and some small cuts of pork and lamb. Most other cuts cook more evenly if microwaved for a longer period of time at a lower power level.

If your oven has a temperature probe, you may want to insert it or use another microwave-safe thermometer. Remove the meat from the microwave after the initial cooking time, and insert the microwave-safe thermometer. Standing time will allow the temperature within the meat to rise and complete the cooking process.

Serve Orange Pork Chops (page 150) proudly to your family. The chops are browned in a microwave browning skillet and coated with an orange juice glaze.

Most meat should be covered with wax paper to prevent spattering in the oven. Pork should be wrapped tightly in heavy-duty plastic wrap or placed in a browning bag or another closed container so that it reaches the safe-eating temperature of 170°F. When done, pork and beef should no longer be pink.

To help meat cook more evenly, it's important to take the time for rearranging, rotating, and turning it over. Some roasts and steaks should be put on a rack to hold the meat out of the juices. Otherwise, the juices will attract the microwaves which will lengthen the cooking time and overcook the meat.

Meat Loaf With Water Chestnuts

Shape the meatloaf mixture into a slightly rounded loaf and place in a baking dish.

1½ pounds ground beef
2 eggs, beaten
½ cup fine, dry breadcrumbs
½ cup finely chopped green onions
½ cup finely chopped green pepper
⅓ cup finely chopped water chestnuts
3 tablespoons catsup
2 tablespoons soy sauce
½ teaspoon salt
¼ teaspoon pepper
3 tablespoons catsup
1 tablespoon soy sauce
1 tablespoon brown sugar

Combine first 10 ingredients, mixing well. Shape mixture into a 10- x 5-inch slightly rounded loaf, and place in a 12- x 8- x 2-inch baking dish. Cover with wax paper and microwave at HIGH for 14 to 18 minutes or until firm, rotating a half-turn after 7 minutes. Drain off excess drippings.

Combine 3 tablespoons catsup, 1 tablespoon soy sauce, and brown sugar; spoon over meat loaf. Reduce to MEDIUM HIGH (70% power), and microwave, uncovered, for 1½ to 2 minutes or until set. Let stand 5 minutes before serving. Yield: 8 servings.

Pizza Meat Loaf

¾ pound ground beef
½ pound bulk pork sausage
1½ cups soft breadcrumbs
1 (8-ounce) can tomato sauce, divided
1 egg, beaten
3 tablespoons finely chopped onion
3 tablespoons finely chopped green pepper
½ teaspoon garlic powder
½ teaspoon dried whole oregano
¼ teaspoon salt
¾ cup (3 ounces) shredded mozzarella cheese

Combine beef, sausage, breadcrumbs, ⅓ cup tomato sauce, egg, onion, green pepper, garlic powder, oregano, and salt in a medium bowl; stir well. Shape mixture into a 9- x 4-inch rounded loaf, and place in a 12- x 8- x 2-inch baking dish. Cover with wax paper and microwave at HIGH for 15 to 17 minutes or until firm, rotating a half-turn after 7 minutes. Drain off excess drippings.

Spread remaining tomato sauce evenly over meat loaf. Microwave, uncovered, at HIGH for 2 minutes. Sprinkle with cheese. Reduce to MEDIUM HIGH (70% power), and microwave, uncovered, 2 to 3 minutes or just until cheese begins to melt. Let stand 5 minutes before serving. Yield: 6 servings.

SHEPHERD'S PIE

1 (10-ounce) package frozen
   mixed vegetables
1 pound ground beef
¼ cup chopped onion
½ cup fine, dry breadcrumbs
½ cup tomato sauce
½ cup milk
1 tablespoon brown sugar
⅛ teaspoon ground allspice
½ teaspoon salt
⅛ teaspoon pepper
3 cups peeled and cubed
   potatoes
¼ cup water
2 tablespoons butter or
   margarine
¼ cup milk
¼ teaspoon salt
⅛ teaspoon pepper
½ cup (2 ounces) shredded
   Cheddar cheese

Place frozen vegetables in a 9-inch pieplate. Microwave, uncovered, at HIGH for 4 to 5 minutes or until thawed; drain and set aside.

Combine beef, onion, breadcrumbs, tomato sauce, ½ cup milk, brown sugar, allspice, ½ teaspoon salt, ⅛ teaspoon pepper, and thawed vegetables in a medium bowl, stirring well. Press beef mixture into a 9-inch pieplate. Cover with wax paper and microwave at HIGH for 10 to 11 minutes or until meat is no longer pink, rotating a quarter-turn after 5 minutes. Let stand, covered, 5 minutes; drain and set aside.

Place potatoes in a deep 2-quart casserole; add water. Cover with heavy-duty plastic wrap and microwave at HIGH for 10 to 12 minutes or until potatoes are tender, stirring after 5 minutes. Drain well.

Combine potatoes, butter, ¼ cup milk, ¼ teaspoon salt, and ⅛ teaspoon pepper in a medium bowl; beat at medium speed of an electric mixer until smooth. Spread potato mixture over beef mixture, sealing to edge of pieplate. Sprinkle with cheese; microwave, uncovered, at HIGH for 3 minutes or until cheese melts. Serve immediately. Yield: 6 to 8 servings.

MEXI-BEEF CASSEROLE

1 pound ground beef
¾ cup chopped onion
½ cup chopped celery
1 (16-ounce) can red kidney
   beans, drained
1 (12-ounce) can whole kernel
   corn, drained
1 (8-ounce) can tomato sauce
1 (2¼-ounce) can sliced ripe
   olives, drained
1½ teaspoons chili powder
½ teaspoon salt
½ teaspoon pepper
½ cup (2 ounces) shredded
   Cheddar cheese
½ cup crushed corn chips

Combine ground beef, onion, and celery in a 2½-quart casserole, stirring well. Cover with wax paper and microwave at HIGH for 5 to 6 minutes or until meat is no longer pink, stirring every 2 minutes. Drain off drippings.

Add beans and next 6 ingredients to meat mixture, stirring well. Cover and microwave at HIGH for 4 to 5 minutes or until thoroughly heated, stirring after 2 minutes. Sprinkle with cheese and chips. Reduce to MEDIUM HIGH (70% power), and microwave, uncovered, for 2 to 3 minutes or until cheese melts. Serve immediately. Yield: 6 servings.

Beefy Enchilada Casserole

1½ pounds ground beef
1 cup chopped onion
1 (4-ounce) can chopped green
 chiles
¼ teaspoon chili powder
¼ teaspoon ground cumin
1 clove garlic, minced
¼ teaspoon salt
¼ teaspoon pepper
¼ cup all-purpose flour
¼ cup undiluted canned beef
 broth
2 (10-ounce) cans enchilada
 sauce
6 (6-inch) corn tortillas
2 (2¼-ounce) cans sliced ripe
 olives, drained
2 cups (8 ounces) shredded
 Cheddar cheese

Combine ground beef, onion, chiles, chili powder, cumin, garlic, salt, and pepper in a 2-quart casserole, stirring well. Cover with wax paper and microwave at HIGH for 7 to 9 minutes or until meat is no longer pink; drain and set aside.

Combine flour and broth in a 2-quart casserole; stir with a wire whisk until smooth. Add enchilada sauce, stirring well. Microwave, uncovered, at HIGH for 5 to 6 minutes or until thickened, stirring every 2 minutes.

Spread ½ cup sauce mixture in a 13- x 9- x 2-inch baking dish; top with 3 tortillas, overlapping edges, if necessary. Spread ½ cup sauce mixture over tortillas; top with half of meat mixture, 1 can olives, and 1 cup cheese. Repeat layers with remaining 3 tortillas, ½ cup sauce mixture, remaining meat mixture, remaining olives, and remaining 1 cup cheese. Top with remaining sauce mixture.

Reduce to MEDIUM HIGH (70% power); cover with wax paper and microwave for 10 to 11 minutes or until thoroughly heated, rotating a half-turn after 5 minutes. Serve immediately. Yield: 8 servings.

Beef Tortillas

1 (1-pound) flank steak
½ cup chopped green onions
¼ cup chopped green pepper
1 tablespoon vinegar
1½ teaspoons chili powder
½ teaspoon dry mustard
¼ teaspoon salt
¼ teaspoon garlic powder
2 teaspoons cornstarch
1 tablespoon water
1 (8-ounce) can tomato sauce
1 teaspoon brown sugar
4 (8-inch) flour tortillas

Partially freeze steak; slice diagonally across grain into 3- x ¼-inch strips, and set aside. Place onions and next 6 ingredients in a 2-quart casserole. Stir in meat. Cover with heavy-duty plastic wrap and microwave at HIGH for 3 minutes; stir well. Reduce to MEDIUM (50% power); cover and microwave for 20 minutes or until meat is tender, stirring after 10 minutes.

Combine cornstarch and water, stirring well. Add cornstarch mixture, tomato sauce, and brown sugar to meat mixture, stirring well. Increase to HIGH power; microwave, uncovered, for 3 to 4 minutes or until thickened, stirring after every minute.

Place about ⅓ cup meat mixture in center of each tortilla. Roll up tortillas, and place seam side down on a serving platter. Spoon any remaining meat mixture over top. Microwave, uncovered, at HIGH for 1 to 2 minutes or until thoroughly heated. Yield: 4 servings.

Ginger Beef

1 (1-pound) flank steak
¼ cup undiluted canned beef
   broth
2 tablespoons soy sauce
2 tablespoons vegetable oil
1½ tablespoons cornstarch
1½ tablespoons grated fresh
   gingerroot
1 tablespoon dry sherry
1 teaspoon sugar
1 clove garlic, minced
1 medium-size green pepper,
   cut into ¾-inch strips
Hot cooked rice
2 green onions, chopped

Partially freeze steak; slice diagonally across grain into ⅛-inch strips, and set aside. Combine broth, soy sauce, oil, cornstarch, gingerroot, sherry, sugar, and garlic in a 2-quart casserole; add meat, tossing well. Cover and refrigerate at least 8 hours.

Place a 10-inch browning skillet in microwave oven; preheat, uncovered, at HIGH for 6 minutes. Add meat mixture and green pepper to hot skillet. Microwave, uncovered, at HIGH for 6 to 9 minutes or until meat is no longer pink, stirring every 3 minutes. Serve over rice, and sprinkle with onions. Yield: 6 servings.

Peppery Beef And Broccoli

¾ pound boneless round steak
¼ cup plus 2 tablespoons
   water
¼ cup soy sauce
3 tablespoons dry sherry
½ to ¾ teaspoon coarsely
   ground black pepper
1 clove garlic, crushed
1 tablespoon vegetable oil
1 (10-ounce) package frozen
   broccoli
2 medium carrots, scraped and
   diagonally sliced
2 teaspoons cornstarch
2 tablespoons water
Hot cooked rice

Partially freeze steak; slice diagonally across grain into 2- x ¼-inch strips; set aside. Combine ¼ cup plus 2 tablespoons water and next 4 ingredients in a medium bowl; add meat, tossing well. Cover and refrigerate at least 2 hours.

Place a 10-inch browning skillet in microwave oven; preheat, uncovered, at HIGH for 5 to 6 minutes. Add oil to hot skillet, tilting to coat surface. Drain meat, reserving liquid. Add meat to skillet, stirring well. Microwave, uncovered, at HIGH for 3½ to 4 minutes or until no longer pink, stirring after 2 minutes; set aside.

Place broccoli in a 2-quart casserole; cover with heavy-duty plastic wrap and microwave at HIGH for 2 to 3 minutes or until partially thawed. Cut broccoli into 2-inch pieces, and return to casserole. Add marinade and carrots to broccoli. Cover and microwave at HIGH for 6 to 7 minutes or until vegetables are crisp-tender. Combine cornstarch and 2 tablespoons water, stirring well. Add cornstarch mixture to vegetable mixture, stirring well. Microwave, uncovered, at HIGH for 5 to 7 minutes or until thickened, stirring after 3 minutes. Add meat; microwave, uncovered, at HIGH for 2 minutes or until thoroughly heated. Serve over rice. Yield: 4 servings.

BEEF WITH PEA PODS

1 pound boneless round steak
¼ cup water
¼ cup sherry
¼ cup soy sauce
2 tablespoons cornstarch
2 teaspoons brown sugar
1 teaspoon grated fresh gingerroot
2 cloves garlic, minced
2 tablespoons vegetable oil
1 (6-ounce) package frozen snow pea pods
1 medium-size sweet red pepper, cut into strips
4 green onions, cut into 1-inch pieces
Green onion fan (optional)

Partially freeze steak; slice diagonally across grain into 2½- x ½-inch strips, and set aside. Combine water and next 6 ingredients, stirring well. Add meat, tossing well. Cover and refrigerate 30 minutes.

Place a 10-inch browning skillet in microwave oven; preheat, uncovered, at HIGH for 6 minutes. Add oil to hot skillet, tilting to coat surface. Drain meat, reserving marinade. Add meat to skillet, stirring well. Microwave, uncovered, at HIGH for 3 to 4 minutes or until no longer pink, stirring after 2 minutes; set aside.

Place reserved marinade in a 1-quart casserole. Microwave, uncovered, at HIGH for 1½ to 2 minutes or until thickened, stirring every 30 seconds. Pour mixture over meat.

Place pea pods in a small bowl; cover with heavy-duty plastic wrap and microwave at HIGH for 1½ to 2 minutes or until partially thawed. Stir pea pods, pepper strips, and 4 green onions into meat mixture. Microwave, uncovered, at HIGH for 3 to 4 minutes or until vegetables are crisp-tender, stirring after 2 minutes. Garnish with a green onion fan, if desired. Yield: 4 servings.

Beef Stroganoff

1½ pounds boneless round
  steak
¾ cup chopped onion
2 teaspoons butter or margarine
¼ cup all-purpose flour
½ teaspoon salt
¼ teaspoon pepper
⅛ teaspoon ground nutmeg
¾ cup undiluted canned beef
  broth
2 tablespoons Chablis or other
  dry white wine
½ pound fresh mushrooms,
  sliced
1 (8-ounce) carton commercial
  sour cream
3 cups hot cooked noodles
½ cup chopped fresh parsley

Partially freeze steak; slice diagonally across grain into 3- x ½-inch strips, and set aside. Combine onion and butter in a 3-quart casserole. Cover with heavy-duty plastic wrap and microwave at HIGH for 2 to 3 minutes or until onion is tender. Combine flour, salt, pepper, and nutmeg in a plastic bag, mixing well; add meat, shaking to coat.

Add meat to onion mixture. Cover and microwave at HIGH for 5 to 7 minutes or until meat is no longer pink. Stir in broth and wine; cover and microwave at HIGH for 7 to 8 minutes or until boiling. Add mushrooms, stirring well. Reduce to MEDIUM (50% power); cover and microwave for 25 to 35 minutes or until meat is tender, stirring every 10 minutes. Stir in sour cream; cover and microwave at MEDIUM for 3 to 5 minutes or just until sour cream is heated.

Combine noodles and parsley, tossing well; arrange on serving platter. Spoon meat mixture over top; serve immediately. Yield: 6 servings.

Delicious Beef Kabobs

¼ cup teriyaki sauce
2 tablespoons orange juice
2 tablespoons honey
1 tablespoon minced onion
1 tablespoon vegetable oil
½ teaspoon garlic powder
½ teaspoon ground ginger
1 pound sirloin tip roast, cut
  into 1-inch pieces
4 small onions, quartered
1 medium zucchini, cut into 16
  slices
Hot cooked rice

Combine teriyaki sauce, orange juice, honey, minced onion, oil, garlic powder, and ginger in a bowl, stirring well. Place meat in a large shallow dish. Pour sauce mixture over meat; cover and refrigerate at least 8 hours. Drain, reserving marinade.

Alternately thread meat, onion, and zucchini on eight 12-inch wooden skewers. Place 4 kabobs on a roasting rack or lay lengthwise across a 12- x 8- x 2-inch baking dish. Microwave, uncovered, at HIGH for 6 to 8 minutes or to desired degree of doneness, turning and basting with marinade every 2 minutes. Repeat procedure with remaining 4 kabobs. Serve over rice. Yield: 4 servings.

Before microwaving a roast, pierce it deeply on all sides with a fork; this allows the steam and moisture to reach the interior.

Flavorful Pot Roast With Gravy

For tender results, place the pot roast in a prepared browning bag in a baking dish. Add water and onion to bag. Tie bag loosely with string before microwaving.

1 tablespoon beef-flavored
  bouillon granules
1½ teaspoons all-purpose flour
¼ teaspoon paprika
¼ teaspoon freshly ground
  pepper
1 (2- to 3-pound) boneless
  chuck roast, uniformly
  shaped and no more than
  2 to 2½ inches thick
¼ cup water
1 medium onion, sliced and
  separated into rings
2 tablespoons butter or
  margarine
2 tablespoons all-purpose flour

Combine first 4 ingredients, stirring well; sprinkle over roast, and rub in gently. Place roast in a large browning bag prepared according to package directions and placed in a 12- x 8- x 2-inch baking dish; add water and onion. Tie bag loosely with string or a ½-inch-wide strip cut from open end of bag.

Microwave at MEDIUM (50% power) for 50 to 60 minutes or until microwave thermometer registers 150°, turning bag over and rotating dish a half-turn every 25 minutes. Let roast stand 10 to 15 minutes in bag or until thermometer registers 160°. Remove roast to serving platter, reserving drippings.

Place butter in a 2-cup glass measure. Microwave, uncovered, at HIGH for 45 seconds or until melted. Add flour; stir until blended. Gradually add reserved drippings, stirring well. Microwave, uncovered, at HIGH for 3 to 4 minutes or until thickened, stirring after 2 minutes. Serve gravy with roast. Yield: 8 servings.

Tangy Sauerbraten

4 whole cloves
1 bay leaf
1 (4-pound) boneless bottom
  round roast, uniformly
  shaped
1 cup Burgundy or other dry
  red wine
½ cup red wine vinegar
½ cup chopped celery
2 carrots, scraped and sliced
2 small onions, sliced
1 clove garlic, minced
½ teaspoon pepper
¼ teaspoon salt
¾ cup finely crushed
  gingersnaps
¼ cup water
1 tablespoon all-purpose flour
½ teaspoon beef-flavored
  bouillon granules
Steamed baby carrots (optional)
Steamed brussels sprouts
  (optional)

Tie cloves and bay leaf together in a cheesecloth bag. Pierce meat several times with a fork, and place in a 3-quart casserole. Add cheesecloth bag. Combine wine and next 7 ingredients, stirring well. Pour over roast. Cover and refrigerate 3 days, turning roast each day.

Remove and discard cheesecloth bag. Sprinkle crushed gingersnaps over roast. Cover with heavy-duty plastic wrap and microwave at HIGH for 16 minutes, turning roast over after 8 minutes. Reduce to MEDIUM (50% power); cover and microwave for 35 to 40 minutes or until microwave thermometer registers 135°, turning roast over and basting after 15 minutes. Let stand, covered, 15 minutes or until thermometer registers 150°. Remove roast to a serving platter, reserving vegetable marinade.

Transfer vegetable marinade to container of an electric blender or food processor. Cover and process until smooth. Pour pureed mixture into a 2-quart bowl.

TANGY SAUERBRATEN

(continued)

Combine water, flour, and bouillon granules, stirring well; add to pureed mixture. Microwave, uncovered, at HIGH for 5 to 7 minutes or until thickened, stirring after 3 minutes. Slice roast with an electric knife, if desired; top with gravy. Garnish with carrots and brussels sprouts, if desired. Yield: 8 to 10 servings.

Tangy Sauerbraten gets its mouth-watering flavor from marinating in a spicy wine and vinegar mixture.

Lemon Veal With Carrots features paper-thin slices of veal that are browned in a microwave browning skillet and served with carrots.

Lemon Veal With Carrots ———————

½ **pound (¼-inch-thick) veal cutlets**
2 **tablespoons all-purpose flour**
¼ **teaspoon salt**
⅛ **teaspoon pepper**
¼ **teaspoon dried whole rosemary, crushed**
¼ **teaspoon garlic powder**
2 **tablespoons butter or margarine**
2 **carrots, scraped and cut into julienne strips**
2 **tablespoons lemon juice**
2 **tablespoons Chablis or other dry white wine**
Lemon wedges (optional)
Sprig of fresh rosemary (optional)

Remove and discard any excess fat from cutlets. Place cutlets between 2 sheets of wax paper; flatten to ⅛-inch thickness, using a meat mallet or rolling pin.

Combine flour and next 4 ingredients; stir well. Dredge cutlets in flour mixture; set aside.

Place a 10-inch browning skillet in microwave oven; preheat, uncovered, at HIGH for 6 to 8 minutes. Add butter to hot skillet, tilting to coat surface. Place cutlets in skillet; cover browning skillet with lid and microwave at HIGH for 2 minutes. Turn cutlets over; add carrot strips, lemon juice, and wine. Reduce to MEDIUM HIGH (70% power); cover and microwave for 6 minutes or until veal is tender and carrots are crisp-tender, rotating a half-turn after 3 minutes. Garnish with lemon wedges and a sprig of rosemary, if desired. Yield: 2 servings.

Simmered Veal And Peppers

2 medium-size green peppers,
   cut into ¼-inch strips
½ cup chopped onion
1 clove garlic, minced
2 tablespoons olive oil
1½ pounds veal cutlets, cut
   into ½-inch strips
¼ cup all-purpose flour
1 cup sliced fresh mushrooms
1 (28-ounce) can whole
   tomatoes, undrained and
   chopped
1 (8-ounce) can tomato sauce
½ teaspoon dried whole basil
½ teaspoon dried whole
   oregano
½ teaspoon salt
¼ teaspoon pepper
Hot cooked spaghetti

Place green pepper, onion, garlic, and oil in a 3-quart casserole. Cover with heavy-duty plastic wrap and microwave at HIGH for 3 to 4 minutes or until vegetables are tender. Dredge meat in flour; add to vegetable mixture. Cover and microwave at HIGH for 10 minutes, stirring after 5 minutes.

Add mushrooms, tomatoes, tomato sauce, basil, oregano, salt, and pepper to meat mixture. Cover and microwave at HIGH for 10 minutes or until boiling, stirring after 5 minutes. Reduce to MEDIUM (50% power); cover and microwave for 30 to 35 minutes or until meat is tender, stirring every 10 minutes. Serve over spaghetti. Yield: 8 servings.

Veal In Mushroom And Dill Gravy

1 tablespoon butter or
   margarine
1 (4-ounce) can sliced
   mushrooms, drained
⅓ cup chopped green onions
⅓ cup water
1 teaspoon beef-flavored
   bouillon granules
1 teaspoon grated lemon rind
1 tablespoon lemon juice
¼ teaspoon dried whole
   dillweed
⅛ teaspoon pepper
1 pound (¼-inch-thick) veal
   cutlets
1½ tablespoons cornstarch
2 tablespoons water

Place butter in a 4-cup glass measure; microwave, uncovered, at HIGH for 35 seconds or until melted. Stir in mushrooms, onions, ⅓ cup water, bouillon granules, lemon rind, lemon juice, dillweed, and pepper; set aside.

Arrange veal in a 12- x 8- x 2-inch baking dish. Pour mushroom mixture over veal. Reduce to MEDIUM (50% power); cover with heavy-duty plastic wrap and microwave for 15 to 18 minutes or until veal is tender, rotating a half-turn every 5 minutes.

Remove veal to a serving platter, reserving mushroom mixture in baking dish. Combine cornstarch and 2 tablespoons water, stirring well; stir into mushroom mixture. Microwave, uncovered, at HIGH for 3 to 4 minutes or until slightly thickened. Serve gravy over veal. Yield: 4 servings.

It is possible to microwave and drain ground beef or sausage at the same time. Crumble the meat into a plastic colander placed inside a 2-quart casserole. Microwave at HIGH until no longer pink. Drippings will drain into the casserole.

Italian Veal Cutlets

3 tablespoons chopped onion
2 teaspoons olive oil
1 (8-ounce) can tomato sauce
½ teaspoon dried whole basil
1 pound (¼-inch-thick) veal
   cutlets (about 4)
3 tablespoons all-purpose flour
½ teaspoon salt
⅛ teaspoon pepper
1 egg
2 tablespoons milk
½ cup seasoned, dry
   breadcrumbs
½ teaspoon paprika
2 tablespoons olive oil
¾ cup (3 ounces) shredded
   mozzarella cheese
1 tablespoon grated Parmesan
   cheese
2 tablespoons chopped fresh
   parsley

Combine onion and 2 teaspoons oil in a 4-cup glass measure. Cover with heavy-duty plastic wrap and microwave at HIGH for 1 to 2 minutes or until onion is tender. Stir in tomato sauce and basil. Microwave, uncovered, at HIGH for 3 to 4 minutes or until thickened; set aside.

Remove and discard any excess fat from cutlets. Place cutlets between 2 sheets of wax paper; flatten to ⅛-inch thickness, using a meat mallet or rolling pin.

Combine flour, salt, and pepper; stir well. Combine egg and milk; stir well. Combine breadcrumbs and paprika; stir well. Dredge cutlets in flour mixture; dip in egg mixture, and coat with breadcrumb mixture.

Place a 10-inch browning skillet in microwave oven; preheat, uncovered, at HIGH for 6 to 8 minutes. Add 2 tablespoons olive oil to hot skillet, tilting to coat surface. Place cutlets in skillet, overlapping edges, if necessary; microwave, uncovered, at HIGH for 2 minutes. Turn cutlets over. Microwave, uncovered, at HIGH for 3 to 4 minutes or until veal is tender. Drain off drippings. Pour tomato sauce mixture over veal. Sprinkle with mozzarella cheese; top with Parmesan cheese. Reduce to MEDIUM HIGH (70% power); microwave, uncovered, for 1½ minutes or until cheese melts. Sprinkle with parsley. Yield: 4 servings.

Orange Pork Chops

4 (1-inch-thick) pork chops
   (about 1¾ pounds)
3 tablespoons seasoned, dry
   breadcrumbs
Pepper to taste
Paprika
2 tablespoons vegetable oil
¾ cup orange juice
2 tablespoons orange
   marmalade
1 tablespoon grated orange
   rind
⅓ cup sugar
1 teaspoon cornstarch
½ teaspoon ground cinnamon
Hot cooked parslied rice with
   lemon rind (optional)

Dredge chops in breadcrumbs; sprinkle with pepper and paprika. Place a 10-inch browning skillet in microwave oven; preheat, uncovered, at HIGH for 6 to 8 minutes. Add oil to hot skillet, tilting to coat surface. Arrange chops in skillet with thickest portions towards outside of dish; microwave, uncovered, at HIGH for 1 minute. Turn chops over and microwave, uncovered, for 1 minute.

Cover browning skillet with lid; reduce to MEDIUM (50% power), and microwave 20 minutes or until chops are tender and no longer pink, turning chops over after 10 minutes.

Combine orange juice, marmalade, and orange rind in a 2-cup glass measure; add sugar, cornstarch, and cinnamon, stirring well. Microwave, uncovered, at HIGH for 3 minutes or until slightly thickened. Serve chops over rice, if desired; spoon sauce over chops before serving. Yield: 4 servings.

SWEET-AND-SOUR PORK

1 (8¼-ounce) can pineapple chunks, undrained
¼ cup sugar
2 tablespoons cornstarch
¼ cup rice vinegar
2 tablespoons catsup
1 tablespoon plus 1½ teaspoons soy sauce
¼ teaspoon grated fresh gingerroot
1 pound boneless pork, trimmed and cut into 1-inch cubes
1 medium-size green pepper, cut into strips
1 medium-size sweet red pepper, cut into strips
2 green onions, sliced diagonally into 1-inch pieces
Hot cooked rice

Drain pineapple chunks, reserving liquid; set pineapple and liquid aside.

Combine sugar and cornstarch in a 2-quart casserole. Stir in vinegar, catsup, soy sauce, and gingerroot. Add pineapple juice and pork. Cover with heavy-duty plastic wrap and microwave at MEDIUM (50% power) for 6 to 7 minutes or until pork is no longer pink, stirring every 3 minutes.

Stir in pineapple chunks, pepper strips, and onions. Cover and microwave at HIGH for 5 minutes or until pepper strips are crisp-tender, stirring after 2½ minutes. Let stand, covered, 5 minutes. Serve over hot cooked rice. Yield: 4 servings.

Tie the split sections of pork loin roast together with string.

HERBED PORK LOIN

2 teaspoons rubbed sage
2 cloves garlic, minced
1 teaspoon ground marjoram
½ teaspoon dried whole oregano
½ teaspoon pepper
1 (4-pound) boneless double pork loin roast, cut for rolling

Combine first 5 ingredients in a small bowl. Trim excess fat from roast; place split sections of roast atop each other. Rub surface of roast with herb mixture. Tie roast at 2- to 3-inch intervals with string.

Place roast in a large browning bag prepared according to package directions and placed in a 12- x 8- x 2-inch baking dish. Tie bag loosely with string or a ½-inch-wide strip cut from open end of bag.

Microwave at MEDIUM (50% power) for 45 to 50 minutes or until microwave thermometer registers 165°, turning bag over and rotating dish a half-turn every 25 minutes. Let roast stand 10 minutes in bag or until thermometer registers 170°. Yield: 8 servings.

Place the roast in a prepared browning bag in a baking dish. A microwave thermometer will register 170° when complete.

Danish Pork Roast

½ teaspoon ground cinnamon
½ teaspoon salt
½ teaspoon pepper
¼ teaspoon ground cloves
¼ teaspoon ground mace
1 (4-pound) boneless double pork loin roast, cut for rolling
12 pitted prunes
½ (6-ounce) package dried apricots
2 tablespoons golden raisins
¼ teaspoon ground cinnamon
¼ cup brandy
2 tablespoons red currant jelly

Combine ½ teaspoon cinnamon, salt, pepper, cloves, and mace; rub over roast. Cover and refrigerate at least 8 hours. Combine prunes, apricots, raisins, ¼ teaspoon cinnamon, and brandy. Cover and refrigerate at least 8 hours.

Drain fruit, discarding brandy. Trim excess fat from roast; place bottom of roast, fat side down. Arrange fruit mixture on roast. Place top of roast, fat side up, atop fruit mixture. Tie roast at 2- to 3-inch intervals with string. Place roast in a large browning bag prepared according to package directions and placed in a 12- x 8- x 2-inch baking dish. Tie bag loosely with string or a ½-inch-wide strip cut from open end of bag. Microwave at MEDIUM (50% power) for 45 to 50 minutes or until microwave thermometer registers 165°, turning bag over and rotating dish a half-turn every 25 minutes. Let roast stand 10 minutes in bag or until thermometer registers 170°.

Place jelly in a 1-cup glass measure. Microwave, uncovered, at HIGH for 30 seconds to 1 minute or until melted. Remove roast from bag; brush with jelly. Yield: 8 to 10 servings.

Grilled Ribs

⅓ cup finely chopped onion
3 tablespoons vegetable oil
1 cup chili sauce
¼ cup firmly packed brown sugar
¼ cup lemon juice
2 tablespoons cider vinegar
1 teaspoon salt
2 dashes of hot sauce
4 pounds spareribs
¼ cup beer or water
Fresh parsley sprigs (optional)

Combine onion and oil in a 4-cup glass measure. Cover with heavy-duty plastic wrap and microwave at HIGH for 2 to 3 minutes or until onion is tender. Stir in chili sauce and next 5 ingredients. Cover and microwave at HIGH for 4 to 5 minutes or until slightly thickened, stirring after 2 minutes; set aside.

Cut ribs into serving-size pieces; place in a 13- x 9- x 2-inch baking dish. Pour beer over ribs. Cover with heavy-duty plastic wrap and microwave at HIGH for 20 minutes, rearranging ribs in dish after 10 minutes.

Transfer ribs to barbecue grill. Grill ribs over medium coals for 15 minutes or to desired degree of doneness, turning and basting frequently with sauce. Garnish with parsley, if desired. Yield: 4 to 6 servings.

Grilled Ribs are partially cooked in the microwave oven and then transferred to the barbecue grill.

CRANBERRY HAM SLICE

1 cup fresh cranberries
½ cup sugar
¼ cup port wine
1 teaspoon grated orange rind
2 teaspoons cornstarch
2 tablespoons water
1 (1-pound) fully cooked ham
  slice

Combine cranberries, sugar, and wine in a 4-cup glass measure. Microwave, uncovered, at HIGH for 4 to 4½ minutes or until cranberry skins pop, stirring after 2 minutes. Stir in orange rind. Combine cornstarch and water; add to cranberry mixture. Microwave, uncovered, at HIGH for 1 to 1½ minutes or until thickened and bubbly; set aside.

Place ham slice on a roasting rack in a shallow baking dish. Reduce to MEDIUM HIGH (70% power); cover with wax paper and microwave for 6 to 8 minutes or until thoroughly heated, turning ham over after 4 minutes. Serve with cranberry sauce. Yield: 4 servings.

SPAGHETTI WITH SAUSAGE MEAT SAUCE

1 pound mild or hot Italian
  sausage
1 cup sliced fresh mushrooms
⅔ cup chopped onion
1 small carrot, scraped and
  shredded
1 tablespoon olive oil
1 clove garlic, minced
1 (14½-ounce) can Italian-style
  tomatoes, undrained and
  chopped
1 (6-ounce) can tomato paste
½ cup water
1 tablespoon dried parsley
  flakes
1 teaspoon beef-flavored
  bouillon granules
½ teaspoon salt
½ teaspoon dried whole basil
¼ teaspoon dried whole
  oregano
¼ teaspoon pepper
Hot cooked spaghetti
Freshly grated Parmesan cheese

Remove casings from sausage; place sausage in a 3-quart casserole, stirring to crumble. Cover with wax paper and microwave at HIGH for 5 to 6 minutes or until meat is no longer pink, stirring after 3 minutes. Drain and set aide.

Place mushrooms, onion, carrot, oil, and garlic in casserole. Cover and microwave at HIGH for 3 to 4 minutes or until vegetables are tender. Add sausage, tomatoes, tomato paste, water, parsley flakes, bouillon granules, salt, basil, oregano, and pepper; stir well. Cover and microwave at HIGH for to 7 to 8 minutes or until slightly thickened, stirring after 4 minutes.

Serve sauce over spaghetti, and sprinkle with cheese. Yield: 4 servings.

Enjoy barbecued flavor all year long, even if you cook outdoors only in the summer—just freeze the barbecued meat, and then reheat it in the microwave.

Sausage Pizza

½ pound Italian sausage
2 tablespoons butter or
  margarine
1 cup water
1 package dry yeast
2½ to 3 cups all-purpose flour
2 teaspoons sugar, divided
2 teaspoons salt, divided
1 tablespoon vegetable oil
1 medium onion, chopped
3 cloves garlic, minced
1 (28-ounce) can whole
  tomatoes, undrained and
  chopped
1 (6-ounce) can tomato paste
1 teaspoon dried whole basil
¾ teaspoon crushed fennel
  seeds
½ cup grated Parmesan cheese
2 (8-ounce) packages shredded
  mozzarella cheese
½ pound fresh mushrooms,
  sliced
1 medium-size green pepper,
  chopped
1 can sliced ripe olives,
  drained

Remove casings from sausage; place sausage in a 1½-quart casserole, stirring to crumble. Cover with wax paper and microwave at HIGH for 4 to 6 minutes or until meat is no longer pink, stirring after 2 minutes. Drain meat, and set aside.

Combine butter and water in a large bowl. Microwave, uncovered, at HIGH for 1½ minutes. Stir to melt butter; cool to lukewarm (110°). Sprinkle yeast over water mixture; let stand 5 minutes. Stir until dissolved.

Gradually add flour, 1 teaspoon sugar, and 1 teaspoon salt to yeast mixture, stirring well (dough may be sticky). Turn dough out onto a lightly floured surface, and knead until smooth and elastic. Shape dough into a ball, and place in a lightly greased bowl, turning to grease top; cover with heavy-duty plastic wrap. Pour 3 cups water into a 4-cup glass measure. Microwave, uncovered, at HIGH for 7 to 8 minutes or until boiling. Move glass measure to back of microwave oven. Place dough in microwave oven with water. Reduce to LOW (10% power), and microwave for 4 minutes. Let rest 15 minutes. Repeat procedure until doubled in bulk.

Combine vegetable oil, onion, and garlic in a 3-quart casserole; microwave, uncovered, at HIGH for 4 to 5 minutes or until onion is tender. Add tomatoes, tomato paste, basil, fennel, remaining 1 teaspoon sugar, and remaining 1 teaspoon salt to onion mixture; stir well. Cover with wax paper and microwave at HIGH for 17 to 20 minutes or until mixture is thickened, stirring every 5 minutes.

Punch dough down, and divide in half. Lightly grease hands, and pat each portion of dough into a lightly greased 12-inch pizza pan. Spoon half of sauce mixture over each; sprinkle each with half of Parmesan cheese and half of mozzarella cheese. Top with sausage, mushrooms, green pepper, and olives. Place pizzas in conventional oven, and bake at 450° for 25 minutes or until crust is golden brown. Serve immediately. Yield: two 12-inch pizzas.

Never reheat meat at HIGH power; use MEDIUM (50% power) to avoid overcooking.

Zucchini, yellow squash, onion, and cherry tomatoes are threaded onto skewers for Lamb and Vegetable Kabobs.

Lamb And Vegetable Kabobs

2 tablespoons butter or
  margarine
½ teaspoon curry powder
¾ pound boneless lamb, cut
  into 1-inch cubes
1 small zucchini, cut into
  ¾-inch slices
1 small yellow squash, cut into
  cubes
1 small onion, halved and
  quartered
8 cherry tomatoes
Hot cooked rice

Place butter in a small bowl; microwave, uncovered, at HIGH for 45 seconds or until melted. Stir in curry powder; set aside.

Alternately thread lamb, zucchini, yellow squash, and onion on four 12-inch wooden skewers. Place kabobs on a roasting rack or lay lengthwise across a 12- x 8- x 2-inch baking dish. Brush with butter mixture. Cover with wax paper and microwave at HIGH for 4 minutes; thread tomatoes on ends of skewers and rearrange kabobs. Cover and microwave at HIGH for 4 to 6 minutes or to desired degree of doneness. Serve over rice. Yield: 4 servings.

Orange Lamb Chops

6 (1-inch-thick) lamb loin chops (about 2 pounds)
1 (11-ounce) can mandarin oranges, undrained
½ cup chutney
3 tablespoons firmly packed brown sugar
2 tablespoons lemon juice
1 tablespoon cornstarch

Trim excess fat from lamb chops. Arrange chops in a 10- x 6- x 2-inch baking dish with thickest portions towards outside of dish. Cover with wax paper and microwave at MEDIUM HIGH (70% power) for 8 minutes, turning chops over and rearranging after 4 minutes. Drain off drippings.

Drain oranges, reserving ½ cup juice; set juice aside. Arrange oranges over chops. Combine ¼ cup reserved orange juice, chutney, brown sugar, and lemon juice; stir well, and pour over chops. Reduce to MEDIUM (50% power); cover with wax paper and microwave for 10 to 12 minutes or until lamb is tender. Transfer chops and oranges to serving platter, reserving drippings in dish. Combine cornstarch and ¼ cup remaining orange juice, stirring well; add to drippings. Microwave, uncovered, at HIGH for 2 to 3 minutes or until thickened, stirring after 1 minute; spoon over chops. Yield: 6 servings.

Herbed Lamb Chops

½ cup Chablis or other dry white wine
2 tablespoons lemon juice
1 tablespoon olive oil
4 cloves garlic, minced
2 teaspoons rubbed sage
1 teaspoon dried whole rosemary
½ teaspoon dried whole oregano
6 (1-inch-thick) lamb loin chops (about 1½ pounds)

Combine wine, lemon juice, oil, garlic, sage, rosemary, and oregano in a 12- x 8- x 2-inch baking dish. Trim excess fat from chops; place chops in baking dish. Cover and refrigerate at least 8 hours, turning chops occasionally.

Arrange chops with thickest portions towards outside of dish. Cover with wax paper and microwave at MEDIUM (50% power) for 8 minutes, turning chops over and rearranging after 4 minutes. Drain chops, reserving marinade.

Transfer chops to barbecue grill. Grill chops over medium coals for 14 minutes or to desired degree of doneness, turning and basting frequently with marinade. Serve immediately. Yield: 6 servings.

For a quicker barbecue, microwave the meat until partially done; then finish cooking it on the grill. Meat will be more moist yet still have plenty of barbecue flavor.

Poultry

The natural moistness of poultry makes it an excellent choice for microwave cooking. In addition to being ready to serve in a fraction of the time required for conventional cooking, poultry cooked in the microwave remains tender, moist, and flavorful.

When testing recipes using chicken pieces, we found that proper arrangement of the pieces was a key to getting overall good results. It is best to place thicker, meatier parts towards the outside of the dish and thinner, bonier parts towards the center. Rearranging the pieces about halfway through microwaving time will promote more even cooking.

We also observed that the weight and size of a whole chicken can affect the cooking time. We feel you will get better results microwaving birds that weigh 10 pounds or less. Remember, the larger the bird, the lower the power, and the longer it must cook.

You can shield small, bony pieces of whole poultry with small pieces of aluminum foil. This is especially helpful on wing tips and legs (see *Shielding*, page 8).

To tell if a bird is done, check it in several places. The drumstick should move easily, no pink should remain, and the juices should run clear. If using a temperature probe, it should register between 180°F and 185°F. Standing time will allow the internal areas to continue to cook upon removal from the oven.

In some of our recipes the poultry will brown slightly as it microwaves. Most of the time the poultry will brown when brushed with melted butter, soy sauce, or another brown sauce. You can also give it a crisp brown look from a coating of breadcrumbs or corn flake crumbs or by cooking it in a browning dish.

Glazed Chicken With Pecan-Rice Dressing (page 161) glistens with an orange marmalade glaze. Green grapes, spiced crab apples, and celery leaves add the finishing touches.

CHICKEN WITH HERBED VEGETABLES

1 (3- to 3½-pound) broiler-fryer
½ cup water
1 tablespoon chopped fresh parsley
2 teaspoons chicken-flavored bouillon granules
1 teaspoon salt
1 teaspoon chopped fresh oregano
¼ teaspoon pepper
2 stalks celery, sliced
1 medium onion, halved and quartered
1 medium zucchini, cut into 1-inch slices
1 medium-size yellow squash, cut into ¼-inch slices

Soak a large clay cooker and lid in cold water for 20 minutes or according to manufacturer's directions.

Remove giblets and neck from chicken; reserve for other uses. Rinse chicken with cold water; pat dry. Lift wingtips up and over back, and tuck under chicken. Tie legs together with nylon tie or string. Place chicken, breast side up, in clay pot; add ½ cup water and next 5 ingredients. Cover with lid, and microwave at HIGH for 15 minutes. Reduce to MEDIUM HIGH (70% power); cover and microwave for 15 minutes. Add celery, onion, zucchini, and squash; cover and microwave at MEDIUM HIGH for 10 minutes or until chicken and vegetables are tender. Let stand, covered, 5 minutes. Yield: 4 servings.

ORANGE-GLAZED CHICKEN

Soak a clay cooker and lid in water before adding the ingredients for Orange-Glazed Chicken.

1 (3- to 3½-pound) broiler-fryer
1 tablespoon butter or margarine
2 cloves garlic, minced
1 medium onion, halved and quartered
2 carrots, scraped and sliced
2 stalks celery, sliced
Grated rind of 1 orange
Juice of 1 orange
¼ cup vermouth
¼ cup undiluted canned chicken broth
½ teaspoon salt
¼ teaspoon white pepper
2 tablespoons water
1 tablespoon cornstarch

Soak a large clay cooker and lid in cold water for 20 minutes or according to manufacturer's directions.

Remove giblets and neck from chicken; reserve for other uses. Rinse chicken with cold water; pat dry. Lift wingtips up and over back, and tuck under chicken. Tie legs together with nylon tie or string. Rub entire chicken with butter; set aside.

Combine garlic, onion, carrots, and celery in clay pot. Place chicken, breast side up, on top of vegetables. Combine orange rind and next 5 ingredients; stir well. Pour over chicken and vegetables.

Cover with lid, and microwave at HIGH for 35 to 40 minutes or until chicken and vegetables are tender. Drain juices into a 4-cup glass measure; microwave, uncovered, at HIGH for 2 minutes or until boiling. Combine 2 tablespoons water and cornstarch, stirring well; add to juices. Microwave, uncovered, at HIGH for 4 to 5 minutes or until thickened. Spoon sauce over chicken, and serve with vegetables. Yield: 4 servings.

Glazed Chicken With Pecan-Rice Dressing

½ cup chopped celery
¼ cup chopped onion
¼ cup plus 1 tablespoon butter
  or margarine, divided
1¾ cups cooked long-grain rice
⅓ cup chopped pecans
1 tablespoon grated orange
  rind
1 tablespoon dried parsley
  flakes
1 (3- to 3½-pound) broiler-fryer
¼ teaspoon salt
⅓ cup orange marmalade
1 tablespoon orange juice
¾ teaspoon browning and
  seasoning sauce
Green grapes (optional)
Spiced crabapples (optional)
Celery leaves (optional)

Combine celery, onion, and 1 tablespoon butter in a 1-quart casserole. Cover with heavy-duty plastic wrap and microwave at HIGH for 3 to 4 minutes or until onion is tender, stirring after 1 minute. Add rice, pecans, orange rind, and parsley flakes, stirring well; set aside.

Remove giblets and neck from chicken; reserve for other uses. Rinse chicken with cold water; pat dry. Sprinkle cavity of chicken with salt. Lift wingtips up and over back, and tuck under chicken. Stuff cavity of chicken with rice mixture. Close cavity, and secure with wooden picks. Tie legs together with nylon tie or string. Place chicken, breast side down, in a 12- x 8- x 2-inch baking dish; set aside.

Place remaining ¼ cup butter in a 2-cup glass measure; microwave, uncovered, at HIGH for 55 seconds or until melted. Stir in marmalade, orange juice, and seasoning sauce. Microwave, uncovered, at HIGH for 45 seconds or until thoroughly heated.

Brush chicken with half of glaze; microwave, uncovered, at HIGH for 3 minutes. Reduce to MEDIUM (50% power), and microwave, uncovered, for 20 minutes. Turn chicken, breast side up, and brush with remaining glaze. Shield wingtips and ends of legs with small pieces of aluminum foil, if needed. Insert microwave thermometer between leg and thigh, if desired. Microwave, uncovered, at MEDIUM for 20 to 25 minutes or until drumsticks are easy to move; thermometer should register 185°. Discard aluminum foil. Serve chicken over rice dressing, and garnish with grapes, crabapples, and celery leaves, if desired. Yield: 4 to 6 servings.

Do not attempt to deep-fry chicken in the microwave oven. The deep, hot oil can reach dangerous temperatures and result in a fire.

CHICKEN IN TERIYAKI SAUCE

When preparing Chicken in Teriyaki Sauce, lift wingtips up and over back and tuck under the bird; tie legs together with string.

⅓ cup sherry
⅓ cup honey
¼ cup soy sauce
1 (3-pound) broiler-fryer
1 tablespoon water
1 teaspoon cornstarch

Combine sherry, honey, and soy sauce; set aside. Remove giblets and neck from chicken; reserve for other use. Rinse chicken with cold water; pat dry. Lift wingtips up and over back, and tuck under chicken. Tie legs together with nylon tie or string.

Place chicken in a large browning bag prepared according to package directions and placed in a 12- x 8- x 2-inch baking dish; pour sherry mixture over chicken. Tie bag loosely with string or a ½-inch-wide strip cut from open end of bag. Turn bag to coat chicken with sherry mixture; refrigerate 1 hour, turning bag once.

Cut 6 slits in top of bag. Microwave at HIGH for 10 minutes; rotate a half-turn, and insert microwave thermometer between leg and thigh, if desired. Microwave at HIGH for 10 minutes. Let chicken stand in bag 5 minutes; thermometer should register 185°.

Remove chicken from bag, reserving drippings. Combine 1 tablespoon water and cornstarch in a 2-cup glass measure; gradually add ½ cup reserved drippings, stirring well. Microwave, uncovered, at HIGH for 2 to 3 minutes or until thickened, stirring after 1 minute. Spoon sauce over chicken. Yield: 4 servings.

CHICKEN WITH SESAME-MUSTARD SAUCE

1 teaspoon sugar
1 teaspoon dry mustard
¼ cup plus 1 tablespoon water
2 tablespoons soy sauce
2 teaspoons rice wine
2 teaspoons dark sesame oil
1 cup chopped green onions
2 tablespoons plus 1½
   teaspoons dark sesame oil
1 (3-pound) broiler-fryer
Green onion fans (optional)

Combine sugar and mustard in a 1-cup glass measure; add ¼ cup plus 1 tablespoon water, stirring well. Stir in soy sauce, wine, and 2 teaspoons sesame oil. Microwave, uncovered, at HIGH for 1 to 2 minutes or until sugar is dissolved; set aside.

Combine chopped onions and 2 tablespoons plus 1½ teaspoons sesame oil in container of an electric blender or food processor; process until smooth. Remove giblets and neck from chicken; reserve for other uses. Rinse chicken with cold water; pat dry. Lift wingtips up and over back, and tuck under chicken. Rub onion mixture over chicken and inside cavity; close cavity, and secure with wooden picks. Tie legs together with nylon tie or string.

CHICKEN WITH SESAME-MUSTARD SAUCE

(continued)

Place chicken, breast side down, on a rack placed inside a 12- x 8- x 2-inch baking dish. Cover with a tent of wax paper; reduce to MEDIUM (50% power), and microwave for 25 minutes. Turn chicken breast side up. Shield wingtips and ends of legs with pieces of aluminum foil, if needed; cover with wax paper, and insert microwave thermometer between leg and thigh, if desired. Microwave at MEDIUM for 25 to 30 minutes or until drumsticks are easy to move. Let stand, covered, 2 minutes; thermometer should register 185°. Discard aluminum foil; transfer to a serving platter, and garnish with green onion fans, if desired. Serve chicken with soy sauce mixture. Yield: 4 servings.

BASIL-STUFFED ROASTED CHICKEN

2 tablespoons butter or margarine
1 stalk celery, diced
2 green onions, chopped
½ cup skim milk
1 egg, slightly beaten
1 teaspoon dried whole basil
½ teaspoon pepper
⅛ teaspoon garlic powder
2 cups cornbread stuffing mix
1 (3-pound) broiler-fryer
2 tablespoons commercial teriyaki glaze
Dried whole basil (optional)

Combine butter, celery, and onions in a 4-cup glass measure. Cover with heavy-duty plastic wrap and microwave at HIGH for 3 minutes. Stir in milk, egg, 1 teaspoon basil, pepper, and garlic powder. Add stuffing mix, stirring well; set aside.

Remove giblets and neck from chicken; reserve for other uses. Rinse chicken with cold water; pat dry. Lift wingtips up and over back, and tuck under chicken. Stuff cavity of chicken with cornbread mixture. Close cavity, and secure with wooden picks. Tie legs together with nylon tie or string. Rub entire surface of chicken with teriyaki glaze.

Place chicken, breast side down, in a 12- x 8- x 2-inch baking dish. Cover with a tent of wax paper; reduce to MEDIUM HIGH (70% power), and microwave for 15 minutes. Turn chicken breast side up. Shield wingtips and ends of legs with pieces of aluminum foil, if needed; cover with wax paper, and insert microwave thermometer between leg and thigh, if desired. Microwave at MEDIUM HIGH for 15 to 20 minutes or until drumsticks are easy to move. Let stand, covered, 10 minutes; thermometer should register 185°. Discard aluminum foil. Sprinkle chicken with basil, if desired. Yield: 4 servings.

Chicken Marengo

⅓ cup seasoned, dry
  breadcrumbs
1 (1.5-ounce) package spaghetti
  sauce mix
1 (2½-to 3-pound) broiler-fryer,
  cut up
1 cup sliced fresh mushrooms
½ cup Chablis or other dry
  white wine
¼ teaspoon dried whole basil
1 (16-ounce) can whole
  tomatoes, undrained and
  chopped
Hot cooked spaghetti

Combine breadcrumbs and spaghetti sauce mix in a plastic bag. Place chicken in bag with crumb mixture, shaking to coat. Arrange chicken pieces in a 3-quart casserole with thickest portions towards outside of casserole. Cover with wax paper and microwave at HIGH for 10 minutes. Rearrange pieces; add mushrooms, wine, and basil. Stir in tomatoes. Reduce to MEDIUM HIGH (70% power); cover and microwave for 10 to 12 minutes or until chicken is tender. Let stand, covered, 3 minutes. Serve over spaghetti. Yield: 4 to 6 servings.

Chicken Tetrazzini

1 (8-ounce) package vermicelli
1 (3-pound) broiler-fryer, cut
  up and skinned
1½ cups water
¼ cup butter or margarine
1 cup sliced fresh mushrooms
1 medium onion, chopped
2 teaspoons lemon juice
⅓ cup all-purpose flour
1 teaspoon salt
⅛ teaspoon ground nutmeg
1 cup half-and-half
¼ cup sliced pimiento-stuffed
  olives
¼ cup grated Parmesan cheese

Cook vermicelli according to package directions; drain and set aside.

Arrange chicken pieces in a 12- x 8- x 2-inch baking dish with thickest portions towards outside of dish. Pour water over chicken. Cover with wax paper and microwave at HIGH for 18 to 20 minutes or until chicken is tender. Let stand, covered, 5 minutes. Remove chicken from dish, reserving 1 cup broth. Bone chicken, and chop into bite-size pieces; set aside.

Combine butter, mushrooms, onion, and lemon juice in a 4-cup glass measure. Cover with heavy-duty plastic wrap and microwave at HIGH for 2½ to 3 minutes or until onion is tender. Stir in flour, salt, and nutmeg. Gradually add 1 cup broth and half-and-half, stirring well. Microwave, uncovered, at HIGH for 4 to 5 minutes or until mixture is thickened, stirring every 2 minutes; set aside.

Place vermicelli in a 12- x 8- x 2-inch baking dish. Top with chopped chicken, sauce, and olives; toss gently. Sprinkle with cheese. Cover with wax paper and microwave at HIGH for 4 to 5 minutes or until thoroughly heated. Let stand, covered, 2 minutes. Yield: 6 servings.

CHICKEN CACCIATORE

1 large onion, sliced and
   separated into rings
2 cloves garlic, minced
1 tablespoon vegetable oil
1 (3-pound) broiler-fryer,
   cut up
1 (8-ounce) can tomato sauce
1 (7½-ounce) can whole
   tomatoes, undrained and
   chopped
¼ cup Chablis or other dry
   white wine
1 teaspoon salt
¾ teaspoon dried whole
   oregano
½ teaspoon celery seeds
¼ teaspoon pepper
2 bay leaves
Hot cooked spaghetti

Place onion, garlic, and oil in a 12- x 8- x 2-inch baking dish. Microwave, uncovered, at HIGH for 4 to 5 minutes or until onion is tender, stirring after 2 minutes. Arrange chicken pieces over onion with thickest portions towards outside of dish.

Combine tomato sauce, tomatoes, wine, salt, oregano, celery seeds, pepper, and bay leaves, stirring well. Pour over chicken. Reduce to MEDIUM HIGH (70% power); cover with wax paper and microwave for 25 to 28 minutes or until chicken is tender, rearranging pieces every 10 minutes. Remove and discard bay leaves. Serve over spaghetti. Yield: 4 to 6 servings.

ORANGE-SAUCED CHICKEN

1 (2½- to 3-pound)
   broiler-fryer, cut up and
   skinned
½ teaspoon salt
⅓ cup frozen orange juice
   concentrate, undiluted
⅓ cup water
2 tablespoons firmly packed
   brown sugar
2 tablespoons chopped fresh
   parsley
2 teaspoons soy sauce
¼ teaspoon ground ginger
1 tablespoon cornstarch
1 tablespoon water
Hot cooked rice
Orange slices (optional)

Arrange chicken pieces in a 12- x 8- x 2-inch baking dish, with thickest portions towards outside of dish. Sprinkle with salt; set aside.

Combine orange juice, water, sugar, parsley, soy sauce, and ginger, stirring well; pour over chicken. Cover with wax paper and microwave at MEDIUM HIGH (70% power) for 25 to 28 minutes or until chicken is tender, rearranging pieces every 10 minutes.

Remove chicken to a serving platter, reserving sauce. Combine cornstarch and water, stirring well; add to reserved sauce. Increase to HIGH power; microwave, uncovered, for 3 minutes or until mixture is thickened. Spoon sauce over chicken. Serve with rice. Garnish with orange slices, if desired. Yield: 4 servings.

Skinning chicken before microwaving it with a sauce allows more flavor from the sauce to be absorbed.

HONEY-PEACH CHICKEN

2 tablespoons butter or
margarine
1 (16-ounce) can sliced peaches,
undrained
¼ cup honey
2 tablespoons lemon juice
1 tablespoon plus 1½
teaspoons cornstarch
1 teaspoon salt
¼ teaspoon curry powder
1 (3- to 3½-pound)
broiler-fryer, cut up and
skinned

Place butter in a 12- x 8- x 2-inch baking dish. Microwave, uncovered, at HIGH for 45 seconds or until melted.

Drain peaches, reserving liquid; set peaches aside. Add peach liquid and honey to melted butter. Combine lemon juice and cornstarch, stirring well; add to butter mixture. Stir in salt and curry powder. Arrange chicken in butter mixture with thickest portions towards outside of dish. Cover with wax paper and microwave at HIGH for 18 to 20 minutes or until chicken is tender, rearranging pieces every 6 minutes.

Remove chicken to a serving platter, reserving sauce. Add peach slices to reserved sauce. Microwave, uncovered, at HIGH for 2 to 3 minutes or until thoroughly heated. Spoon sauce and peaches over chicken. Yield: 4 servings.

OLD-FASHIONED BARBECUE CHICKEN

¼ cup firmly packed brown
sugar
¼ cup catsup
1 tablespoon cider vinegar
1 tablespoon Worcestershire
sauce
2 teaspoons lemon juice
1 teaspoon salt
¼ teaspoon pepper
1 (2½- to 3-pound)
broiler-fryer, cut up and
skinned
Green onion fan

Combine first 7 ingredients in a 2-cup glass measure; stir well. Microwave, uncovered, at HIGH for 1½ minutes or until boiling; set aside.

Arrange chicken pieces in a 12- x 8- x 2-inch baking dish with thickest portions towards outside of dish. Cover with wax paper and microwave at HIGH for 10 minutes; drain off drippings, and rearrange chicken. Brush chicken with sauce. Cover and microwave at HIGH for 9 to 10 minutes or until chicken is tender, rearranging pieces and brushing with sauce after 5 minutes. Let stand, covered, 2 minutes. Garnish with a green onion fan, if desired. Yield: 4 servings.

Old-Fashioned Barbecue Chicken is saucy and moist—just right for a picnic.

Spicy Crumb-Coated Chicken rivals conventional oven-fried chicken.

SPICY CRUMB-COATED CHICKEN

2 tablespoons sesame seeds
¼ cup plus 2 tablespoons
   butter or margarine
1½ tablespoons dry mustard
1 cup seasoned, dry
   breadcrumbs
1½ teaspoons chili powder
1 teaspoon dried parsley flakes
¼ teaspoon salt
¼ teaspoon pepper
1 (2½- to 3-pound)
   broiler-fryer, cut up and
   skinned
Celery leaves (optional)
Cherry tomatoes (optional)

Spread sesame seeds in a pieplate; microwave, uncovered, at HIGH for 4 to 6 minutes or until lightly toasted. Set aside.

Place butter in a small bowl; microwave at HIGH for 1 minute or until melted. Stir in dry mustard; set aside.

Combine sesame seeds, breadcrumbs, chili powder, parsley flakes, salt, and pepper in a shallow container. Dip chicken in butter mixture, and coat in breadcrumb mixture.

Arrange chicken on a rack placed inside a baking dish with thickest portions towards outside of dish. Cover with wax paper and microwave at HIGH for 18 to 20 minutes or until chicken is tender, rearranging after 9 minutes. Garnish with celery leaves and cherry tomatoes, if desired. Yield: 4 servings.

CHICKEN AND VEGETABLES COOKED IN WINE

1 (3-pound) broiler-fryer, cut
  up and skinned
½ teaspoon salt
¼ teaspoon pepper
2 carrots, scraped and sliced
½ cup chopped celery
½ cup uncooked long-grain
  rice
1 medium onion, chopped
¾ teaspoon dried whole
  oregano
1 clove garlic, minced
1½ cups Chablis or other dry
  white wine
1 cup water

Arrange chicken pieces in a 3-quart casserole with thickest portions towards outside of casserole. Sprinkle with salt and pepper. Cover with wax paper and microwave at HIGH for 5 minutes; drain.

Add carrots, celery, rice, onion, oregano, and garlic; pour wine and water over vegetables. Cover and microwave at HIGH for 12 minutes, stirring after 6 minutes. Reduce to MEDIUM HIGH (70% power); cover and microwave for 10 to 12 minutes or until chicken, rice, and vegetables are tender. Let stand, covered, 2 minutes. Serve immediately. Yield: 4 servings.

GINGER CHICKEN WITH HAM-FRIED RICE

½ cup soy sauce
⅓ cup sugar
1 teaspoon minced fresh
  gingerroot
1 clove garlic, minced
1 (3-pound) broiler-fryer,
  cut up
Ham-Fried Rice

Combine soy sauce, sugar, gingerroot, and garlic in a large zip top heavy-duty plastic bag. Place chicken in bag, and secure tightly; refrigerate at least 8 hours, turning bag occasionally.

Remove chicken, reserving marinade; arrange chicken pieces in a 12- x 8- x 2-inch baking dish with thickest portions towards outside of dish. Cover with wax paper and microwave at HIGH for 5 minutes. Reduce to MEDIUM HIGH (70% power); cover and microwave for 20 minutes, rearranging pieces and topping with marinade after 10 minutes. Serve over Ham-Fried Rice. Yield: 4 servings.

HAM-FRIED RICE:

2 eggs, beaten
1 tablespoon water
⅓ cup chopped green onions
1 tablespoon vegetable oil
3 cups cooked long-grain rice
½ cup diced cooked ham
½ cup frozen green peas,
  thawed
2 tablespoons teriyaki sauce

Combine eggs and water in a small bowl. Cover with heavy-duty plastic wrap and microwave at HIGH for 1½ to 2 minutes or until eggs are set, stirring after 1 minute. Chop eggs, and set aside.

Combine green onions and oil in a 2-quart casserole. Microwave, uncovered, at HIGH for 1 to 2 minutes or until crisp-tender. Add rice, ham, peas, teriyaki sauce, and chopped eggs. Cover with heavy-duty plastic wrap and microwave at HIGH for 2 to 4 minutes or until thoroughly heated. Yield: 4 servings.

FRUITED CHICKEN SALAD

1 cup water
1 stalk celery, sliced
1 small onion, sliced
2 chicken-flavored bouillon
  cubes
1 (3-pound) broiler-fryer,
  cut up
1 (15¼-ounce) can pineapple
  chunks, undrained
1 cup seedless green grapes,
  halved
1 small apple, unpeeled and
  diced
1 cup chopped celery
½ cup commercial sour cream
½ cup mayonnaise
Curly leaf lettuce
¼ cup chopped unsalted
  cashews

The chicken for Fruited Chicken Salad is microwaved quickly and easily in a mixture of bouillon, onion, and celery. When tender, skin, bone, and chop the chicken.

Combine water, sliced celery, onion, and bouillon cubes in a 4-cup glass measure. Microwave, uncovered, at HIGH for 5 minutes or until boiling. Arrange chicken pieces in a 3-quart deep casserole with thickest portions towards outside of dish. Pour bouillon mixture over chicken; cover with heavy-duty plastic wrap and microwave at HIGH for 13 to 15 minutes or until chicken is tender. Let stand, covered, until cool. Strain broth, and reserve for use in other recipes; skin, bone, and chop chicken to equal 2½ cups.

Drain pineapple, reserving 2 tablespoons juice. Combine chopped chicken, pineapple, grapes, apple, and 1 cup celery in a large bowl; toss gently, and set aside. Combine sour cream, mayonnaise, and 2 tablespoons pineapple juice in a 2-cup glass measure. Pour over chicken mixture, stirring to combine. Cover and refrigerate at least 2 hours. Serve on a bed of lettuce, and sprinkle with cashews. Yield: 6 servings.

HONEY-MUSTARD CHICKEN

2 tablespoons butter or
  margarine
½ cup honey
3 tablespoons Dijon mustard
2 tablespoons lemon juice
4 (8-ounce) chicken breast
  halves, skinned
¼ teaspoon salt
¼ teaspoon pepper
2 tablespoons water
1 tablespoon cornstarch
Lemon wedge (optional)
Fresh lemon balm sprigs
  (optional)

Place butter in a 12- x 8- x 2-inch baking dish. Microwave, uncovered, at HIGH for 45 seconds or until melted. Stir in honey, mustard, and lemon juice. Add chicken, turning to coat well. Sprinkle with salt and pepper. Cover and refrigerate at least 3 hours, turning occasionally.

Arrange chicken with thickest portions towards outside of dish. Cover with wax paper and microwave at HIGH for 10 minutes, rotating a half-turn after 5 minutes. Reduce to MEDIUM HIGH (70% power); cover and microwave for 10 to 12 minutes or until chicken is tender, turning and basting chicken after 5 minutes. Remove chicken to a serving platter, reserving honey mixture in baking dish.

Combine water and cornstarch, stirring well; add to honey mixture. Microwave, uncovered, at HIGH for 2 to 2½ minutes or until thickened. Spoon sauce over chicken, and garnish with a lemon wedge and lemon balm sprigs, if desired. Yield: 4 servings.

MEXICAN CHEESE AND CHICKEN BAKE

¼ cup butter or margarine
½ teaspoon salt
¼ teaspoon pepper
6 (3- to 4-ounce) skinned and
  boned chicken breast halves
1 (2.8-ounce) can French-fried
  onion rings, crushed
1 tablespoon olive oil
1 large tomato, seeded and
  chopped
1 (4-ounce) can sliced
  mushrooms, drained
⅓ cup chopped yellow pepper
⅓ cup sliced pimiento-stuffed
  olives
½ teaspoon dried whole
  oregano
½ cup (2 ounces) shredded
  Monterey Jack cheese

Place butter in a 10- x 6- x 2-inch baking dish. Microwave, uncovered, at HIGH for 55 seconds or until melted. Stir in salt and pepper. Dip each chicken piece in butter mixture; roll in crushed onion rings. Arrange chicken in baking dish with thickest portions towards outside of dish. Cover with wax paper and microwave at HIGH for 10 to 12 minutes or until chicken is tender; set aside.

Place oil, tomato, mushrooms, pepper, olives, and oregano in a 1-quart glass measure. Cover with heavy-duty plastic wrap and microwave at HIGH for 4 to 6 minutes or until pepper is tender; drain.

Spoon vegetable mixture over chicken. Sprinkle with cheese; cover and microwave at HIGH for 2 to 3 minutes or until cheese melts. Let stand, uncovered, 2 minutes before serving. Yield: 6 servings.

Moist, tender chicken breasts get a coating of sweet and tangy sauce for Honey-Mustard Chicken.

RED PEPPER-CITRUS CHICKEN

4 (4½- to 5-ounce) skinned and
    boned chicken breast halves
1 teaspoon grated lemon rind
¼ cup lemon juice
¼ cup water
⅛ teaspoon curry powder
⅛ teaspoon garlic powder
⅛ teaspoon paprika
Hot cooked parslied rice
    (optional)
1 tablespoon water
2 teaspoons cornstarch
½ large sweet red pepper, cut
    into strips
Lemon slices (optional)

Place chicken in a 12- x 8- x 2-inch baking dish with thickest portions towards outside of dish. Combine lemon rind, juice, water, and curry powder; pour over chicken. Sprinkle with garlic powder. Cover with wax paper and microwave at HIGH for 3 minutes. Remove chicken from dish, and place on cutting board. Holding a sharp knife at an angle, slice each chicken breast against the grain into ¾-inch slices, cutting to, but not through the opposite side. Reassemble each chicken breast; return to baking dish. Sprinkle with paprika. Cover and microwave at HIGH for 3 to 4 minutes or until tender.

Remove chicken, reserving liquid. Arrange chicken over rice on serving platter, if desired. Strain reserved liquid; return to baking dish.

Combine water and cornstarch, stirring well. Stir into reserved liquid. Add pepper strips; microwave, uncovered, at HIGH for 2 minutes or until mixture thickens slightly. Spoon sauce and pepper strips over chicken; garnish with lemon slices, if desired. Yield: 4 servings.

MARSALA CHICKEN SUPREME

4 (3-ounce) skinned and boned chicken breast halves
¼ cup butter or margarine
2 teaspoons lemon juice
¼ teaspoon salt
⅛ teaspoon white pepper
¼ cup whipping cream
2 tablespoons Marsala wine
1½ teaspoons cornstarch
⅛ teaspoon chicken-flavored bouillon granules
Chopped fresh chives

Place chicken between 2 sheets of wax paper. Flatten to ⅛-inch thickness, using a meat mallet or rolling pin.

Place butter in a 12- x 8- x 2-inch baking dish. Microwave, uncovered, at HIGH for 55 seconds or until melted. Dip chicken in butter, turning to coat. Sprinkle with lemon juice, salt, and pepper. Arrange chicken with thickest portions towards outside of dish. Reduce to MEDIUM (50% power); cover with wax paper and microwave for 12 to 15 minutes or until chicken is tender, rearranging after 6 minutes.

Remove chicken to a serving platter, reserving ¼ cup butter mixture. Combine butter mixture, whipping cream, wine, cornstarch, and bouillon granules in a 2-cup glass measure, stirring well. Microwave, uncovered, at HIGH for 2 to 3 minutes or until thickened. Spoon over chicken. Sprinkle with chives. Yield: 4 servings.

EASY CORDON BLEU

4 (4-ounce) skinned and boned chicken breast halves
4 thin slices prosciutto ham
2 (1-ounce) slices Swiss cheese, cut in half
1 tablespoon plus 1½ teaspoons butter or margarine
4 ounces fresh mushrooms, sliced
3 tablespoons Chablis or other dry white wine
1 teaspoon lemon-herb seasoned salt
½ cup (2 ounces) shredded Swiss cheese

Place chicken between 2 sheets of wax paper. Flatten to ¼-inch thickness, using a meat mallet or rolling pin. Place a slice of ham and cheese on each piece. Roll up lengthwise; secure with wooden picks.

Place butter in a 9-inch pieplate. Microwave, uncovered, at HIGH for 45 seconds or until melted. Stir in mushrooms. Microwave, uncovered, at HIGH for 1½ to 2 minutes or until tender. Stir in wine and salt. Add chicken, turning to coat. Place chicken, seam side down, in pieplate; cover with wax paper and microwave at HIGH for 2 minutes. Reduce to MEDIUM (50% power); cover and microwave for 7 to 9 minutes or until chicken is tender, basting with butter mixture after 4 minutes. Sprinkle with ½ cup cheese. Cover and microwave at MEDIUM for 2 minutes or until cheese melts. Let stand, covered, 1 minute. Yield: 4 servings.

Elegant Stuffed Chicken Breasts

4 (4- to 5-ounce) skinned and boned chicken breast halves
¾ cup water
¼ cup uncooked long-grain rice
1 small carrot, scraped and grated
1 (2-ounce) jar diced pimiento, drained
1 tablespoon chopped green onions
1 teaspoon grated orange rind
1 teaspoon beef-flavored bouillon granules
¼ teaspoon pepper
1 cup orange juice
1 tablespoon cornstarch

Place chicken between 2 sheets of wax paper. Flatten to ⅛-inch thickness, using a meat mallet or rolling pin.

Combine water and next 7 ingredients in a 1-quart casserole. Cover with heavy-duty plastic wrap and microwave at HIGH for 5 minutes. Reduce to MEDIUM (50% power); cover and microwave for 7 minutes or until all liquid is absorbed.

Spoon about ¼ cup rice mixture over each piece of chicken, spreading to within ½-inch from edge. Roll up lengthwise, and secure with wooden picks. Place chicken, seam side down, in a 9-inch square baking dish. Cover with wax paper and microwave at MEDIUM for 12 to 14 minutes or until chicken is tender, rotating a half-turn after 5 minutes.

Combine orange juice and cornstarch in a 2-cup glass measure. Microwave, uncovered, at HIGH for 4 to 5 minutes or until thickened. Let stand 2 minutes. Serve sauce over chicken. Yield: 4 servings.

Chicken Alla Romano

Roll up thin slices of ham and cheese in flattened chicken breasts for Chicken Alla Romano. Secure rolls with wooden picks.

2 (4-ounce) skinned and boned chicken breast halves
1 (1-ounce) slice Swiss cheese, halved
1 thin slice prosciutto or smoked ham, halved
3 tablespoons fine, dry breadcrumbs
1 tablespoon grated Parmesan cheese
½ teaspoon garlic salt
1 teaspoon paprika
Pinch of dried whole tarragon
2 tablespoons butter or margarine

Place chicken between 2 sheets of wax paper. Flatten to ¼-inch thickness, using a meat mallet or rolling pin. Place a slice of Swiss cheese and prosciutto in center of each piece of chicken. Roll up lengthwise; secure with wooden picks.

Combine breadcrumbs, Parmesan cheese, salt, paprika, and tarragon; set aside. Place butter in a 1-cup glass measure; microwave, uncovered, at HIGH for 45 seconds or until melted.

Dip each piece of chicken in butter; roll in breadcrumb mixture. Place chicken, seam side down, in a 1-quart casserole. Cover with wax paper and microwave at HIGH for 5 to 6 minutes or until chicken is tender, rotating a half-turn after 3 minutes. Slice before serving, if desired. Yield: 2 servings.

When sliced, Chicken Alla Romano can be arranged to show off the spiral ham and cheese filling.

ORIENTAL CHICKEN AND SPINACH

¼ cup undiluted canned
  chicken broth
¼ cup soy sauce
2 tablespoons rice wine
1 tablespoon brown sugar
1 tablespoon cornstarch
½ pound skinned and boned
  chicken breast halves, cut
  into thin strips
½ pound fresh spinach
½ cup sliced fresh mushrooms
½ cup fresh bean sprouts
¼ pound fresh snow pea pods,
  trimmed
½ (8-ounce) can sliced water
  chestnuts, drained
2 green onions, sliced into
  1-inch pieces
Hot cooked rice

Combine chicken broth, soy sauce, wine, sugar, and cornstarch in a 1-quart casserole. Cover with heavy-duty plastic wrap and microwave at HIGH for 5 to 6 minutes or until slightly thickened.

Add chicken strips, spinach, mushrooms, bean sprouts, snow peas, water chestnuts, and onions to sauce mixture. Cover and microwave at HIGH for 10 to 12 minutes or until chicken is tender, stirring every 4 minutes. Serve over rice. Yield: 4 servings.

CHINESE CHICKEN STIR-FRY

1 tablespoon vegetable oil
¾ pound skinned and boned
  chicken breast halves, cut
  into 1-inch pieces
½ cup sliced fresh mushrooms
2 stalks celery, diagonally
  sliced
1 carrot, scraped and cut into
  thin strips
1 (8-ounce) can sliced water
  chestnuts, drained
1 (8-ounce) can bamboo shoots,
  drained
1 cup undiluted canned
  chicken broth
1 tablespoon cornstarch
2 tablespoons soy sauce
Hot cooked rice
Sliced almonds

Place a 10-inch browning skillet in microwave oven; preheat, uncovered, at HIGH for 6 minutes. Add 1 tablespoon oil to hot skillet, tilting to coat surface. Add chicken to skillet, stirring well. Microwave, uncovered, at HIGH for 3 to 3½ minutes or until chicken is no longer pink, stirring after 2 minutes.

Add mushrooms and next 4 ingredients to chicken; microwave, uncovered, at HIGH for 6 to 6½ minutes or until vegetables are crisp-tender, stirring every 2 minutes. Set aside.

Combine chicken broth, cornstarch, and soy sauce, stirring well. Add to chicken mixture, and microwave, uncovered, at HIGH for 5 minutes or until slightly thickened. Cover and let stand 5 minutes. Serve over rice, and sprinkle with almonds. Yield: 4 servings.

MARINATED CHICKEN KABOBS

¾ to 1 pound skinned and
  boned chicken breast halves,
  cut into 1-inch pieces
3 tablespoons soy sauce
3 tablespoons commercial
  Italian salad dressing
2 teaspoons sesame seeds
2 teaspoons lemon juice
½ teaspoon ground ginger
⅛ teaspoon garlic powder
1 small green pepper, cut into
  eighths
1 small sweet red pepper, cut
  into eighths
1 medium onion, cut into
  eighths
⅓ cup water
Hot cooked rice

Place chicken pieces in a shallow container; set aside. Combine soy sauce and next 5 ingredients in a jar; cover tightly, and shake vigorously. Pour marinade over chicken; cover and refrigerate at least 2 hours.

Combine green and red pepper, onion, and water in a large bowl. Cover with heavy-duty plastic wrap, and microwave at HIGH for 4 to 5 minutes or until vegetables are crisp-tender. Drain well.

Remove chicken, reserving marinade. Alternately thread chicken and vegetables on four 12-inch wooden skewers. Place kabobs in a 12- x 8- x 2-inch baking dish. Brush with reserved marinade. Cover with wax paper and microwave at HIGH for 4 minutes. Rearrange kabobs; cover and microwave at HIGH for 3 to 4 minutes or until chicken is tender. Serve over rice. Yield: 4 servings.

GINGERED CHICKEN AND CASHEWS

½ cup cashews
1 tablespoon plus 1 teaspoon
  soy sauce
1 tablespoon water
1 teaspoon cornstarch
1 teaspoon sugar
⅛ teaspoon salt
⅛ teaspoon pepper
1½ pounds skinned and boned
  chicken breast halves, cut
  into 1-inch pieces
1 tablespoon vegetable oil
1 (8-ounce) can bamboo shoots,
  drained
1 small sweet red pepper, cut
  into strips
3 green onions, cut into 1-inch
  pieces
1½ teaspoons grated fresh
  gingerroot
1 tablespoon soy sauce
2 teaspoons dry sherry
Hot cooked rice

Spread cashews in a 9-inch pieplate. Microwave, uncovered, at HIGH for 3 to 4 minutes or until lightly toasted, stirring after every minute; set aside.

Combine 1 tablespoon plus 1 teaspoon soy sauce and next 5 ingredients in a medium bowl; stir well. Add chicken, tossing well; refrigerate 15 minutes. Place a 10-inch browning skillet in microwave oven; preheat, uncovered, at HIGH for 6 minutes. Add oil to hot skillet, tilting to coat surface. Add chicken to skillet, stirring well. Microwave, uncovered, at HIGH for 4 to 4½ minutes or until chicken is no longer pink, stirring after 2 minutes; set aside.

Combine bamboo shoots, pepper strips, green onions, and gingerroot in a 1½-quart casserole. Cover with heavy-duty plastic wrap and microwave at HIGH for 2 to 3 minutes or until vegetables are crisp-tender; add to chicken. Stir in cashews and 1 tablespoon soy sauce. Microwave, uncovered, at HIGH for 1 to 1½ minutes or until thoroughly heated. Stir in sherry. Serve over rice. Yield: 6 servings.

PEANUT-CURRY CHICKEN

1 pound skinned and boned
   chicken breast halves, cut
   into 1-inch pieces
¼ cup all-purpose flour
⅓ cup crunchy peanut butter
⅓ cup buttermilk
1 egg, beaten
2 teaspoons lemon juice
1 teaspoon curry powder
½ teaspoon salt
⅛ teaspoon red pepper
⅛ teaspoon pepper
¾ cup seasoned, dry
   breadcrumbs
¼ cup butter or margarine
¾ cup chutney

Dredge chicken pieces in flour. Combine peanut butter and next 7 ingredients in a medium bowl; stir well. Dip chicken in peanut butter mixture; roll in breadcrumbs.

Place butter in a 12- x 8- x 2-inch baking dish. Microwave, uncovered, at HIGH for 55 seconds or until melted. Add chicken, tossing gently. Microwave, uncovered, at HIGH for 10 to 12 minutes or until chicken is tender, stirring after 5 minutes.

Place chutney in a 2-cup glass measure. Microwave, uncovered, at HIGH for 2 to 3 minutes or until thoroughly heated. Serve chutney as a dipping sauce for chicken. Yield: 4 to 6 servings.

MESQUITE-GRILLED CHICKEN

½ cup vinegar
½ cup soy sauce
2 tablespoons lemon juice
1 clove garlic
1 (2½- to 3-pound)
   broiler-fryer, split

Soak 1 cup mesquite chips in water for 1 to 24 hours; set aside.

Combine vinegar, soy sauce, lemon juice, and garlic in container of an electric blender; process 10 seconds. Place chicken in a large zip top heavy-duty plastic bag. Pour marinade into bag, and secure tightly; refrigerate at least 8 hours, turning bag occasionally.

Remove chicken, reserving marinade; arrange chicken on a rack placed inside a baking dish with thickest portions towards outside of dish. Cover with wax paper and microwave at HIGH for 18 to 20 minutes or until chicken is tender, rotating a half-turn after 10 minutes.

Drain mesquite chips, and place directly on hot coals. Transfer chicken to barbecue grill. Cook over medium coals for 15 to 20 minutes or to desired degree of doneness, turning and brushing with marinade after 10 minutes. Serve immediately. Yield: 4 servings.

When wax paper is used as a cover in the microwave, the oven fan sometimes blows it off. Crumpling it slightly helps keep it in place.

For a pretty golden finish, brush Sassy Spinach-Stuffed Chicken with butter and sprinkle with paprika before it microwaves.

SASSY SPINACH-STUFFED CHICKEN

1 (10-ounce) package frozen spinach
1 medium onion, chopped
1 egg
½ cup ricotta cheese
¼ cup chopped fresh parsley
1½ teaspoons chopped fresh basil
¼ teaspoon white pepper
¼ teaspoon ground nutmeg
4 (10-ounce) chicken leg quarters
2 tablespoons butter or margarine
Paprika
1 lemon, thinly sliced
Fresh spinach leaves (optional)

Remove wrapper from spinach package; place package in a medium baking dish. Microwave at HIGH for 3 to 5 minutes or until thawed. Drain spinach well, pressing between layers of paper towels. Combine spinach, onion, egg, cheese, parsley, basil, pepper, and nutmeg; set aside.

Place chicken pieces, skin side up, on a rack placed inside a baking dish. Gently separate chicken skin from flesh, forming a pocket. Stuff pockets evenly with spinach mixture.

Place butter in a small bowl; microwave, uncovered, for 45 seconds or until melted. Brush chicken with butter; sprinkle with paprika. Reduce to MEDIUM HIGH (70% power); cover with wax paper and microwave for 25 to 30 minutes or until chicken is tender and no longer pink. Let stand, covered, 5 minutes. Garnish with lemon slices and fresh spinach leaves, if desired. Yield: 4 servings.

Gently separate the chicken skin from flesh; fill pockets with a tasty spinach mixture.

SOY-LIME CHICKEN THIGHS

2 tablespoons water
1 tablespoon plus 1 teaspoon
   cornstarch
¼ cup lime juice
3 tablespoons soy sauce
2 tablespoons dry sherry
½ teaspoon ground ginger
¼ teaspoon red pepper
⅓ cup water
¼ cup pineapple preserves
6 (4-ounce) boned and skinned
   chicken thighs
Grated lime rind

Combine 2 tablespoons water and cornstarch, stirring well; add lime juice and next 4 ingredients, stirring well. Combine ⅓ cup water and preserves in a 2-cup glass measure. Microwave, uncovered, at HIGH for 3 minutes or until preserves are melted. Stir in cornstarch mixture.

Place chicken pieces in a 12- x 8- x 2-inch baking dish. Pour sauce over chicken. Cover with wax paper and microwave at HIGH for 12 to 14 minutes or until chicken is tender, basting with sauce every 4 minutes. Sprinkle with lime rind before serving. Yield: 6 servings.

DRUMSTICKS ITALIAN STYLE

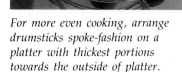

8 (3- to 4-ounce) chicken
   drumsticks, skinned
1 (15½-ounce) jar commercial
   pizza sauce
1 (4-ounce) can sliced
   mushrooms, drained
1 teaspoon dried parsley flakes
1 teaspoon dried whole basil
⅛ teaspoon garlic powder
½ cup grated Parmesan cheese
4 (1-ounce) slices mozzarella
   cheese, cut in half diagonally

Arrange drumsticks spoke-fashion on a 12-inch round glass platter with thickest portions towards outside of platter. Cover with wax paper and microwave at HIGH for 10 minutes; drain off liquid. Combine pizza sauce and next 4 ingredients; pour over drumsticks. Cover with wax paper and microwave at HIGH for 5 to 7 minutes or until chicken is tender. Sprinkle with Parmesan cheese; arrange mozzarella cheese over top. Microwave, uncovered, at HIGH for 2 to 3 minutes or until cheese melts. Serve immediately. Yield: 4 servings.

For more even cooking, arrange drumsticks spoke-fashion on a platter with thickest portions towards the outside of platter.

CHICKEN LIVERS IN ITALIAN SAUCE

1 pound chicken livers,
   quartered
2 tablespoons vegetable oil
½ cup minced onion
½ cup minced celery
1 (8-ounce) can tomato sauce
1 (6-ounce) can tomato paste
1 (4-ounce) can sliced
   mushrooms, undrained
¼ cup water
¼ teaspoon garlic powder
½ teaspoon salt
⅛ teaspoon pepper
¼ teaspoon dried whole basil
Hot cooked egg noodles
2 tablespoons grated Parmesan
   cheese

Place chicken livers and oil in a 2-quart casserole. Cover with wax paper and microwave at HIGH for 6 to 7 minutes or until livers are tender. Drain; remove livers from casserole, and set aside.

Add onion and celery to casserole; cover and microwave at HIGH for 2 minutes. Return livers to casserole; add tomato sauce, tomato paste, mushrooms, water, garlic powder, salt, pepper, and basil, stirring gently. Reduce to MEDIUM HIGH (70% power); cover and microwave for 10 to 12 minutes or until slightly thickened. Serve over noodles, and sprinkle with cheese. Yield: 4 to 6 servings.

Cornish Dinner Duo

2 (1¼- to 1½-pound) Cornish
  hens
2 teaspoons butter or margarine
¼ cup finely chopped onion
¼ cup chopped celery
½ cup diluted canned chicken
  broth
¼ cup chopped pecans
¼ teaspoon salt
¼ teaspoon dried whole thyme
⅛ teaspoon pepper
1 teaspoon paprika
1 cup cooked long-grain rice
1 (4-ounce) can sliced
  mushrooms, drained
¼ cup shredded carrot

Remove giblets from hens; reserve for other uses. Rinse hens with cold water, and pat dry. Tie legs together with nylon tie or string.

Place butter in a 12- x 8- x 2-inch baking dish. Microwave, uncovered, at HIGH for 35 seconds or until melted. Add onion and celery; cover with heavy-duty plastic wrap and microwave at HIGH for 2 minutes or until crisp-tender. Stir in broth and next 4 ingredients.

Place hens, breast side down, in baking dish. Cover with wax paper and microwave at HIGH for 15 minutes. Turn hens breast side up; sprinkle with paprika. Cover and microwave at HIGH for 12 to 15 minutes or until juices run clear when thigh is pierced with a fork. Remove hens to a serving platter, reserving liquid in baking dish. Add rice, mushrooms, and carrot to liquid in baking dish. Cover with wax paper and microwave at HIGH for 3 minutes or until thoroughly heated. Serve with hens. Yield: 2 servings.

Brown Dressed Hens

¼ cup finely chopped onion
1 tablespoon butter or
  margarine
⅓ cup golden raisins
1 teaspoon dry sherry
¾ cup cooked long-grain and
  wild rice mix
¼ cup slivered almonds
1 tablespoon chopped fresh
  parsley
1 teaspoon grated orange rind
2 (1- to 1¼-pound) Cornish
  hens
¼ teaspoon salt
¼ teaspoon pepper
2 tablespoons butter or
  margarine
1 teaspoon browning and
  seasoning sauce

Combine onion and 1 tablespoon butter in a small bowl; microwave, uncovered, at HIGH for 1 to 2 minutes or until onion is tender. Add raisins and sherry; microwave, uncovered, at HIGH for 1 minute. Add rice, almonds, parsley, and orange rind; toss gently, and set aside.

Remove giblets from hens; reserve for other uses. Rinse hens with cold water, and pat dry. Sprinkle cavities of hens with salt and pepper. Stuff hens lightly with rice mixture, and close cavities. Secure with wooden picks. Tie legs together with nylon tie or string. Place hens, breast side down, on a rack placed inside a baking dish, and set aside.

Place 2 tablespoons butter in a small bowl; microwave, uncovered, at HIGH for 45 seconds or until melted. Add seasoning sauce, stirring well. Brush hens with butter mixture; cover with wax paper and microwave at HIGH for 10 minutes. Turn hens breast side up; brush with remaining butter mixture. Cover and microwave at HIGH for 10 to 11 minutes or until juices run clear when thigh is pierced with a fork. Let stand, covered, 5 minutes. Serve immediately. Yield: 2 servings.

Cornish hens can microwave to perfection as seen in Cornish Hens With Zesty Orange Rice.

CORNISH HENS WITH ZESTY ORANGE RICE

½ cup hot water
½ cup uncooked instant rice
2 tablespoons butter or
    margarine
1 tablespoon finely chopped
    celery
1 large orange
2 tablespoons minced onion
2 tablespoons chopped walnuts
¼ teaspoon ground ginger
⅛ teaspoon ground allspice
2 (1½-pound) Cornish hens
½ cup orange juice
1 tablespoon cornstarch
2 tablespoons dry sherry
1 tablespoon brown sugar
1 tablespoon soy sauce
Pinch of ground allspice
Orange slices (optional)

Place water in a 4-cup glass measure. Microwave, uncovered, at HIGH for 1½ minutes or until boiling. Stir in rice; let stand, covered, until all liquid is absorbed.

Place butter and celery in a 1-cup glass measure. Microwave, uncovered, at HIGH for 45 seconds or until butter is melted; add to rice. Grate ¼ teaspoon orange rind; add to rice mixture. Peel and section orange, discarding remaining rind. Coarsely chop orange segments; add to rice mixture. Stir in onion, walnuts, ginger, and ⅛ teaspoon allspice.

Remove giblets from hens; reserve for other uses. Rinse hens with cold water, and pat dry. Stuff hens lightly with rice mixture, and close cavities. Secure with wooden picks. Tie legs together with nylon tie or string. Place hens, breast side down, on a rack placed inside a baking dish.

CORNISH HENS WITH ZESTY ORANGE RICE
(continued)

Combine orange juice and cornstarch in a 1-cup glass measure, stirring well. Stir in sherry, sugar, soy sauce, and a pinch of allspice. Microwave, uncovered, at HIGH for 1½ to 2 minutes or until thickened. Brush hens with half of orange juice mixture; cover with wax paper and microwave at HIGH for 8 minutes, rotating a half-turn after 4 minutes. Turn hens breast side up. Brush with remaining orange juice mixture. Cover and microwave at HIGH for 10 to 12 minutes or until juices run clear when thigh is pierced with a fork. Let stand, covered, 5 minutes. Garnish with orange slices, if desired. Yield: 2 servings.

GRILLED FRUITED CORNISH HENS

2 tablespoons butter or
   margarine
¼ pound hot bulk pork
   sausage, crumbled
4 slices raisin bread, cubed
   and toasted
¼ teaspoon ground cinnamon
1 medium apple, unpeeled,
   cored, and chopped
2 tablespoons orange juice
4 (1- to 1½-pound) Cornish
   hens
¼ cup vegetable oil, divided

Soak 4 cups mesquite chips in water for 1 to 24 hours; set aside.

Place butter in a 1-cup glass measure. Microwave, uncovered, at HIGH for 45 seconds or until melted; set aside. Place sausage in a 2-cup glass measure. Microwave, uncovered, at HIGH for 2 minutes or until no longer pink; drain. Combine toasted bread cubes and cinnamon in a medium bowl, stirring well. Add sausage and apple. Sprinkle with orange juice, and stir in melted butter; set aside.

Remove giblets from hens; reserve for other uses. Rinse hens with cold water, and pat dry. Stuff hens lightly with sausage mixture, and close cavities. Secure with wooden picks. Tie legs together with string. Place 2 hens, breast side down, on a rack placed inside a baking dish; brush lightly with 1 tablespoon oil. Cover with wax paper, and microwave at HIGH for 14 to 18 minutes or until juices run clear when thigh is pierced with a fork, rotating a half-turn after 7 minutes. Repeat procedure with remaining hens and 1 tablespoon oil.

Drain mesquite chips, and place directly on hot coals. Transfer hens to barbecue grill, placing breast side up. Cook over hot coals for 10 minutes on each side or to desired degree of doneness, basting often with remaining 2 tablespoons oil. Yield: 4 servings.

Lime-Grilled Cornish Hens

2 (1½-pound) Cornish hens, split
2 limes, quartered
½ cup chopped onion
2 tablespoons Chablis or other dry white wine
2 tablespoons lime juice
2 cloves garlic, crushed
1 tablespoon plus 1 teaspoon chopped fresh mint leaves
1 tablespoon chopped fresh parsley
½ teaspoon salt
¼ teaspoon white pepper
¼ teaspoon Worcestershire sauce

Remove giblets from hens; reserve for other uses. Rinse hens with cold water; pat dry. Place hens in a large zip top heavy-duty plastic bag.

Combine lime quarters and remaining ingredients in a medium bowl; pour over hens and secure bag tightly. Refrigerate at least 2 hours, turning bag occasionally.

Remove hens, reserving marinade. Place hens on a rack placed inside a baking dish. Cover with wax paper and microwave at HIGH for 14 to 18 minutes or until juices run clear when thigh is pierced with a fork, rotating a half-turn after 7 minutes.

Transfer hens to barbecue grill. Cook over medium-hot coals for 20 minutes or to desired degree of doneness, turning and brushing hens with reserved marinade every 5 minutes. Yield: 4 servings.

Roast Turkey With Sausage-Bread Stuffing

1 (10-pound) turkey
½ pound bulk pork sausage
1 cup chopped onion
1 cup chopped celery
2 cups herb-seasoned stuffing mix
2 cups cornbread stuffing mix
1 medium apple, peeled and chopped
1 (8-ounce) can crushed pineapple, drained
½ cup chopped fresh mushrooms
½ cup chopped pecans
⅓ cup brandy
¼ cup apricot preserves
2 tablespoons vegetable oil
½ teaspoon browning and seasoning sauce
½ cup water
Dried apricot roses (optional)
Celery leaves (optional)

Remove giblets and neck from turkey, and reserve for other uses. Rinse turkey with cold water, and pat dry.

Crumble sausage in a 1-quart casserole; add onion and celery. Cover with wax paper and microwave at HIGH for 3 to 4 minutes or until sausage is no longer pink. Drain. Place in a large bowl; add herb-seasoned stuffing mix and next 7 ingredients, mixing well.

Lightly stuff dressing into cavity of turkey. Tie ends of legs together with nylon tie or string; lift wingtips up and over back, and tuck under bird.

Combine vegetable oil and seasoning sauce in a small bowl; brush surface of turkey. Place turkey, breast side up, in a large browning bag prepared according to package directions and placed on a 12-inch round glass platter. Add water; tie bag loosely with string or a ½-inch-wide strip cut from open end of bag. Reduce to MEDIUM (50% power); microwave for 1 hour, rotating a half-turn every 15 minutes. Shield wingtips and ends of legs with small pieces of aluminum foil, if needed. Insert microwave

ROAST TURKEY WITH SAUSAGE-BREAD STUFFING

(continued)

thermometer between leg and thigh, if desired. Microwave at MEDIUM for 30 to 45 minutes or until drumsticks are easy to move, rotating a half-turn every 15 minutes; thermometer should register 180°. Let stand, in bag, 15 minutes or until thermometer registers 185°. Discard aluminum foil. Garnish with apricot roses and celery leaves, if desired. Yield: 12 servings.

When festive holidays roll around, consider preparing Roast Turkey With Sausage-Bread Stuffing.

Turkey Kabobs With Indonesian Sauce

½ cup vermouth
⅓ cup peanut oil
¼ cup soy sauce
3 cloves garlic, crushed
1 tablespoon plus 1½ teaspoons grated fresh gingerroot
1 tablespoon lemon juice
2 teaspoons coarsely ground black pepper
1 (2-pound) boneless turkey breast, cut into 1-inch cubes
Indonesian Sauce

Combine first 7 ingredients in a large bowl, stirring well; add turkey. Cover and refrigerate 4 to 6 hours.

Drain turkey, reserving marinade. Loosely thread turkey onto eight 12-inch wooden skewers. Place kabobs in a 12- x 8- x 2-inch baking dish. Cover with wax paper and microwave at HIGH for 9 to 10 minutes or until turkey is tender, rearranging kabobs and basting with marinade every 3 minutes. Serve with Indonesian Sauce. Yield: 8 servings.

Indonesian Sauce:

½ cup chopped onion
1 clove garlic, minced
1 tablespoon peanut oil
½ cup undiluted canned chicken broth
⅔ cup crunchy peanut butter
3 tablespoons soy sauce
2 tablespoons catsup
1 tablespoon dark brown sugar
1 tablespoon lime juice
¼ teaspoon crushed red pepper

Combine onion, garlic, and oil in a 4-cup glass measure. Microwave, uncovered, at HIGH for 2 minutes. Stir in broth; microwave, uncovered, at HIGH for 2 to 3 minutes or until boiling. Stir in peanut butter, soy sauce, catsup, dark brown sugar, lime juice, and crushed red pepper, stirring well. Yield: 1½ cups.

Teriyaki Turkey

½ pound boneless turkey breast, skinned
¼ cup teriyaki sauce
2 teaspoons sherry
1 teaspoon chicken-flavored bouillon granules
1 teaspoon grated fresh gingerroot
½ teaspoon sugar
1 medium onion, cut into 8 wedges
1 medium-size green pepper, cut into strips
⅔ cup sliced celery
2 tablespoons water
1½ teaspoons cornstarch
1 tomato, cut into wedges
Hot cooked rice

Slice turkey into thin strips. Combine teriyaki sauce and next 4 ingredients in a 1-quart casserole. Add turkey; refrigerate 30 minutes.

Place onion, green pepper strips, and celery in a 2-quart casserole. Cover with heavy-duty plastic wrap and microwave at HIGH for 3½ to 4½ minutes or until crisp-tender, stirring after 2 minutes; set aside.

Cover turkey with heavy-duty plastic wrap and microwave at HIGH for 3½ to 4½ minutes or until turkey is tender, stirring after 2 minutes; add to vegetable mixture.

Combine water and cornstarch; add to turkey mixture, stirring well. Cover and microwave at HIGH for 3 to 4 minutes or until thickened, stirring after 2 minutes. Stir in tomato wedges. Let stand, covered, 5 minutes. Serve over rice. Yield: 4 servings.

Lemon Turkey Cutlets

4 (4-ounce) turkey breast
  cutlets
1 egg, slightly beaten
½ cup seasoned, dry
  breadcrumbs
½ cup water
2 tablespoons lemon juice
2 teaspoons cornstarch
1 teaspoon chicken-flavored
  bouillon granules
1 tablespoon chopped fresh
  chives
Lemon slices (optional)

Place turkey between 2 sheets of wax paper. Flatten to ¼-inch thickness, using a meat mallet or rolling pin.

Coat each cutlet in egg, and dredge in breadcrumbs; place on a rack placed inside a baking dish. Cover with wax paper and microwave at MEDIUM HIGH (70% power) for 9 to 10 minutes or until turkey is tender. Let stand, covered, while preparing sauce.

Combine water, lemon juice, cornstarch, and bouillon granules in a 1-cup glass measure. Microwave, uncovered, at HIGH for 3 minutes or until slightly thickened. Stir in chopped chives. Spoon sauce over cutlets. Garnish with lemon slices, if desired. Yield: 4 servings.

Turkey-Spinach Rollups With Saffron Sauce

1 tablespoon butter or
  margarine
1 (10-ounce) package frozen
  chopped spinach
½ cup finely chopped onion
⅓ cup seasoned, dry
  breadcrumbs
1 egg, beaten
2 tablespoons grated Parmesan
  cheese
1 teaspoon lemon juice
¼ teaspoon garlic powder
¼ teaspoon pepper
Dash of hot sauce
6 (4-ounce) turkey cutlets
2 eggs, beaten
⅔ cup seasoned, dry
  breadcrumbs
Saffron Sauce

Place butter in a medium bowl; microwave, uncovered, at HIGH for 35 seconds or until melted. Remove wrapper from spinach package; place package in a medium baking dish. Microwave at HIGH for 3 to 5 minutes or until thawed. Drain spinach; press between layers of paper towels. Add spinach and next 8 ingredients to butter, stirring well; set aside.

Place turkey between 2 sheets of wax paper. Flatten to ⅛-inch thickness, using a meat mallet or rolling pin. Top each cutlet with spinach mixture, spreading evenly. Roll up lengthwise, and secure with wooden picks. Coat turkey rolls in egg, and dredge in ⅔ cup breadcrumbs.

Place rolls, seam side down, in a 12- x 8- x 2-inch baking dish. Cover with wax paper; microwave at HIGH for 9 to 12 minutes or until tender, rearranging rolls and rotating a half-turn after 4 minutes. Serve rolls with Saffron Sauce. Yield: 6 servings.

Saffron Sauce:

2 tablespoons butter
⅛ teaspoon saffron threads
1 tablespoon all-purpose
  flour
2 tablespoons orange juice
½ cup plus 2 tablespoons
  half-and-half
2 tablespoons water
¼ teaspoon salt

Place butter and saffron in a 1-quart casserole. Microwave, uncovered, at HIGH for 45 seconds or until butter melts. Stir in flour. Gradually add orange juice, stirring well. Microwave, uncovered, at HIGH for 1 minute. Stir in half-and-half and remaining ingredients; microwave, uncovered, at HIGH for 2 to 3 minutes or until sauce is thickened, stirring after every minute. Yield: about 1 cup.

DUCKLING BORDEAUX

1 (3½- to 4½-pound) dressed
  duckling
½ cup orange marmalade,
  divided
1 tablespoon soy sauce,
  divided
1 tablespoon butter
2 tablespoons Chablis or other
  dry white wine
2 tablespoons vinegar
¼ teaspoon pepper
Watercress (optional)
Apple slices (optional)
Grapes (optional)

Remove giblets and neck from duckling; reserve for other uses. Close cavity of duckling with wooden picks. Tie ends of legs with nylon tie or string. Place duckling on a rack placed inside a baking dish. Prick skin with a fork at 2-inch intervals. Cover with wax paper and microwave at HIGH for 10 minutes, rotating a half-turn after 5 minutes. Drain off drippings.

Combine ¼ cup orange marmalade, and 1½ teaspoons soy sauce; stir well. Brush duckling with sauce. Shield wingtips and ends of legs with small pieces of aluminum foil, if needed. Cover with wax paper; insert microwave thermometer between leg and thigh, if desired. Microwave at HIGH for 10 to 12 minutes or until drumsticks are easy to move, rotating a half-turn after 5 minutes; thermometer should register 180°. Drain off drippings.

Place butter in a 2-cup glass measure; microwave, uncovered, at HIGH for 35 seconds or until melted. Add wine, vinegar, pepper, remaining ¼ cup marmalade, and remaining 1½ teaspoons soy sauce; microwave, uncovered, at HIGH for 2½ minutes, stirring after 1 minute. Spoon sauce over duckling; microwave, uncovered, at HIGH for 5 minutes. Let stand 5 minutes or until thermometer registers 185°. Discard aluminum foil. Garnish with watercress, apple slices, and grapes, if desired. Yield: 2 to 4 servings.

HONEY-GRILLED DUCKLING

1 (5-pound) dressed duckling
½ cup soy sauce
¼ cup chopped fresh parsley
2 tablespoons lemon juice
2 tablespoons honey
1 clove garlic, minced

Remove giblets and neck from duckling; reserve for other uses. Split duckling lengthwise, using an electric knife.

Place duckling, breast side down, on a rack placed inside a 12- x 8- x 2-inch baking dish. Prick skin with a fork at 2-inch intervals. Cover with wax paper and microwave at HIGH for 11 minutes. Drain off drippings. Turn duckling breast side up. Microwave at HIGH for 12 to 15 minutes or until juices run clear when thigh is pierced with a fork.

Combine soy sauce, parsley, lemon juice, honey, and garlic, stirring well. Transfer duckling to barbecue grill. Cook over medium coals for 15 to 20 minutes or to desired degree of doneness, turning and basting often with soy sauce mixture. Yield: 4 servings.

Garnished with apple slices, grapes, and watercress,
Duckling Bordeaux makes a lovely presentation.

Sauces

If you've ever made a sauce in your microwave, you already know that it's one of the best ways to use the oven. Microwave sauces are actually easier to make than conventional sauces because you don't have the problems of lumping, scorching, and constant stirring.

Our recipes offer a variety of savory and dessert sauces. The savory sauces are perfect spooned over meat, poultry, fish, or vegetables while the dessert sauces are delicious served over pound cake or ice cream.

You will find a glass measure or casserole dish ideal for making sauces in the microwave oven. Just be sure to use a container large enough to prevent the sauce from bubbling over. In most cases, you will need to use a container that will hold about twice the volume of the sauce.

Watch the sauce carefully as it cooks. If you see that it is about to bubble over, just open the microwave door and stir the sauce. Occasional stirring will help mix the cooked portion near the outside of the dish with the uncooked portion in the center.

Sour Cream-Dill Sauce (page 193) adds interesting flavor when spooned over a variety of cooked fresh vegetables.

BASIC WHITE SAUCE

Make sure Basic White Sauce isn't lumpy by blending flour into the melted butter; gradually add milk, stirring well.

2 tablespoons butter or
   margarine
2 tablespoons all-purpose flour
1 cup milk
¼ teaspoon salt

Place butter in a 4-cup glass measure. Microwave, uncovered, at HIGH for 45 seconds or until melted. Blend in flour. Gradually add milk, stirring well. Microwave, uncovered, at HIGH for 3 to 4 minutes or until thickened, stirring after every minute. Stir in salt. Serve immediately over fish, poultry, or vegetables. Yield: 1 cup.

CHEESE SAUCE:

Add ¾ cup (3 ounces) shredded Cheddar cheese and ⅛ teaspoon dry mustard to hot white sauce. Stir sauce until cheese melts. Yield: 1¼ cups.

CURRY SAUCE:

Add 2 teaspoons curry powder to hot white sauce. Stir until blended. Yield: 1 cup.

GARLIC-CHEESE SAUCE

1 tablespoon butter or
   margarine
1 tablespoon all-purpose flour
½ cup milk
¼ cup (1 ounce) shredded
   Cheddar cheese
¼ teaspoon garlic powder
Dash of pepper

Place butter in a 2-cup glass measure. Microwave, uncovered, at HIGH for 35 seconds or until melted. Blend in flour. Gradually add milk, stirring well. Microwave, uncovered, at HIGH for 1½ to 2 minutes or until thickened, stirring after 1 minute. Add cheese, garlic powder, and pepper; stir well. Microwave, uncovered, at HIGH for 20 to 30 seconds or until cheese melts. Serve immediately over fish, poultry, or vegetables. Yield: ⅔ cup.

ZUCCHINI-MUSHROOM-CHEESE SAUCE

½ cup finely chopped zucchini
½ cup sliced fresh mushrooms
1 tablespoon butter or
   margarine
2 cloves garlic, minced
2 tablespoons all-purpose flour
½ cup undiluted canned
   chicken broth
½ cup half-and-half
⅓ cup grated Parmesan cheese
¼ teaspoon white pepper

Combine first 4 ingredients in a 2-cup glass measure; microwave, uncovered, at HIGH for 2 to 4 minutes or until vegetables are tender, stirring after 1 minute. Blend in flour. Gradually add chicken broth and half-and-half, stirring well. Microwave, uncovered, at HIGH for 4 to 6 minutes or until slightly thickened, stirring after every minute. Stir in Parmesan cheese and white pepper; microwave, uncovered, at HIGH for 30 seconds. Serve immediately over meats or vegetables. Yield: 1½ cups.

MUSHROOM-SHERRY SAUCE

2 tablespoons butter or
  margarine
¾ pound fresh mushrooms,
  sliced
3 tablespoons finely chopped
  green onions
1 teaspoon paprika
¼ cup dry sherry
2 tablespoons cornstarch
¾ cup half-and-half
¼ teaspoon salt
⅛ teaspoon pepper
⅛ teaspoon red pepper

Place butter in a 1½-quart casserole. Microwave, uncovered, at HIGH for 45 seconds or until melted. Stir in mushrooms, green onions, and paprika; microwave, uncovered, at HIGH for 4 minutes or until vegetables are tender. Set vegetables aside.

Combine sherry and cornstarch, stirring well; add to mushroom mixture. Stir in half-and-half, salt, pepper, and red pepper; microwave, uncovered, at HIGH for 3 to 3½ minutes or until thickened, stirring after every minute. Serve immediately over meats. Yield: about 3 cups.

SOUR CREAM-DILL SAUCE

2 tablespoons butter or
  margarine
3 tablespoons all-purpose flour
1 cup undiluted canned
  chicken broth
¼ cup commercial sour cream
2 teaspoons dried whole
  dillweed

Place butter in a 2-cup glass measure. Microwave, uncovered, at HIGH for 45 seconds or until melted. Blend in flour. Gradually add broth, stirring well. Microwave at HIGH for 4 to 5 minutes or until thickened, stirring after every minute. Let stand 3 minutes. Add sour cream and dillweed; stir until smooth. Serve immediately over vegetables. Yield: about 1¼ cups.

MORNAY SAUCE

3 tablespoons butter or
  margarine
3 tablespoons all-purpose flour
¾ cup undiluted canned
  chicken broth
¾ cup milk
3 tablespoons grated Parmesan
  cheese
⅛ teaspoon salt

Place butter in a 4-cup glass measure. Microwave, uncovered, at HIGH for 50 seconds or until melted. Blend in flour. Gradually add broth, milk, and cheese, stirring well. Microwave, uncovered, at HIGH for 4 minutes or until thickened, stirring after every minute. Stir in salt. Serve immediately over fish, poultry, or vegetables. Yield: 1¾ cups.

Once a sauce begins to thicken, you may need to stir every 30 seconds with a wire whisk to prevent bubbling over. Opening the door to the microwave will stop the sauce from bubbling any higher.

Hollandaise Sauce

3 egg yolks
2 tablespoons lemon juice
¼ teaspoon salt
½ cup butter

Combine egg yolks, lemon juice, and salt in a small bowl; beat with a wire whisk until blended. Set aside.

Place butter in a 2-cup glass measure. Microwave, uncovered, at HIGH for 1 minute or just until melted (do not allow butter to boil).

Gradually add butter to yolk mixture, stirring constantly with a wire whisk. Reduce to MEDIUM (50% power); microwave, uncovered, for 1 to 1½ minutes or until thickened, stirring with a wire whisk every 30 seconds. Serve immediately over meats or vegetables. Yield: ⅔ cup.

Prevent Hollandaise Sauce from curdling by gradually adding melted butter to yolk mixture; stir constantly with a whisk.

Tangy Lemon Sauce

½ cup mayonnaise
2 tablespoons milk
1 tablespoon lemon juice
½ teaspoon grated onion
⅛ teaspoon dried whole thyme
1 teaspoon grated lemon rind

Combine first 5 ingredients in a 1-cup glass measure, stirring well. Microwave, uncovered, at HIGH for 1 minute or just until thoroughly heated. Stir in lemon rind, and serve immediately over vegetables. Yield: about ¾ cup.

Red Pepper Sauce

1 small sweet red pepper, chopped
2 teaspoons butter or margarine
1 clove garlic, crushed
2 tomatoes, peeled, seeded, and chopped (about 1 cup)
1 teaspoon minced fresh basil or ¼ teaspoon dried whole basil
⅛ teaspoon salt
⅛ teaspoon pepper

Combine red pepper, butter, and garlic in a 4-cup glass measure. Microwave, uncovered, at HIGH for 2 minutes. Add tomatoes, stirring well. Microwave, uncovered, at HIGH for 2 to 3 minutes or until tomatoes are softened.

Position knife blade in bowl of food processor; add tomato mixture. Process 30 seconds or until pureed. Return puree to glass measure; add basil, salt, and pepper. Microwave, uncovered, at HIGH for 4 to 6 minutes or until slightly thickened, stirring after 2 minutes. Serve hot or cold over fish, meats, poultry, or vegetables. Yield: 1 cup.

Most sauces can be reheated at HIGH, stirring every 30 seconds. The length of time will vary depending on the amount of sauce. Sauces that contain eggs or whipping cream should be reheated at MEDIUM (50% power).

Give ribs or chicken a generous coating of Fireside Barbecue Sauce for lots of warm flavor.

FIRESIDE BARBECUE SAUCE

2 tablespoons vegetable oil
1 tablespoon instant minced
  onion
¼ teaspoon garlic powder
1 cup catsup
⅓ cup water
¼ cup firmly packed brown
  sugar
3 tablespoons cider vinegar
3 tablespoons lemon juice
2 tablespoons soy sauce
2 tablespoons prepared
  mustard
1 tablespoon Worcestershire
  sauce
¼ teaspoon celery seeds
2 to 3 drops of hot sauce

Combine oil, onion, and garlic powder in a 4-cup glass measure. Microwave, uncovered, at HIGH for 1 minute. Stir in catsup, water, brown sugar, vinegar, lemon juice, soy sauce, mustard, Worcestershire sauce, celery seeds, and hot sauce. Microwave, uncovered, at HIGH for 5 to 7 minutes or until boiling, stirring after 3 minutes. Brush sauce over grilled ribs or chicken. Yield: 2½ cups.

CHOCOLATE-MINT SAUCE

1 (6-ounce) package chocolate-covered mint wafer candies
⅓ cup whipping cream

Combine mint wafer candies and whipping cream in a 4-cup glass measure. Cover with heavy-duty plastic wrap and microwave at MEDIUM (50% power) for 3 to 4 minutes or until melted, stirring after every minute. Serve immediately over ice cream. Yield: 1 cup.

PRALINE SAUCE

¼ cup butter or margarine
1¼ cups firmly packed brown sugar
3 tablespoons all-purpose flour
¾ cup light corn syrup
¾ cup chopped pecans
1 (5-ounce) can evaporated milk

Place butter in a large bowl. Microwave, uncovered, at HIGH for 55 seconds or until melted. Stir in brown sugar and flour. Gradually add corn syrup, stirring well. Microwave, uncovered, at HIGH for 6 to 7 minutes or until mixture comes to a boil and thickens, stirring every 2 minutes. Let cool to lukewarm.

Spread pecans in a 9-inch pieplate. Microwave, uncovered, at HIGH for 4 to 5 minutes or until lightly toasted, stirring every 2 minutes.

Gradually add toasted pecans and milk to lukewarm sauce, stirring well. Serve sauce immediately over ice cream or pound cake. Yield: about 2 cups.

STRAWBERRY SUNDAE SAUCE

3 (10-ounce) packages frozen sliced strawberries
1 tablespoon cornstarch
1 tablespoon lemon juice
½ cup red currant jelly
3 tablespoons grenadine syrup

Remove frozen strawberries from packages, and place in a large bowl. Microwave, uncovered, at HIGH for 4 to 7 minutes or just until thawed. Drain strawberries, reserving ½ cup juice. Set strawberries aside. Combine strawberry juice and cornstarch in a large bowl, stirring until smooth. Add lemon juice; stir well. Set aside.

Place jelly in a 1-cup glass measure. Microwave, uncovered, at HIGH for 1½ to 2 minutes or until melted. Stir jelly into strawberry juice mixture. Microwave, uncovered, at HIGH for 2½ minutes or until slightly thickened, stirring after 1½ minutes. Add strawberries and grenadine syrup, stirring well. Microwave, uncovered, at HIGH for 1 minute or until thoroughly heated. Serve immediately over ice cream. Yield: about 2 cups.

Chocolate-Mint Sauce is guaranteed to be a winner when served over ice cream.

Soups and Stews

With the help of the microwave oven, you can serve a bowl of refreshing dessert soup or a steaming bowl of nourishing soup in no time at all. Most of our soups are easy to prepare—they are just cooked and stirred until done. But a few of the soups are thickened with a cream sauce base which requires a bit more attention.

Speed isn't the only reason for preparing soups and stews in the microwave oven. Vegetables in these mixtures look brighter and taste fresher than those that simmer conventionally for hours.

Some of the soups and stews may call for preparation in what may seem like an extra-large container. This is because soups with lots of liquid need plenty of room for simmering and stirring.

COOL RASPBERRY SOUP

2 (10-ounce) packages frozen raspberries
2½ cups water
1½ cups Burgundy or other dry red wine
¼ cup plus 1 tablespoon sugar
1 (3-inch) stick cinnamon
2 tablespoons plus 1½ teaspoons cornstarch
Whipped cream (optional)
Grated semisweet chocolate (optional)

Place raspberries in a medium bowl; microwave, uncovered, at MEDIUM (50% power) for 5 to 6 minutes or until thawed. Combine next 4 ingredients in a deep 2-quart casserole. Increase to HIGH power and microwave, uncovered, for 6 to 8 minutes or until mixture comes to a boil. Press raspberry mixture through a sieve or food mill, and return to casserole; discard raspberry seeds and cinnamon stick. Combine ¼ cup raspberry liquid and cornstarch; stir well. Add to remaining raspberry liquid in casserole, stirring well. Microwave, uncovered, at HIGH for 6 to 9 minutes or until slightly thickened, stirring every 3 minutes. Cover and chill thoroughly. Garnish each serving with a dollop of whipped cream, and sprinkle with grated chocolate, if desired. Yield: 4½ cups.

Serve steaming Gumbo (page 211) over rice. Add a sprinkling of filé to each serving, if desired.

Swirl whipped cream into Elegant Chocolate-Apricot Dessert Soup.

ELEGANT CHOCOLATE-APRICOT DESSERT SOUP

1 (14½-ounce) can apricot
    halves in light syrup,
    drained
1 (6-ounce) package semisweet
    chocolate morsels
1 cup milk
1½ cups whipping cream
1 tablespoon apricot-flavored
    brandy
¼ teaspoon ground cardamom
Whipped cream
Chocolate curls (optional)

Place apricots in container of an electric blender or food processor; process until smooth. Set aside.

Combine chocolate morsels and milk in a deep 2-quart casserole; cover with heavy-duty plastic wrap and microwave at MEDIUM HIGH (70% power) for 3 to 4 minutes or until chocolate is melted. Stir with a wire whisk until smooth.

Add chocolate mixture to apricot puree in container of an electric blender. Add whipping cream, brandy, and cardamom; process until smooth. Cover and chill thoroughly. Ladle into dessert bowls; garnish each serving with a dollop of whipped cream, gently swirling with a knife. Top with chocolate curls, if desired. Yield: 4 cups.

FRESH BROCCOLI SOUP

3 tablespoons butter or
  margarine
¼ cup chopped onion
3 tablespoons all-purpose flour
1 (10¾-ounce) can chicken
  broth, diluted
1 cup finely chopped fresh
  broccoli
1 small bay leaf
½ cup half-and-half
½ teaspoon pepper

Place butter in a deep 1½-quart casserole. Microwave, uncovered, at HIGH for 50 seconds or until melted. Add onion; microwave, uncovered, at HIGH for 2½ to 3 minutes or until onion is tender. Stir in flour. Gradually add chicken broth, broccoli, and bay leaf, stirring well. Cover with heavy-duty plastic wrap and microwave at HIGH for 5 to 7 minutes or until broccoli is tender, stirring every 2 minutes. Remove and discard bay leaf. Stir in half-and-half and pepper. Reduce to MEDIUM (50% power); cover and microwave for 2 to 3 minutes or until slightly thickened and thoroughly heated. Serve immediately. Yield: 4 cups.

CELERY SOUP

2 slices bacon, cut into ½-inch
  pieces
1½ cups thinly sliced celery
¼ cup chopped onion
¼ cup water
¼ cup all-purpose flour
½ teaspoon salt
½ teaspoon dried whole basil
⅛ teaspoon celery seeds
⅛ teaspoon pepper
2¼ cups milk
½ cup half-and-half

Place bacon in a deep 2-quart casserole; cover with heavy-duty plastic wrap and microwave at HIGH for 2 minutes or until partially cooked. Add celery, onion, and water. Cover with heavy-duty plastic wrap and microwave at HIGH for 6 to 9 minutes or until celery is tender, stirring after 3 minutes.

Stir in flour and next 4 ingredients. Gradually add milk; stir well. Microwave, uncovered, at HIGH for 8 to 10 minutes or until thickened, stirring after 4 minutes. Gradually stir in half-and-half. Place mixture in container of an electric blender; process until smooth. Serve immediately. Yield: 3½ cups.

CREAM OF MUSHROOM SOUP

2 cups sliced fresh mushrooms
¾ cup chopped green onions
2 tablespoons butter or
  margarine
3 tablespoons all-purpose flour
Pinch of white pepper
Pinch of ground nutmeg
2 cups diluted canned beef
  broth
1 cup whipping cream
Minced fresh parsley (optional)

Combine mushrooms, onions, and butter in a deep 2-quart casserole. Microwave, uncovered, at HIGH for 6 to 7 minutes or until vegetables are tender, stirring after 3 minutes. Stir in flour, pepper, and nutmeg. Gradually add broth and whipping cream, stirring well. Microwave, uncovered, at HIGH for 15 to 20 minutes or until slightly thickened and thoroughly heated, stirring every 5 minutes. Garnish with parsley, if desired. Serve immediately. Yield: 3 cups.

CREAM OF ASPARAGUS SOUP

¼ cup sliced almonds
2 (10-ounce) packages frozen
   asparagus spears
1 cup water
¼ cup chopped onion
2 tablespoons chopped fresh
   parsley
2 tablespoons butter or
   margarine
3 tablespoons all-purpose flour
2 cups half-and-half
1 cup milk
½ teaspoon salt
⅛ teaspoon white pepper
Additional chopped fresh
   parsley

Spread almonds in a 9-inch pieplate. Microwave, uncovered, at HIGH for 2 to 4 minutes or until lightly toasted, stirring after every minute. Set aside.

Combine asparagus, water, onion, and 2 tablespoons chopped parsley in a deep 3-quart casserole; cover with heavy-duty plastic wrap and microwave at HIGH for 5 minutes. Separate asparagus spears with a fork; cover and microwave at HIGH for 4 to 5 minutes or until asparagus is tender.

Place asparagus and cooking liquid in container of an electric blender; process until smooth. Set aside.

Place butter in 3-quart casserole; microwave, uncovered, at HIGH for 45 seconds or until melted. Stir in flour. Gradually add half-and-half and milk, stirring well. Microwave, uncovered, at HIGH for 8 to 9 minutes or until slightly thickened, stirring every 2 minutes. Stir in asparagus puree, salt, and pepper. Cover and microwave at HIGH for 2 to 3 minutes or until thoroughly heated, stirring after every minute. Garnish each serving with almonds and additional parsley. Yield: 6 cups.

BORSCHT

1¾ pounds medium beets
   without tops, peeled and
   grated
½ small cabbage (about ½
   pound), thinly sliced
2 medium carrots, scraped and
   thinly sliced
1 medium onion, chopped
1 stalk celery, thinly sliced
2 (10½-ounce) cans beef broth,
   diluted
1 tablespoon lemon juice
¼ teaspoon sugar
¼ teaspoon pepper
Commercial sour cream
   (optional)

Combine first 6 ingredients in a deep 5-quart casserole; cover with heavy-duty plastic wrap and microwave at HIGH for 30 minutes, stirring every 10 minutes. Stir in lemon juice, sugar, and pepper; cover and microwave at HIGH for 8 to 10 minutes or until beets are tender, stirring every 5 minutes.

Place half of beet mixture in container of an electric blender; process until smooth. Repeat procedure with remaining beet mixture. Return mixture to casserole. Cover with heavy-duty plastic wrap and microwave at HIGH for 3 to 4 minutes or until thoroughly heated. Garnish each serving with a dollop of sour cream, if desired. Serve hot or cold. Yield: 9 cups.

Cream of Asparagus Soup looks inviting when topped with parsley and microwave-toasted almonds.

FRENCH ONION SOUP

¼ cup plus 2 tablespoons
    butter or margarine
4 medium onions, thinly sliced
    and separated into rings
1 clove garlic, minced
2 teaspoons all-purpose flour
1 teaspoon dry mustard
2 (10¾-ounce) cans beef broth,
    undiluted
¼ cup Chablis or other dry
    white wine
2 teaspoons Worcestershire
    sauce
4 (½-inch-thick) slices French
    bread, toasted
1 cup (4 ounces) shredded
    Swiss cheese
¼ cup grated Parmesan cheese

Place butter in a deep 3-quart casserole. Microwave, uncovered, at HIGH for 1 minute or until melted. Stir in onion and garlic. Microwave, uncovered, at HIGH for 20 to 30 minutes or until onion is tender, stirring every 10 minutes. Stir in flour and dry mustard. Gradually add broth, wine, and Worcestershire sauce, stirring well. Microwave, uncovered, at HIGH for 9 to 10 minutes or until slightly thickened, stirring after 5 minutes.

Pour soup into bowls. Top each serving with a slice of toasted French bread; sprinkle with cheeses. Reduce to LOW (10% power); microwave, uncovered, for 1 to 3 minutes or until cheeses melt. Serve immediately. Yield: 5 cups.

VICHYSSOISE

1 tablespoon butter or
    margarine
1 small onion, chopped
3 medium leeks, trimmed
    and thinly sliced
1 (10¾-ounce) can chicken
    broth, diluted
3 medium potatoes, peeled
    and diced
½ teaspoon salt
⅛ teaspoon pepper
1 cup milk
1 cup half-and-half
¼ cup commercial sour cream
Chopped fresh chives

Place butter in a deep 3-quart casserole; microwave, uncovered, at HIGH for 35 seconds or until melted. Add onion and leeks; microwave, uncovered, at HIGH for 4 to 5 minutes or until vegetables are tender, stirring after 2 minutes. Add broth, potatoes, salt, and pepper. Cover with heavy-duty plastic wrap and microwave at HIGH for 12 to 15 minutes or until potatoes are tender, stirring every 4 minutes. Cool slightly.

Spoon one-third of mixture into container of an electric blender; process until smooth. Repeat procedure with remaining mixture.

Stir in milk, half-and-half, and sour cream. Cover and refrigerate until thoroughly chilled. Sprinkle each serving with chives. Yield: 8 cups.

When microwaving soups or stews, be sure the vegetables are cut into evenly shaped pieces. Starting with warm water will also decrease cooking time.

SUMMER VEGETABLE SOUP

2 cups water
1 cup peeled and diced
  potatoes
1 cup thinly sliced carrots
2½ teaspoons salt
1 (16-ounce) package frozen
  green peas
1 cup fresh cauliflower
  flowerets
1 cup fresh broccoli flowerets
3 tablespoons butter or
  margarine
3 tablespoons all-purpose flour
3 cups milk
¼ teaspoon white pepper

Combine water, potatoes, carrots, and salt in a deep 3-quart casserole; cover with heavy-duty plastic wrap and microwave at HIGH for 15 to 17 minutes or until potatoes are tender, stirring after 8 minutes. Add peas, cauliflower, and broccoli; cover and microwave at HIGH for 9 to 12 minutes or until vegetables are tender. Do not drain; set aside.

Place butter in a 2-quart glass measure; microwave, uncovered, at HIGH for 50 seconds or until melted. Stir in flour. Gradually add milk, stirring well. Microwave, uncovered, at HIGH for 8 to 9 minutes or until thickened, stirring every 3 minutes. Stir in pepper.

Add sauce to undrained vegetable mixture, stirring well. Cover and microwave at HIGH for 2 minutes or until thoroughly heated. Serve immediately. Yield: about 10 cups.

CREAM OF TOMATO SOUP

3 tablespoons butter or
  margarine
¼ cup grated onion
3 tablespoons all-purpose flour
¾ teaspoon salt
¼ teaspoon pepper
1 small bay leaf
4 cups tomato juice
1 cup milk

Place butter in a deep 3-quart casserole; microwave, uncovered, at HIGH for 50 seconds or until melted. Stir in onion. Cover with heavy-duty plastic wrap; microwave at HIGH for 2 to 3 minutes or until tender. Stir in flour, salt, pepper, and bay leaf. Gradually add tomato juice and milk, stirring well. Cover and microwave at HIGH for 25 to 30 minutes or until slightly thickened. Discard bay leaf. Yield: 4 cups.

BEER-CHEESE SOUP

3 cups milk
1 (12-ounce) can beer, divided
1 (16-ounce) jar process cheese
  spread
1 (8-ounce) jar process cheese
  spread
½ (10¾-ounce) can chicken
  broth, undiluted
1 teaspoon Worcestershire
  sauce
2 dashes of hot sauce
3 tablespoons cornstarch

Combine milk and ¾ cup beer in a deep 3-quart casserole. Cover with heavy-duty plastic wrap and microwave at HIGH for 4 to 5 minutes or just until thoroughly heated. Add cheese spread, chicken broth, Worcestershire sauce, and hot sauce, stirring well. Cover and microwave at HIGH for 4 to 5 minutes or until cheese melts, stirring after 2 minutes.

Combine remaining beer and 3 tablespoons cornstarch; add to cheese mixture, stirring well. Cover and microwave at HIGH for 10 to 12 minutes or until soup is thickened, stirring every 3 minutes. Yield: 8 cups.

Sharp Cheddar Cheese Soup

3 tablespoons butter or
  margarine
¼ cup plus 2 tablespoons
  all-purpose flour
2 (10¾-ounce) cans chicken
  broth, undiluted
1 cup milk
1 cup half-and-half
¼ cup plus 2 tablespoons
  Chablis or other dry white
  wine
1 tablespoon finely chopped
  sweet red pepper (optional)
1 tablespoon finely chopped
  green pepper
½ teaspoon golden
  Worcestershire sauce
¼ teaspoon white pepper
¼ teaspoon hot sauce
2 cups (8 ounces) shredded
  sharp Cheddar cheese

Place butter in a deep 3-quart casserole; microwave, uncovered, at HIGH for 50 seconds or until melted. Stir in flour.

Gradually add chicken broth, milk, and half-and-half, stirring well. Cover and microwave at HIGH for 12 minutes or until thickened, stirring every 4 minutes. Add wine, red pepper, if desired, green pepper, Worcestershire sauce, white pepper, and hot sauce, stirring well. Cover and microwave at HIGH for 3 minutes or until thoroughly heated. Add cheese, stirring until melted. Serve immediately. Yield: 6 cups.

Peanut Soup

1 cup sliced celery
1 small onion, chopped
2 tablespoons butter or
  margarine
2 tablespoons all-purpose flour
1 (10¾-ounce) can chicken
  broth, diluted
1 cup creamy peanut butter
1 cup half-and-half
Dash of white pepper
2 tablespoons chopped peanuts
  (optional)

Combine celery, onion, and butter in a deep 3-quart casserole. Cover with heavy-duty plastic wrap and microwave at HIGH for 3 to 3½ minutes or until vegetables are tender. Stir in flour. Gradually add chicken broth, stirring well. Cover and microwave at HIGH for 6 to 8 minutes or until slightly thickened, stirring every 2 minutes. Add peanut butter, half-and-half, and pepper, stirring well. Reduce to MEDIUM (50% power); cover and microwave for 14 to 16 minutes or until slightly thickened and thoroughly heated. Sprinkle with chopped peanuts, if desired. Yield: 6 cups.

Split Pea Soup

1½ cups dried green split peas
5 cups water
¾ pound smoked ham hock
½ cup chopped onion
½ cup chopped carrot
½ teaspoon salt
⅛ teaspoon pepper

Sort and wash peas; place in a deep 3-quart casserole. Cover with water 2 inches above peas; let soak overnight. Drain and rinse peas.

Return peas to casserole, and add 5 cups water. Microwave, uncovered, at HIGH for 50 minutes. Add ham hock, and remaining ingredients. Reduce to MEDIUM HIGH (70% power);

SPLIT PEA SOUP

(continued)

cover with heavy-duty plastic wrap and micro-wave for 20 minutes. Remove ham hock, and remove meat from bone. Chop meat, and stir into soup. Increase to HIGH power; cover and microwave for 5 to 10 minutes or until peas are tender. Pour soup into container of an electric blender, and process until smooth. Serve imme-diately. Yield: 5 cups.

LENTIL SOUP

4½ cups water
1 (14½-ounce) can whole
  tomatoes, undrained and
  chopped
½ cup dried lentils
½ cup chopped celery
2 small potatoes, peeled and
  cubed
1 small onion, finely chopped
1 small carrot, scraped and
  thinly sliced
1 tablespoon dried parsley
  flakes
1½ teaspoons beef-flavored
  bouillon granules
1 bay leaf
¼ teaspoon salt
⅛ teaspoon pepper
1 clove garlic, crushed

Combine all ingredients in a deep 3-quart casserole. Microwave, uncovered, at HIGH for 10 to 12 minutes or until boiling. Reduce to MEDIUM HIGH (70% power); cover with heavy-duty plastic wrap and microwave for 40 to 50 minutes or until lentils are tender, stirring after 20 minutes. Remove and discard bay leaf. Serve immediately. Yield: 7½ cups.

EGG DROP SOUP

4 cups water
1 (10¾-ounce) can chicken
  broth, undiluted
1 (4-ounce) can sliced
  mushrooms, drained
2 cloves garlic
1 teaspoon soy sauce
1 teaspoon chicken-flavored
  bouillon granules
⅛ teaspoon white pepper
2 eggs, beaten
⅓ cup sliced green onions

Combine hot water, chicken broth, mush-rooms, garlic, soy sauce, and bouillon granules in a deep 3-quart casserole. Cover with heavy-duty plastic wrap and microwave at HIGH for 10 to 12 minutes or until boiling. Add pepper, stirring well. Gradually pour beaten eggs in a thin stream into soup, stirring constantly. Cover and let stand 3 minutes. Remove garlic; sprinkle soup with green onions. Yield: 6 cups.

Egg Drop Soup gets its characteristic appearance when beaten eggs are slowly stirred into the hot, broth-based soup.

Garden Chicken Noodle Soup

2 (8-ounce) chicken breast
 halves, skinned
1½ quarts water
1 cup frozen green peas
1 medium-size yellow squash,
 thinly sliced
½ cup thinly sliced carrot
½ cup chopped celery
½ cup chopped onion
1 tablespoon chicken-flavored
 bouillon granules
1 teaspoon salt
¼ teaspoon pepper
2 cups uncooked medium egg
 noodles

Arrange chicken in a deep 3-quart casserole; add water. Stir in peas and next 7 ingredients; cover with heavy-duty plastic wrap and microwave at HIGH for 20 to 25 minutes or until boiling. Stir in noodles. Reduce to MEDIUM (50% power); cover and microwave for 20 to 30 minutes or until noodles and chicken are tender, stirring every 10 minutes.

Remove chicken from soup; let cool. Skim excess fat from soup. Remove chicken from bones, and cut into bite-size pieces; return chicken to soup. Cover and microwave at HIGH for 5 to 6 minutes or until soup is thoroughly heated. Serve immediately. Yield: 8 cups.

Sausage-Bean Soup

1 pound bulk pork sausage
1 quart water
1 (28-ounce) can whole
 tomatoes, undrained and
 chopped
2 (16-ounce) cans kidney beans,
 undrained
1 large onion, chopped
1 medium-size green pepper
1 cup peeled and diced
 potatoes
½ teaspoon salt
½ teaspoon garlic salt
½ teaspoon dried whole thyme
½ teaspoon black pepper

Crumble sausage into a deep 5-quart casserole; microwave, uncovered, at HIGH for 6 to 7 minutes or until sausage is no longer pink, stirring every 2 minutes. Drain off drippings; stir in water, tomatoes, beans, onion, green pepper, potatoes, salt, garlic salt, thyme, and pepper. Cover with heavy-duty plastic wrap and microwave at HIGH for 45 to 50 minutes or until potatoes are tender, stirring every 15 minutes. Serve immediately. Yield: 14 cups.

Garden Chicken Noodle Soup, filled with colorful fresh vegetables and tasty egg noodles, looks good and is good for you.

NAVY BEAN SOUP

1 cup dried navy beans
⅛ teaspoon baking soda
5 cups water
½ cup chopped celery
½ cup chopped onion
½ cup chopped carrot
1 tablespoon chopped fresh
  parsley
1 chicken-flavored bouillon
  cube
½ cup diced cooked ham
1 bay leaf

Sort and wash beans; combine beans and soda in a deep 3-quart casserole. Cover with water 2 inches above beans; let soak overnight. Drain beans; combine beans, 5 cups water, and next 5 ingredients. Cover with heavy-duty plastic wrap and microwave at HIGH for 15 minutes or until boiling. Add ham and bay leaf. Reduce to MEDIUM LOW (30% power); cover and microwave for 2½ hours or until beans are tender. Remove and discard bay leaf. Serve immediately. Yield: 6½ cups.

The end results are worth the time it takes to microwave this hearty Navy Bean Soup.

Red Pepper Chili

1½ pounds ground chuck
1 (4-ounce) can chopped green chiles, drained
1 small green pepper, chopped
1 small onion, chopped
1 clove garlic, minced
1 (28-ounce) can whole tomatoes, undrained and chopped
1 (8-ounce) can tomato sauce
1 cup water
2 tablespoons chili powder
1 teaspoon salt
½ teaspoon ground cumin
½ teaspoon dried whole oregano
¼ teaspoon red pepper
1 (15-ounce) can kidney beans, drained

Combine first 5 ingredients in a deep 3-quart casserole, stirring to crumble beef. Cover with heavy-duty plastic wrap and microwave at HIGH for 7 to 8 minutes or until beef is no longer pink, stirring after 4 minutes. Drain off drippings.

Add chopped tomatoes, tomato sauce, water, chili powder, salt, cumin, oregano, and red pepper. Cover and microwave at HIGH for 10 minutes, stirring after 5 minutes. Stir in beans; cover and microwave at HIGH for 10 to 12 minutes or until beans are tender, stirring after 5 minutes. Serve immediately. Yield: 8 cups.

Gumbo

⅔ cup vegetable oil
⅔ cup all-purpose flour
2 cups sliced okra
1 cup chopped onion
1 cup chopped celery
½ cup chopped green pepper
2 cloves garlic, minced
2 (10¾-ounce) cans chicken broth, undiluted
1½ cups water
1 (14½-ounce) can whole tomatoes, drained and chopped
2 tablespoons Worcestershire sauce
1 to 2 teaspoons hot sauce
½ teaspoon paprika
½ teaspoon dried whole thyme
¼ teaspoon ground mace
1 pound unpeeled medium-size fresh shrimp, peeled and deveined
2 cups cubed cooked chicken or turkey
1 (12-ounce) container fresh oysters, drained
Hot cooked rice
Gumbo filé (optional)

Combine oil and flour in a deep 3-quart casserole, stirring well. Microwave, uncovered, at HIGH for 6 minutes, stirring after 3 minutes. Stir well. Microwave, uncovered, at HIGH for 2 to 4 minutes or until roux is the color of a copper penny, stirring every 30 seconds.

Stir in okra, onion, celery, green pepper, and garlic. Cover with heavy-duty plastic wrap and microwave at HIGH for 4 to 5 minutes or until vegetables are tender.

Stir in broth, water, tomatoes, Worcestershire sauce, hot sauce, paprika, thyme, and mace. Cover and microwave at HIGH for 13 to 15 minutes or until boiling, stirring after 8 minutes. Stir in shrimp, chicken, and oysters. Reduce to MEDIUM HIGH (70% power); cover and microwave for 8 to 10 minutes or until shrimp are pink and edges of oysters begin to curl. Serve gumbo over rice; sprinkle with filé, if desired. Yield: about 12 cups.

Manhattan Clam Chowder

4 slices bacon, cut into 1-inch
  pieces
1⅓ cups water
1 medium-size sweet potato,
  peeled and diced
1 (28-ounce) can whole
  tomatoes, undrained and
  chopped
1 (6-ounce) can tomato paste
⅔ cup chopped celery
⅓ cup chopped green pepper
1½ teaspoons Worcestershire
  sauce
¾ teaspoon dried Italian
  seasoning
1 bay leaf
⅛ teaspoon dried whole thyme
2 (6½-ounce) cans minced
  clams, undrained

Place bacon in a deep 3-quart casserole. Microwave, uncovered, at HIGH for 3½ to 4½ minutes or until bacon is crisp. Remove bacon, and set aside. Drain off drippings.

Add water and sweet potato to casserole; cover with heavy-duty plastic wrap and microwave at HIGH for 8 minutes. Add tomatoes, tomato paste, celery, green pepper, Worcestershire sauce, Italian seasoning, bay leaf, and thyme, stirring well. Cover and microwave at HIGH for 7 to 8 minutes or until vegetables are tender, stirring after 4 minutes. Stir in clams. Reduce to MEDIUM HIGH (70% power); cover and microwave for 2 minutes or until thoroughly heated. Remove and discard bay leaf. Sprinkle with bacon, and serve immediately. Yield: 8 cups.

Mexican Cheddar-Corn Chowder

1 tablespoon butter or
  margarine
½ cup chopped onion
2 cups peeled and diced
  potatoes
1 cup water
½ teaspoon dried whole basil
2 cups milk
2 (17-ounce) cans cream-style
  corn
1 (14½-ounce) can whole
  tomatoes, drained and
  chopped
1 (4-ounce) can chopped green
  chiles, undrained
½ cup diced sweet red pepper
½ teaspoon salt
⅛ teaspoon pepper
1 cup (4 ounces) shredded
  sharp Cheddar cheese

Place butter in a deep 3-quart casserole; microwave, uncovered, at HIGH for 35 seconds or until melted. Stir in onion; microwave, uncovered, at HIGH for 3 to 4 minutes or until onion is tender. Add potatoes, water, and basil; cover with heavy-duty plastic wrap and microwave at HIGH for 12 to 15 minutes or until potatoes are tender, stirring every 5 minutes.

Stir in milk, corn, chopped tomatoes, green chiles, red pepper, salt, and pepper. Cover and microwave at HIGH for 5 to 6 minutes or until thoroughly heated, stirring after 3 minutes. Stir in cheese. Reduce to MEDIUM LOW (30% power); cover and microwave for 5 to 6 minutes or until cheese melts, stirring after 3 minutes. Serve immediately. Yield: 10 cups.

Even though Mexican Cheddar-Corn Chowder is prepared in a matter of minutes, it's still packed with the hearty flavor of corn, potatoes, chiles, and cheese.

Fish Chowder With Celery Croutons

2 slices bacon, chopped
1 medium onion, chopped
1 pound cod fillets
1 large potato, peeled and
   diced
2½ cups water
1½ teaspoons salt
¼ teaspoon pepper
3 tablespoons butter or
   margarine
¼ cup all-purpose flour
2 cups evaporated milk
Celery Croutons
Chopped fresh parsley

Place bacon in a deep 3-quart casserole. Microwave, uncovered, at HIGH for 3½ to 4 minutes or until bacon is crisp. Add onion; microwave, uncovered, at HIGH for 2 to 3 minutes or until onion is tender.

Cut fish fillets into bite-size pieces. Add fish, potato, water, salt, and pepper to bacon and onion mixture. Cover with heavy-duty plastic wrap and microwave at HIGH for 5 minutes. Reduce to MEDIUM HIGH (70% power); cover and microwave for 10 to 12 minutes or until potato is tender, stirring after 5 minutes.

Place butter in a 4-cup glass measure. Microwave, uncovered, at HIGH for 50 seconds or until melted. Stir in flour. Gradually add milk, stirring well. Microwave, uncovered, at HIGH for 5 to 6 minutes or until thickened, stirring after every minute. Add sauce to fish mixture, stirring well. Cover and microwave at HIGH for 6 to 8 minutes or until chowder is slightly thickened. Sprinkle with Celery Croutons and parsley before serving. Yield: 8 cups.

Celery Croutons:

1 tablespoon plus 1½
   teaspoons butter or
   margarine
3 slices white bread, cut into
   ¼-inch cubes (about 1 cup)
½ teaspoon celery salt

Place butter in a 9-inch pieplate. Microwave, uncovered, at HIGH for 40 seconds or until melted. Add bread cubes and celery salt, tossing gently to coat well. Microwave, uncovered, at HIGH for 3 to 4 minutes or until bread cubes are dry, stirring after every minute. Yield: 1 cup.

Hamburger Stew

¾ pound ground chuck
1 small onion, chopped
1 (7½-ounce) can whole
   tomatoes, undrained and
   chopped
1 (10-ounce) package frozen
   mixed vegetables
1½ cups diluted canned beef
   broth
3 medium potatoes, peeled
   and cubed
¼ teaspoon celery seeds
¼ teaspoon dried whole basil
¼ teaspoon chili powder
¼ teaspoon salt
⅛ teaspoon pepper

Crumble beef into a deep 3-quart casserole; stir in onion. Cover with wax paper and microwave at HIGH for 5 to 6 minutes or until beef is no longer pink, stirring after 3 minutes. Drain off drippings.

Add tomatoes, vegetables, broth, potatoes, celery seeds, basil, chili powder, salt, and pepper, stirring well. Reduce to MEDIUM HIGH (70% power); cover with heavy-duty plastic wrap and microwave for 30 to 35 minutes or until vegetables are tender, stirring every 10 minutes. Serve immediately. Yield: 6 cups.

CHICKEN BRUNSWICK STEW

4 (4-ounce) skinned and boned
  chicken breast halves
¾ cup water
1 (28-ounce) can whole
  tomatoes, undrained and
  chopped
1 (8-ounce) can tomato sauce
1 large onion, finely chopped
1 small green pepper, seeded
  and chopped
⅓ cup vinegar
2 tablespoons sugar
½ cup water
2 tablespoons flour
1 tablespoon hot sauce
1 teaspoon salt
¼ teaspoon pepper
1 (8¾-ounce) can whole kernel
  corn, drained

Place chicken and ¾ cup water in a 1½-quart casserole. Cover with heavy-duty plastic wrap and microwave at HIGH for 13 to 14 minutes or until chicken is tender, rearranging after 7 minutes. Drain chicken, and let cool. Position knife blade in food processor bowl; add chicken. Cover and process until coarsely shredded.

Combine chicken, tomatoes, tomato sauce, onion, green pepper, vinegar, and sugar in a deep 3-quart casserole. Combine ½ cup water and flour, stirring well. Add to chicken mixture. Stir in hot sauce, salt, and pepper. Cover and microwave at HIGH for 15 minutes. Stir well. Reduce to MEDIUM LOW (30% power); cover and microwave for 30 minutes, stirring after 15 minutes. Stir in corn. Increase to HIGH; cover and microwave for 8 to 10 minutes or until thoroughly heated. Serve immediately. Yield: about 8 cups.

WHITE WINE STEW WITH DUMPLINGS

¼ cup plus 1 tablespoon flour
1 teaspoon salt
½ teaspoon pepper
1¼ pounds boneless beef
  chuck, cut into 1-inch cubes
3 tablespoons butter or
  margarine
2 cups water
1½ cups Chablis or other dry
  white wine
1 cup chopped onion
2 cloves garlic, minced
2 teaspoons beef-flavored
  bouillon granules
1 bay leaf
⅛ teaspoon dried whole thyme
2 medium carrots, scraped and
  sliced
1 large potato, peeled and
  cubed
1 cup frozen green peas
¼ cup sliced celery
1 cup biscuit mix
1 egg, beaten
3 tablespoons milk
1 tablespoon plus 1 teaspoon
  minced fresh parsley

Combine flour, salt, and pepper; dredge beef in flour mixture. Place a 10-inch browning skillet in microwave oven; preheat, uncovered, at HIGH for 6 minutes. Add butter to hot skillet, tilting to coat surface. Add beef to skillet, stirring well. Microwave, uncovered, at HIGH for 6 minutes or until beef is browned, stirring after 3 minutes.

Combine beef, water, wine, onion, garlic, bouillon granules, bay leaf, and thyme in a deep 3-quart casserole. Cover with heavy-duty plastic wrap and microwave at HIGH for 5 minutes. Stir in carrots, potato, peas, and celery. Reduce to MEDIUM (50% power); cover and microwave for 75 to 80 minutes or until vegetables and beef are tender, stirring every 20 minutes. Remove and discard bay leaf.

Combine biscuit mix, egg, milk, and parsley, stirring well. Drop mixture by heaping tablespoonfuls on top of stew. Increase to HIGH; cover and microwave for 3½ to 4 minutes or until dumplings are set, but still moist. Let stand, covered, 5 minutes. Yield: 8 cups.

White Wine Stew is topped with heaping tablespoonfuls of dumpling batter. Cover and microwave until set.

Vegetables

Fresh vegetables are at their best when cooked in the microwave oven. Besides speeding preparation, the microwave oven retains more of the vegetables' crisp texture and color and keeps flavors at their peak.

You'll find vegetables need only a small amount of water in which to cook in the microwave. The oven uses the natural moisture of the vegetable to provide most of the cooking liquid. From a few tablespoons to one-half cup of additional liquid is all that is needed. Cover the vegetables to hold in steam and heat as they cook.

Vegetables cook more evenly in the microwave oven if all the pieces are the same size. So, for cut-up vegetables, cut or dice into even-size pieces. Also remember to place tougher ends of vegetables toward the outside of the container. This procedure allows the the entire asparagus or broccoli spear, for example, to be cooked just right.

Be sure to pierce vegetables, such as new potatoes, baking potatoes, spaghetti squash, or acorn squash, that are microwaved whole in their skins. This allows steam to escape; otherwise, they may burst.

As a general rule, most vegetables are microwaved on HIGH power and are done when crisp-tender. There are some fresh vegetables—green peas, potatoes, corn kernels—that should be cooked a little longer than others to eliminate any starchy flavor. Also, standing time allows vegetables to become tender without losing their texture. If large vegetables are microwaved until the center is tender, the outside will be mushy.

Remember that if salt is sprinkled on vegetables before cooking, it will result in brown spots. You may add salt to the cooking liquid before microwaving, or you may wait until the vegetables have completed cooking.

Zucchini-Yellow Squash Flower (page 249) is a simple, but dramatic dish that emphasizes the fresh flavor of summer squash.

ARTICHOKES PARMESAN

4 medium artichokes (2 to 2½
  pounds)
Lemon juice
½ cup water
2 tablespoons chopped green
  onions
2 cloves garlic, minced
½ cup butter or margarine
3 cups soft breadcrumbs
½ cup grated Parmesan cheese
¼ cup chopped fresh parsley
Lemon twists (optional)

Wash artichokes by plunging up and down in cold water. Cut off stem end, and trim about ½ inch from top of each artichoke. Remove any loose bottom leaves. Trim away about a fourth of each outer leaf with scissors. Rub lemon juice over top of artichokes and edges of leaves to prevent discoloration.

Place artichokes in a 12- x 8- x 2-inch baking dish; add water. Cover with heavy-duty plastic wrap and microwave at HIGH for 10 to 15 minutes or until lower leaves pull out easily, rearranging every 5 minutes. Drain. Spread leaves apart; scrape out the fuzzy thistle center (choke) with a spoon.

Combine onions, garlic, and butter in a large bowl; microwave, uncovered, at HIGH for 2 to 3 minutes or until onions are tender. Add breadcrumbs, cheese, and parsley; stir until blended. Spoon about ½ cup breadcrumb mixture into center of each artichoke. Stuff remaining mixture evenly between artichoke leaves.

Return artichokes to baking dish; microwave, uncovered, at HIGH for 2 minutes or until thoroughly heated. Transfer to a serving platter; garnish with lemon twists, if desired. Serve immediately. Yield: 4 servings.

ARTICHOKES IN LEMON-HERB BUTTER

4 medium artichokes (2 to 2½
  pounds)
Lemon juice
½ cup water
Lemon-Herb Butter

Wash artichokes by plunging up and down in cold water. Cut off stem end, and trim about ½ inch from top of each artichoke. Remove any loose bottom leaves. Trim away about a fourth of each outer leaf with scissors. Rub lemon juice over top of artichokes and edges of leaves to prevent discoloration.

Place artichokes in a 12- x 8- x 2-inch baking dish; add water. Cover with heavy-duty plastic wrap and microwave at HIGH for 10 to 15 minutes or until lower leaves pull out easily, rearranging every 5 minutes. Drain. Serve with Lemon-Herb Butter. Yield: 4 servings.

LEMON-HERB BUTTER:

½ cup butter
3 tablespoons lemon juice
1 tablespoon chopped fresh
  thyme or 1 teaspoon dried
  whole thyme

Place butter in a 1-cup glass measure. Microwave, uncovered, at HIGH for 1 minute or until melted. Add lemon juice and thyme, stirring until blended. Yield: ⅔ cup.

Asparagus With Mustard Sauce

1 pound fresh asparagus spears
¼ cup water
⅓ cup commercial sour cream
2 tablespoons white wine
  vinegar
1½ tablespoons Dijon mustard

Snap off tough ends of asparagus. Remove scales from spears with a knife or vegetable peeler, if desired. Arrange spears in a 10- x 6- x 2-inch baking dish with stem ends towards outside of dish; add water. Cover with heavy-duty plastic wrap and microwave at HIGH for 6 to 7 minutes or until crisp-tender. Let stand, covered, 1 minute; drain.

Combine sour cream, vinegar, and mustard in a 1-cup glass measure. Reduce to MEDIUM HIGH (70% power); microwave, uncovered, for 1 to 1½ minutes or until thoroughly heated (do not boil), stirring every 30 seconds. Arrange asparagus on a serving platter. Top with mustard sauce. Yield: 4 servings.

Asparagus Goldenrod

1 egg
1 pound fresh asparagus spears
¼ cup water
2 tablespoons butter or
  margarine
2 tablespoons lemon juice
2 tablespoons grated Parmesan
  cheese
1 tablespoon chopped fresh
  basil or 1 teaspoon dried
  whole basil

Gently break egg into a 6-ounce custard cup. Pierce yolk several times with a wooden pick or fork. Cover with heavy-duty plastic wrap and microwave at MEDIUM (50% power) for 1½ to 2½ minutes or until set. Let stand, covered, 2 minutes. Chop egg, and set aside.

Snap off tough ends of asparagus. Remove scales from spears with a knife or vegetable peeler, if desired. Arrange spears in a 10- x 6- x 2-inch baking dish with stem ends towards outside of dish; add water. Cover with heavy-duty plastic wrap and microwave at HIGH for 6 to 7 minutes or until crisp-tender. Let stand, covered, 1 minute; drain. Arrange asparagus on a serving platter.

Combine butter and lemon juice in a 1-cup glass measure. Microwave, uncovered, at HIGH for 45 seconds to 1 minute or until hot and bubbly. Stir well, and pour over asparagus. Sprinkle with cheese, basil, and chopped egg. Serve immediately. Yield: 4 servings.

Avoid adding salt directly to vegetables before microwaving; salt draws moisture out of vegetables, leaving them dry and spotted.

Asparagus With Easy Hollandaise Sauce

For best results, arrange the tender tips of asparagus spears towards the center of the dish.

1 pound fresh asparagus spears
¼ cup water
Easy Hollandaise Sauce
Lemon slices (optional)
Lemon zest (optional)

Snap off tough ends of asparagus. Remove scales from spears with a knife or vegetable peeler, if desired. Arrange spears in a 10- x- 6- x 2-inch baking dish with stem ends towards outside of dish; add water. Cover with heavy-duty plastic wrap and microwave at HIGH for 6 to 7 minutes or until crisp-tender. Let stand, covered, 1 minute; drain. Arrange asparagus on a serving platter; top with Easy Hollandaise Sauce. Garnish with lemon slices and lemon zest, if desired. Yield: 4 servings.

Easy Hollandaise Sauce:

2 egg yolks
1 tablespoon lemon juice
½ teaspoon dry mustard
⅛ teaspoon white pepper
½ cup butter

Combine first 4 ingredients in container of an electric blender; set aside. Place butter in a 1-cup glass measure. Microwave, uncovered, at HIGH for 1 minute or until melted. With blender on high speed, gradually add melted butter to yolk mixture in a slow steady stream; process until thick. Yield: ¾ cup.

One of the best ways to enjoy fresh asparagus is Asparagus With Easy Hollandaise Sauce.

Zesty Lima Beans

1 pound fresh lima beans,
   shelled (about 2 cups)
1 cup water
⅓ cup chopped celery
⅓ cup commercial Italian salad
   dressing
2 green onions, chopped
2 tablespoons chopped green
   pepper
2 tablespoons chopped
   pimiento
1 tablespoon chopped fresh
   parsley

Combine lima beans and water in a 1½-quart casserole. Cover with heavy-duty plastic wrap and microwave at HIGH for 5 minutes. Reduce to MEDIUM HIGH (70% power); cover and microwave for 25 to 30 minutes or until tender, stirring every 5 minutes. Let stand, covered, 3 minutes; drain.

Add celery and remaining ingredients to beans. Microwave, uncovered, at HIGH for 1 minute or until thoroughly heated. Serve with a slotted spoon. Yield: 4 servings.

Wax Beans With Basil Butter

1 pound fresh wax beans
½ cup water
2 tablespoons chopped onion
2 tablespoons chopped celery
2 tablespoons butter or
   margarine
1½ teaspoons minced fresh
   basil or ½ teaspoon dried
   whole basil
¼ teaspoon salt

Wash beans; trim ends, and remove strings. Cut beans diagonally into 1½-inch pieces. Combine beans, water, onion, and celery in a 1-quart casserole. Cover with heavy-duty plastic wrap and microwave at HIGH for 10 to 11 minutes or until beans are crisp-tender; drain. Stir in butter, basil, and salt. Cover and microwave at HIGH for 2 to 3 minutes or until thoroughly heated. Let stand, covered, 1 minute. Serve immediately. Yield: 4 servings.

Herbed Green Beans

½ pound fresh green beans
½ cup water
⅓ cup chopped green pepper
¼ cup sliced green onions
1 tablespoon vegetable oil
1 medium tomato, peeled and
   diced
¾ teaspoon minced fresh basil
   or ¼ teaspoon dried whole
   basil
½ teaspoon salt
¼ teaspoon sugar
¼ teaspoon minced fresh
   rosemary or ⅛ teaspoon
   dried whole rosemary

Wash beans; trim ends, and remove strings. Cut beans into 1½-inch pieces. Combine beans and water in a 1½-quart casserole. Cover with heavy-duty plastic wrap and microwave at HIGH for 9 to 10 minutes or until crisp-tender, stirring every 3 minutes. Let stand, covered, 2 minutes; drain.

Place green pepper, onions, and oil in a small bowl. Cover with heavy-duty plastic wrap and microwave at HIGH for 3 to 4 minutes or until vegetables are tender.

Add green pepper mixture, tomato, and remaining ingredients to beans; mix well. Cover and microwave at HIGH for 2 to 3 minutes or until thoroughly heated. Serve immediately. Yield: 4 servings.

Arrange Marinated Italian Beans into serving-size bundles. Top with pimiento strips.

MARINATED ITALIAN BEANS

1½ pounds fresh green beans
¾ cup water
1½ cups commercial Italian salad dressing
⅓ cup Chablis or other dry white wine
2 tablespoons tarragon vinegar
½ teaspoon dried whole basil
¼ teaspoon pepper
⅛ teaspoon dried whole oregano
2 cloves garlic, crushed
Pimiento strips
Lemon slices (optional)
Sprigs of fresh basil (optional)

Wash beans; trim ends, and remove strings. Place beans in a 12- x 8- x 2-inch baking dish; add water. Cover with heavy-duty plastic wrap and microwave at HIGH for 12 to 14 minutes or until crisp-tender, stirring after 6 minutes. Let stand, covered, 2 minutes; drain.

Combine dressing and next 6 ingredients in a small bowl, stirring well. Pour dressing mixture over beans; cover and refrigerate 6 to 8 hours. Remove beans with a slotted spoon, and arrange into individual servings. Top each serving with pimiento strips. Garnish with lemon slices and sprigs of basil, if desired. Yield: 8 servings.

Orange-Glazed Beets

1 pound medium beets, tops
  removed
½ cup water
¼ cup orange marmalade
2 tablespoons butter or
  margarine
1 tablespoon orange juice
Orange slices (optional)

Wash beets. Combine beets and water in a 1½-quart casserole. Cover with heavy-duty plastic wrap and microwave at HIGH for 12 to 14 minutes or until tender. Drain and cool to touch. Peel beets, and cut into cubes; transfer to a serving bowl.

Combine marmalade, butter, and orange juice in a 1-cup glass measure. Microwave, uncovered, at HIGH for 1 to 1½ minutes or until marmalade melts; stir well. Pour marmalade mixture over beets, and toss gently. Garnish with orange slices, if desired. Serve immediately. Yield: 4 servings.

Place beets in a casserole and add water. Cover and microwave until tender, then drain, cool, and peel.

Harvest Beet Platter

½ pound fresh brussels sprouts
¼ cup water
1 tablespoon butter or
  margarine
½ small butternut squash
1 medium turnip
¼ cup water
2 tablespoons butter or
  margarine
2 teaspoons grated orange rind
2 teaspoons dry sherry
¼ teaspoon sugar
⅛ teaspoon ground cinnamon
Salt and pepper to taste
½ pound medium beets, tops
  removed
¼ cup water
1 tablespoon butter or
  margarine
1 tablespoon port wine
¼ teaspoon sugar
⅛ teaspoon ground ginger

Wash brussels sprouts; remove discolored leaves. Trim stems, and slash bottom of each sprout with a shallow X. Combine sprouts and ¼ cup water in a 1-quart casserole. Cover with heavy-duty plastic wrap and microwave at HIGH for 5 to 7 minutes or until crisp-tender. Let stand, covered, 3 minutes; drain and toss with 1 tablespoon butter. Set aside.

Peel squash, and cut into ¼-inch julienne strips. Peel turnip, and cut into ¼-inch julienne strips. Combine squash, turnip, and ¼ cup water in a 1½-quart casserole. Cover with heavy-duty plastic wrap and microwave at HIGH for 5 to 6 minutes or until crisp-tender. Let stand, covered, 2 minutes. Drain and toss with 2 tablespoons butter, orange rind, sherry, ¼ teaspoon sugar, cinnamon, salt, and pepper. Cover and microwave at HIGH for 45 seconds or until butter melts; set aside.

Wash beets. Combine beets and ¼ cup water in a 1-quart casserole. Cover with heavy-duty plastic wrap and microwave at HIGH for 6 to 7 minutes or until tender. Drain and cool to touch; peel beets. Position knife blade in food processor. Combine beets and 1 tablespoon butter in food processor bowl; process until smooth. Add wine, ¼ teaspoon sugar, and ginger; mix well.

Mound beet puree in center of serving platter. Arrange brussels sprouts around beet puree. Surround sprouts with squash and turnip strips. Yield: 6 to 8 servings.

COLORFUL STEAMED BOK CHOY

1¾ pounds bok choy
1 medium-size sweet red
  pepper, chopped
2 tablespoons soy sauce
1 cup fresh bean sprouts,
  washed and drained

Wash bok choy; drain. Trim base of bok choy; shred leaves, and cut stalks into ½-inch pieces. Place bok choy and red pepper in a 2-quart casserole. Cover with heavy-duty plastic wrap and microwave at HIGH for 4 to 6 minutes or until crisp-tender. Stir soy sauce and bean sprouts into bok choy mixture. Cover and microwave at HIGH for 1 minute or until thoroughly heated. Serve immediately. Yield: 6 to 8 servings.

To prepare bok choy, begin by shredding the leaves and cutting the stalks into small pieces.

FESTIVE BROCCOLI

1½ pounds fresh broccoli
½ cup water
½ cup sliced green onions
2 tablespoons butter or
  margarine
¼ cup chopped pimiento
2 teaspoons grated lemon rind
2 tablespoons lemon juice
1 teaspoon salt
⅛ teaspoon pepper

Remove tough ends of lower stalks from broccoli. Wash broccoli, and separate into spears. Arrange spears in a 12- x 8- x 2-inch baking dish with stem ends towards outside of dish; add water. Cover with heavy-duty plastic wrap and microwave at HIGH for 7 to 8 minutes or until tender. Drain.

Combine onions and butter in a 1-cup glass measure. Microwave, uncovered, at HIGH for 2 minutes or until onions are tender. Stir in pimiento and remaining ingredients. Microwave, uncovered, at HIGH for 1 minute or until thoroughly heated. Pour onion mixture over broccoli before serving. Yield: 6 to 8 servings.

BROCCOLI TIMBALES

Vegetable cooking spray
¾ cup fine, dry breadcrumbs,
  divided
½ pound fresh broccoli, finely
  chopped (2 cups)
½ cup finely chopped onion
1 tablespoon butter or
  margarine
1 cup (4 ounces) shredded
  sharp Cheddar cheese
1 cup half-and-half
4 eggs, beaten
1 teaspoon salt
⅛ teaspoon ground nutmeg
Pinch of red pepper
Coarsely ground black pepper
  to taste
Pimiento strips (optional)
Broccoli flowerets (optional)

Coat six 6-ounce custard cups with cooking spray. Divide ¼ cup breadcrumbs among cups, coating cups well. Set aside.

Place chopped broccoli, onion, and butter in a 2-quart casserole; cover with heavy-duty plastic wrap and microwave at HIGH for 6 minutes or until broccoli is tender, stirring after 3 minutes. Add remaining ½ cup breadcrumbs, cheese, half-and-half, eggs, salt, nutmeg, red pepper, and pepper, stirring well. Spoon mixture evenly into prepared custard cups. Cover each cup with heavy-duty plastic wrap; arrange cups in a circle in microwave oven. Reduce to MEDIUM (50% power); microwave for 12 to 14 minutes or until centers are nearly set and a knife inserted near center comes out clean, rearranging cups every 5 minutes. Unmold cups; garnish with pimiento and broccoli flowerets, if desired. Serve immediately. Yield: 6 servings.

Fresh broccoli lends itself to being prepared many ways. Two new recipes to try are Festive Broccoli and Broccoli Timbales.

Broccoli Oriental

1½ pounds fresh broccoli
1 tablespoon peanut oil
1 green onion, chopped
1 clove garlic, minced
½ teaspoon grated fresh
   gingerroot
½ cup undiluted canned
   chicken broth
1 tablespoon oyster sauce
1 tablespoon water
1 teaspoon cornstarch
½ teaspoon sugar

Remove tough ends of lower stalks from broccoli. Wash broccoli, and separate into flowerets; cut stalks into 1-inch pieces. Set aside.

Place oil, onion, garlic, and gingerroot in a 2-quart casserole. Cover with heavy-duty plastic wrap and microwave at HIGH for 1 minute. Add broccoli; cover and microwave at HIGH for 5 to 6 minutes or until broccoli is crisp-tender. Set aside.

Combine broth, oyster sauce, water, cornstarch, and sugar, stirring well; pour over broccoli. Cover and microwave at HIGH for 2 minutes or until slightly thickened. Serve immediately. Yield: 6 servings.

Pimiento-Topped Brussels Sprouts

1 pound fresh brussels sprouts
   (about 4 cups)
¼ cup water
2 tablespoons butter or
   margarine
2 whole pimientos, drained
   and sliced

Wash brussels sprouts, and remove discolored leaves. Trim stems, and slash bottom of each sprout with a shallow X. Combine sprouts and water in a 1½-quart casserole. Cover with heavy-duty plastic wrap and microwave at HIGH for 6 to 8 minutes or until crisp-tender, stirring after 3 minutes. Let stand, covered, 3 minutes; drain.

Place butter in a 1-cup glass measure. Microwave, uncovered, at HIGH for 45 seconds or until melted. Drizzle butter over sprouts, and toss gently. Sprinkle with pimiento before serving. Yield: 4 servings.

To ready brussels sprouts for microwaving, slash bottom of each sprout with a shallow X.

Brussels Sprouts In Browned Butter And Pecans

1 pound fresh brussels sprouts
   (about 4 cups)
¼ cup water
3 tablespoons butter or
   margarine
¼ cup chopped pecans

Wash brussels sprouts, and remove discolored leaves. Trim stems, and slash bottom of each sprout with a shallow X. Combine sprouts and water in a 1½-quart casserole. Cover with heavy-duty plastic wrap and microwave at HIGH for 6 to 8 minutes or until crisp-tender, stirring after 3 minutes. Let stand, covered, 3 minutes; drain.

Place butter in a 1-cup glass measure. Microwave, uncovered, at HIGH for 50 seconds or until melted. Add pecans to butter; microwave, uncovered, at HIGH for 1 minute. Pour pecan mixture over sprouts, and toss gently before serving. Yield: 4 servings.

CABBAGE WEDGES WITH CHEESE-MUSTARD SAUCE

½ medium cabbage (about 1¼
  pounds)
¼ cup water
1 tablespoon butter or
  margarine
1 tablespoon all-purpose flour
⅛ teaspoon salt
Dash of celery salt
1 cup milk
½ cup (2 ounces) shredded
  sharp Cheddar cheese
¼ teaspoon dry mustard
Paprika (optional)

Wash cabbage, and remove tough outer leaves; drain. Cut cabbage into 4 wedges, and core. Place cabbage wedges and water in a 10- x 6- x 2-inch baking dish. Cover with heavy-duty plastic wrap and microwave at HIGH for 11 to 13 minutes or until tender; drain.

Place butter in a 4-cup glass measure. Microwave, uncovered, at HIGH for 35 seconds or until melted. Stir in flour, salt, and celery salt. Gradually add milk, stirring well. Microwave, uncovered, at HIGH for 3 to 4 minutes or until slightly thickened, stirring after every minute. Add cheese and mustard; microwave, uncovered, at HIGH for 30 seconds or until cheese begins to melt; stir well.

Pour sauce over cabbage wedges; sprinkle with paprika, if desired. Serve immediately. Yield: 4 servings.

Festival Cabbage

1 small cabbage (about 1¼ pounds)
2 tablespoons butter or margarine
1 medium onion, thinly sliced
1 medium-size green pepper, coarsely chopped
2 (14½-ounce) cans tomato wedges, drained
½ teaspoon salt
½ teaspoon pepper
1 cup (4 ounces) shredded Cheddar cheese

Wash cabbage, and remove tough outer leaves; do not drain. Cut cabbage into 6 wedges, and remove core. Arrange cabbage wedges spoke-fashion on a 12-inch round glass platter. Cover with heavy-duty plastic wrap and microwave at HIGH for 11 to 13 minutes or until tender; drain and set aside.

Place butter in a small bowl. Microwave, uncovered, at HIGH for 45 seconds or until melted. Add onion, green pepper, tomatoes, salt, and pepper, stirring well. Spoon vegetable mixture evenly over cabbage. Cover and microwave at HIGH for 7 minutes or until thoroughly heated. Sprinkle cheese over cabbage; cover and microwave at HIGH for 30 seconds or until cheese begins to melt. Serve immediately, using a slotted spoon. Yield: 6 servings.

Hot Red Cabbage

1 small red cabbage (about 1¼ pounds)
1 tablespoon vegetable oil
⅛ teaspoon caraway seeds
1½ tablespoons red wine vinegar
1½ tablespoons red currant jelly
¼ teaspoon salt

Wash cabbage, and remove tough outer leaves; drain. Shred cabbage into thin strips. Combine cabbage, oil, and caraway seeds in a 1½-quart casserole; toss well. Cover with heavy-duty plastic wrap and microwave at HIGH for 8 minutes or until crisp-tender; drain.

Combine vinegar and jelly in a small bowl, stirring well; pour over cabbage, tossing gently. Cover and microwave at HIGH for 30 seconds or until thoroughly heated. Sprinkle with salt; serve immediately. Yield: 4 to 6 servings.

Stir-Fried Chinese Cabbage And Vegetables

1 small Chinese cabbage (about 1 pound)
2 tablespoons peanut oil
1 clove garlic, minced
¼ pound fresh mushrooms, sliced
8 green onions, cut into 1-inch pieces
1 tablespoon soy sauce
1½ teaspoons sherry
½ teaspoon grated fresh gingerroot

Wash cabbage; drain. Cut cabbage crosswise into thin strips; set aside.

Place oil and garlic in a 2-quart casserole; microwave, uncovered, at HIGH for 2 minutes. Stir in cabbage, mushrooms, and onions. Cover with heavy-duty plastic wrap and microwave at HIGH for 4 minutes, stirring after 2 minutes. Stir in soy sauce, sherry, and gingerroot; cover and microwave at HIGH for 2 to 3 minutes or until cabbage is crisp-tender and vegetables are thoroughly heated, stirring after 1 minute. Serve immediately. Yield: 4 to 6 servings.

GOLDEN GRATED CARROTS

1 pound carrots, scraped and shredded
2 tablespoons Chablis or other dry white wine
1 tablespoon butter or margarine
1 tablespoon honey
2 teaspoons lemon juice
⅓ cup golden raisins
1½ teaspoons brown sugar
1 teaspoon curry powder

Place carrots in a 1½-quart casserole. Add wine, butter, honey, and lemon juice. Cover with heavy-duty plastic wrap and microwave at HIGH for 5 to 6 minutes or until crisp-tender. Stir in raisins, brown sugar, and curry powder. Cover and microwave at HIGH for 1 to 2 minutes or until thoroughly heated. Let stand, covered, 2 minutes. Stir well; serve immediately. Yield: 6 servings.

SUNSHINE CARROT STRIPS

1 pound carrots, scraped and cut into julienne strips
¾ cup orange juice, divided
1 tablespoon sugar
2 teaspoons cornstarch
½ teaspoon salt

Combine carrots, ¼ cup orange juice, and sugar in a 10- x 6- x 2-inch baking dish; cover with heavy-duty plastic wrap and microwave at HIGH for 8 to 9 minutes or until crisp-tender.

Combine cornstarch and salt in a small bowl. Add remaining ½ cup orange juice, stirring well. Add cornstarch mixture to carrots; cover and microwave at HIGH for 2 to 2½ minutes or until thickened, stirring after every minute. Serve immediately. Yield: 4 to 6 servings.

CARROTS WITH HORSERADISH

3 cups diagonally sliced carrots
   (about 1 pound)
¼ cup water
1 tablespoon butter or
   margarine
1 tablespoon all-purpose flour
½ cup half-and-half
¼ cup commercial sour cream
2 teaspoons prepared
   horseradish
¼ teaspoon salt
⅛ teaspoon pepper
⅛ teaspoon dry mustard
1 tablespoon fine, dry
   breadcrumbs

Combine carrots and water in a 1-quart casse-role. Cover with heavy-duty plastic wrap and microwave at HIGH for 9 to 10 minutes or until crisp-tender. Let stand, covered, 2 minutes; drain and set aside.

Place butter in a 2-cup glass measure. Micro-wave, uncovered, at HIGH for 35 seconds or until melted. Stir in flour. Gradually add half-and-half, stirring well. Microwave, uncovered, at HIGH for 2 to 3 minutes or until thickened, stirring after every minute. Stir in sour cream, horseradish, salt, pepper, and mustard.

Pour sauce over carrots in casserole, stirring gently. Sprinkle with breadcrumbs. Microwave, uncovered, at HIGH for 4 to 5 minutes or until thoroughly heated. Serve immediately. Yield: 4 servings.

GOLDEN CAULIFLOWER

1 medium head cauliflower
   (about 1½ pounds)
¼ cup water
1 tablespoon butter or
   margarine
1 tablespoon all-purpose flour
½ teaspoon dry mustard
Dash of coarsely ground black
   pepper
½ cup canned diluted chicken
   broth
1 cup (4 ounces) shredded
   sharp Cheddar cheese
4 drops of hot sauce
Paprika
Fresh parsley sprigs (optional)

Wash cauliflower; leave head whole. Place cauliflower in a 1½-quart casserole; add water. Cover with heavy-duty plastic wrap and micro-wave at HIGH for 8 to 9 minutes or until cauli-flower is crisp-tender. Let stand, covered, while preparing sauce.

Place butter in a 2-cup glass measure; micro-wave, uncovered, at HIGH for 35 seconds or until melted. Stir in flour, mustard, and pepper. Gradually add chicken broth, stirring well. Mi-crowave, uncovered, at HIGH for 2 to 3 minutes or until thickened, stirring after every minute. Add cheese and hot sauce, stirring until cheese melts. Drain cauliflower; place on serving plat-ter. Pour sauce over top, and sprinkle with paprika; garnish with parsley, if desired. Yield: 4 to 6 servings.

To cook ½ cup chopped onion, place it in a 1-cup glass measure with one tablespoon of butter or margarine and microwave, uncovered, at HIGH for 2 to 3 minutes.

Colorful Dilled Cauliflower is the ideal vegetable accompaniment for your next picnic.

DILLED CAULIFLOWER

1 medium head cauliflower (1½ to 2 pounds)
½ cup water
¾ cup commercial Italian salad dressing
1 (2-ounce) jar diced pimiento, drained
2 tablespoons chopped green onions
½ teaspoon dried whole dillweed
¼ teaspoon salt

Wash cauliflower; separate into flowerets. Combine flowerets and water in a 1½-quart casserole. Cover with heavy-duty plastic wrap and microwave at HIGH for 10 to 11 minutes or until cauliflower is crisp-tender, stirring after 5 minutes. Let stand, covered, 2 minutes; drain. Transfer cauliflower to a shallow serving dish.

Combine dressing and remaining ingredients, stirring well. Pour over cauliflower, and toss gently. Cover and refrigerate at least 2 hours, stirring occasionally. Yield: 6 servings.

CELERY-ONION-PEPPER TOSS

2 to 2½ cups diagonally sliced
  celery
1 clove garlic, minced
¼ cup water
4 green onions, cut into 1-inch
  pieces
1 medium zucchini, cubed
1 sweet red pepper, cut into
  ¼-inch strips
1 tablespoon soy sauce
⅛ teaspoon pepper
Celery leaves (optional)

Combine celery, garlic, and water in a 2-quart casserole. Cover with heavy-duty plastic wrap and microwave at HIGH for 5 minutes; stir well. Add onions, zucchini, and red pepper. Cover and microwave at HIGH for 5 to 7 minutes or until vegetables are crisp-tender; drain.

Add soy sauce and pepper to vegetable mixture; toss gently. Garnish with celery leaves, if desired. Yield: 6 servings.

CELERY PARMESAN

4 cups diagonally sliced celery
1 small onion, chopped
¼ cup water
3 tablespoons grated Parmesan
  cheese
2 tablespoons minced fresh
  parsley
1 (2-ounce) jar diced pimiento,
  drained
¼ teaspoon coarsely ground
  black pepper

Combine celery, onion, and water in a 1½-quart casserole. Cover with heavy-duty plastic wrap and microwave at HIGH for 10 to 12 minutes or until celery is tender. Let stand, covered, 2 minutes; drain well.

Add cheese, parsley, pimiento, and pepper to celery mixture, stirring well. Cover and microwave at HIGH for 1 to 2 minutes or until thoroughly heated. Serve immediately. Yield: 4 to 6 servings.

BASIC CORN ON THE COB

For Basic Corn on the Cob, wrap ears of corn in heavy-duty plastic wrap, and place in a baking dish.

Large ears fresh corn
Butter or margarine
Salt and pepper
Chopped fresh parsley
  (optional)

Remove husks and silks from corn. Rinse corn, and pat dry. Spread 1½ teaspoons butter on each ear of corn. Wrap each ear of corn in a 12-inch sheet of heavy-duty plastic wrap, twisting ends to seal.

Place wrapped corn in a 12- x 8- x 2-inch baking dish. Microwave at HIGH according to the following times until tender, rearranging corn halfway through cooking time. Let stand 5 minutes. Serve with salt and pepper to taste; sprinkle with parsley, if desired.

LARGE EARS FRESH CORN	TIME AT HIGH
1	2 to 4 minutes
2	5 to 9 minutes
3	7 to 12 minutes
4	8 to 15 minutes

Corn On The Cob In Husks

Large ears fresh corn
Butter or margarine
Salt and pepper

Pull back husks from corn, leaving husks attached at base of cob; remove silks. Rinse corn, and pat dry. Spread 1½ teaspoons butter on each ear of corn; pull husks up over corn. Rinse corn in husks; do not drain. Arrange corn on paper towels in microwave oven.

Microwave at HIGH according to the following times until tender, rearranging corn halfway through cooking time. Let stand 5 minutes; remove husks. Sprinkle with salt and pepper.

LARGE EARS FRESH CORN	TIME AT HIGH
1	3 to 5 minutes
2	6 to 9 minutes
3	9 to 12 minutes
4	12 to 16 minutes

For Corn on the Cob in Husks, remove the silks, rinse the corn, and pull husks back over each ear.

Herbed Parmesan Corn On The Cob

4 medium ears fresh corn
¾ cup water, divided
2 tablespoons grated Parmesan cheese
2 teaspoons all-purpose flour
½ teaspoon dried whole rosemary, crushed
½ teaspoon salt
⅛ teaspoon pepper
¼ cup butter or margarine

Remove husks and silks from corn. Rinse corn, and place in a 12- x 8- x 2-inch baking dish; add ¼ cup water. Cover with heavy-duty plastic wrap and microwave at HIGH for 10 to 12 minutes or until tender; drain.

Combine cheese, flour, rosemary, salt, pepper, and butter in a 2-cup glass measure; add remaining ½ cup water, stirring well. Microwave, uncovered, at HIGH for 2½ to 3 minutes or until slightly thickened, stirring after 1 minute. Spoon butter mixture over corn; serve immediately. Yield: 4 servings.

To make Herbed Parmesan Corn on the Cob, place the ears of corn in a baking dish with water.

Fresh Mexicali Corn

4 medium ears fresh corn
¼ cup water
2 tablespoons butter or margarine
1 medium-size sweet red pepper, chopped
2 tablespoons chopped green chiles
¼ teaspoon salt

Remove husks and silks from corn. Rinse corn, and pat dry. Cut corn from cobs (about 2 cups). Combine corn, water, and butter in a 1-quart casserole. Cover with heavy-duty plastic wrap and microwave at HIGH for 8 minutes, stirring after 4 minutes. Add red pepper, chiles, and salt, stirring well. Cover and microwave at HIGH for 1 to 2 minutes or until corn is tender. Let stand, covered, 1 minute. Serve immediately. Yield: 4 servings.

Fresh Corn With Bacon And Peppers

4 slices bacon, cut into 1-inch
  pieces
4 large ears fresh corn
½ cup chopped green pepper
½ cup chopped sweet red
  pepper
¼ cup chopped onion
¼ teaspoon salt
Dash of red pepper
Red pepper rings (optional)

Place bacon in a 1-quart casserole. Cover with wax paper and microwave at HIGH for 3½ to 4½ minutes or until crisp. Remove bacon, and set aside, reserving 2 teaspoons drippings in casserole.

Remove husks and silks from corn. Rinse corn, and pat dry. Cut corn from cobs (about 2 cups); add to drippings in casserole. Cover with heavy-duty plastic wrap and microwave at HIGH for 5 minutes. Add green pepper, sweet red pepper, chopped onion, salt, and a dash of red pepper; stir well. Cover and microwave at HIGH for 3½ to 5½ minutes or until vegetables are tender, stirring after 2 minutes. Stir in bacon. Garnish with red pepper rings, if desired. Yield: 4 servings.

Old-Fashioned Creamed Corn

6 medium ears fresh corn
¼ cup butter or margarine
¼ cup water
1 teaspoon sugar
½ cup whipping cream
½ teaspoon salt
¼ teaspoon pepper

Remove husks and silks from corn. Rinse corn, and pat dry. Cut corn from cobs (about 3 cups); set aside. Place butter in a 1½-quart casserole; microwave, uncovered, at HIGH for 55 seconds or until melted. Add corn, water, and sugar, stirring well. Cover with heavy-duty plastic wrap and microwave at HIGH for 8 to 9 minutes or until corn is tender, stirring after 4 minutes.

Combine whipping cream, salt, and pepper in a small bowl; add to corn, stirring well. Cover and microwave at HIGH for 3 minutes or just until mixture is thoroughly heated and slightly thickened, stirring after every minute. Serve immediately. Yield: 6 servings.

Do not be tempted to increase the amount of seasonings called for in a microwave recipe. You can easily overdo it because there is usually less liquid to reduce their flavor. You can always add more seasonings later.

CUCUMBERS IN DILL CREAM

2 large cucumbers
½ teaspoon salt
1 cup whipping cream
1 tablespoon minced fresh
dillweed or 1 teaspoon dried
whole dillweed
Coarsely ground black
pepper to taste
1 tablespoon butter or
margarine
Sprig of fresh dillweed
(optional)

Wash and peel cucumbers. Cut cucumbers in half lengthwise; scoop out seeds and discard. Cut cucumbers into julienne strips or crosswise slices. Place cucumbers in a colander, and sprinkle with salt; let drain 20 minutes.

Combine whipping cream, 1 tablespoon dillweed, and pepper in a medium bowl. Microwave, uncovered, at HIGH for 8 to 10 minutes or until mixture is reduced by half, stirring after 4 minutes. Add butter, stirring well; set aside.

Rinse cucumbers under cold running water; pat dry. Place cucumbers in a 1-quart casserole. Microwave, uncovered, at HIGH for 3 to 4 minutes or until crisp-tender. Drain well. Stir in cream mixture; garnish with a sprig of fresh dillweed, if desired. Serve hot or chilled. Yield: 4 servings.

EGGPLANT RATATOUILLE

2 medium onions, thinly sliced
1 tablespoon olive oil
1 clove garlic, crushed
1 medium eggplant (about 1
pound)
1 medium zucchini, sliced
1 medium-size sweet red
pepper, cut into strips
2 medium tomatoes, peeled
and cut into wedges
1 cup sliced fresh mushrooms
2 teaspoons dried whole basil
2 teaspoons dried whole
marjoram
½ teaspoon salt
½ teaspoon coarsely ground
black pepper

Combine onion, oil, and garlic in a 13- x 9- x 2-inch baking dish. Cover with heavy-duty plastic wrap and microwave at HIGH for 1 to 2 minutes or until onion is crisp-tender.

Peel eggplant, and cut into ½-inch cubes. Add eggplant, zucchini, and red pepper to onion mixture. Cover and microwave at HIGH for 10 minutes or until vegetables are tender, stirring after 5 minutes. Stir in tomatoes, mushrooms, basil, marjoram, salt, and pepper. Cover and microwave at HIGH for 2 to 4 minutes or until thoroughly heated. Serve immediately. Yield: 8 servings.

You can dry fresh parsley and other herbs in the microwave; just spread them out on a layer of paper towels and microwave at HIGH for 2 to 4 minutes. Crumble and place in an airtight container to store.

Glossy eggplant shells are natural containers for colorful Eggplant Italiano.

EGGPLANT ITALIANO

3 tablespoons butter or
   margarine
2½ cups seasoned croutons
1 (16-ounce) can whole
   tomatoes, drained and
   chopped
4 green onions, chopped
1 small yellow squash, diced
½ cup chopped green pepper
1 teaspoon dried Italian
   seasoning
¼ teaspoon pepper
3 small eggplant (¾- to
   1-pound each)
3 tablespoons grated Parmesan
   cheese
Sprigs of fresh basil (optional)

Place butter in a large bowl. Microwave, uncovered, at HIGH for 50 seconds or until melted. Add croutons and next 6 ingredients; stir well, and set aside.

Pierce skin of each eggplant with a fork 2 or 3 times. Arrange eggplant in a circle on a double layer of paper towels in microwave oven. Microwave, uncovered, at HIGH for 6 minutes, rearranging after 3 minutes. Let stand 2 minutes. Cut each eggplant in half lengthwise; remove pulp, leaving a ¼-inch shell. Chop pulp; add to vegetable mixture, stirring well.

Place eggplant shells on a 12-inch round glass platter; mound vegetable mixture into shells. Cover with wax paper and microwave at HIGH for 6 to 8 minutes or until thoroughly heated. Sprinkle with cheese. Let stand, covered, 3 minutes. Garnish with sprigs of basil, if desired. Yield: 6 servings.

Lemon-Honey Leeks

6 medium leeks (about 2 pounds)
¼ cup butter or margarine
¼ cup honey
2 tablespoons lemon juice

Wash leeks. Remove roots, tough outer leaves, and tops, leaving 1½ inches of dark leaves. Split leeks in half lengthwise; cut crosswise into 1-inch pieces.

Place leeks in a 2½-quart casserole. Cover with heavy-duty plastic wrap and microwave at HIGH for 7 to 8 minutes or until tender. Drain and set aside.

Place butter in a 2-cup glass measure; microwave, uncovered, at HIGH for 55 seconds or until melted. Stir in honey and lemon juice. Pour over leeks, tossing gently. Cover and microwave at HIGH for 1 to 2 minutes or until thoroughly heated. Serve immediately. Yield: 8 servings.

Marinated Mushrooms

¾ to 1 pound small mushrooms
¾ cup Chablis or other dry white wine
⅓ cup white wine vinegar
⅓ cup finely chopped onion
¼ cup vegetable oil
2 tablespoons chopped fresh parsley
2 cloves garlic, crushed
1 teaspoon salt
1 teaspoon minced fresh thyme or ¼ teaspoon dried whole thyme
⅛ teaspoon coarsely ground black pepper
1 (2-ounce) jar diced pimiento, drained
Lettuce leaves (optional)
Sprigs of fresh thyme (optional)

Clean mushrooms with damp paper towels. Remove stems, and reserve for other uses. Set caps aside.

Combine wine, vinegar, onion, oil, parsley, garlic, salt, thyme, and pepper in a 1-quart casserole, stirring well. Microwave, uncovered, at HIGH for 5 minutes or until boiling. Add mushroom caps, stirring gently. Cover with heavy-duty plastic wrap and microwave at HIGH for 4 to 5 minutes or just until mushrooms are tender, stirring after 2 minutes. Let cool; stir in pimiento. Cover and refrigerate at least 6 hours. Serve with a slotted spoon over lettuce leaves, and garnish with sprigs of thyme, if desired. Yield: 6 to 8 servings.

Do not throw away mushroom stems when working with mushrooms. Slice the stems and place in a glass measure with a teaspoon of butter. Cover and microwave at HIGH for 1 to 1½ minutes per cup. Serve over meat.

WALNUT-STUFFED MUSHROOMS

1¼ pounds large fresh
  mushrooms (about 2 dozen)
2 tablespoons finely chopped
  onion
1 tablespoon butter or
  margarine
½ cup chopped walnuts
½ cup fine, dry breadcrumbs
2 tablespoons chopped fresh
  parsley
¼ teaspoon salt
⅛ teaspoon pepper
Grated Parmesan cheese

Clean mushrooms with damp paper towels. Remove stems, and finely chop; set caps aside.

Combine mushroom stems, onion, and butter in a small bowl. Microwave, uncovered, at HIGH for 2 to 3 minutes or until stems are tender. Stir in walnuts, breadcrumbs, parsley, salt, and pepper.

Spoon breadcrumb mixture into mushroom caps. Arrange half of caps in a circle on a 12-inch round glass platter. Microwave, uncovered, at HIGH for 1½ to 2 minutes. Sprinkle with cheese. Microwave, uncovered, at HIGH for 1½ to 2 minutes or until thoroughly heated. Repeat procedure with remaining mushrooms and cheese. Serve immediately. Yield: 2 dozen.

HOT AND TANGY MUSTARD GREENS

1 pound fresh mustard greens
4 slices bacon, cut into 1-inch
  pieces
1 tablespoon all-purpose flour
1 tablespoon brown sugar
¼ teaspoon salt
¼ teaspoon dry mustard
Dash of hot sauce
⅓ cup milk
1 tablespoon cider vinegar

Wash greens; tear into bite-size pieces. Set aside. Place bacon in a 2-quart casserole. Cover with wax paper and microwave at HIGH for 3½ to 4½ minutes or until crisp. Remove bacon, and drain on paper towels, reserving 1 tablespoon drippings in casserole.

Stir flour and next 4 ingredients into reserved drippings. Gradually add milk, stirring well. Microwave, uncovered, at HIGH for 1½ to 2 minutes or until thickened, stirring after every minute. Add vinegar and greens to sauce mixture; toss gently. Cover with heavy-duty plastic wrap and microwave at HIGH for 2 to 3 minutes or until greens are crisp-tender. Sprinkle with bacon before serving. Yield: 3 to 4 servings.

OKRA AND TOMATOES

1 pound okra
¼ cup chopped onion
¼ cup chopped green pepper
½ cup water
4 medium-size ripe tomatoes,
  peeled, seeded, and coarsely
  chopped
1 teaspoon sugar
¾ teaspoon salt
¼ teaspoon pepper

Wash okra; remove stems, and cut pods into ½-inch slices. Combine okra, onion, green pepper, and water in a 2-quart casserole; stir well. Cover with heavy-duty plastic wrap and microwave at HIGH for 9 to 10 minutes or until okra is tender, stirring every 3 minutes. Drain well.

Add tomatoes, sugar, salt, and pepper to okra mixture; mix well. Cover and microwave at HIGH for 3 minutes. Serve immediately. Yield: 6 servings.

SAUSAGE-STUFFED ONIONS

3 large onions (about 2
  pounds)
¼ pound bulk pork sausage
1 cup dry breadcrumbs
2 tablespoons finely chopped
  fresh parsley
Fresh parsley sprigs (optional)
Lemon wedges (optional)

Peel onions, and cut in half crosswise. Arrange halves, cut side up, in a 12- x 8- x 2-inch baking dish. Cover with heavy-duty plastic wrap and microwave at HIGH for 3 to 4 minutes or until crisp-tender. Let stand, covered, while preparing stuffing.

Crumble sausage into a large bowl. Cover with wax paper and microwave at HIGH for 2 to 3 minutes or until sausage is no longer pink, stirring after every minute. Drain well. Remove centers of onions, leaving ½-inch-thick shells. Chop onion centers, reserving 1 cup. Combine sausage, chopped onion, breadcrumbs, and 2 tablespoons chopped parsley. Fill onion shells with sausage mixture.

Arrange stuffed onions in baking dish. Cover with wax paper and microwave at HIGH for 6 minutes, rotating a half-turn after 3 minutes. Let stand, covered, 2 minutes before serving. Garnish with parsley sprigs and lemon wedges, if desired. Yield: 6 servings.

PEARL ONIONS IN CREAM SAUCE

1½ pounds pearl onions
2 tablespoons water
2 tablespoons butter or
  margarine
2 tablespoons all-purpose flour
1 cup milk
1 teaspoon chicken-flavored
  bouillon granules
½ teaspoon Worcestershire
  sauce
⅛ teaspoon red pepper
½ cup commercial sour cream
3 tablespoons sliced almonds

Peel onions. Combine onions and water in a 1½-quart casserole. Cover with heavy-duty plastic wrap and microwave at HIGH for 7 to 8 minutes or until tender. Drain.

Place butter in casserole with onions; microwave, uncovered, at HIGH for 45 seconds or until butter melts. Stir in flour. Gradually add milk, stirring well. Stir in bouillon granules, Worcestershire sauce, and red pepper. Microwave, uncovered, at HIGH for 2½ to 3½ minutes or until thickened, stirring after every minute. Add sour cream to onion mixture, stirring well.

Spread almonds in a 9-inch pieplate; microwave, uncovered, at HIGH for 2 to 4 minutes or until lightly toasted, stirring after every minute. Sprinkle over onion mixture. Yield: 6 servings.

PARSNIP-CARROT PUREE IN ZUCCHINI SHELLS

2 medium zucchini (about 1
  pound)
3 medium parsnips (about ¼
  pound)
2 large carrots (about ¼ pound)
2 tablespoons water
¼ cup commercial sour cream
2 tablespoons grated Parmesan
  cheese, divided
1 tablespoon butter or
  margarine
½ teaspoon salt

Pierce zucchini several times with a fork. Arrange in microwave oven on paper towels; microwave, uncovered, at HIGH for 4 minutes, rearranging after 2 minutes. Let stand 5 minutes. Cut zucchini in half lengthwise; scoop out pulp and discard, leaving ½-inch-thick shells. Invert shells, and set aside.

Scrape parsnips and carrots, and cut into 2-inch pieces. Combine parsnips, carrots, and water in a 1-quart casserole. Cover with heavy-duty plastic wrap and microwave at HIGH for 5½ to 6 minutes or until vegetables are tender, stirring after 3 minutes. Drain.

Position knife blade in food processor bowl. Place parsnips and carrots in food processor; process until pureed. Add sour cream, 1 tablespoon plus 1 teaspoon cheese, butter, and salt. Process until blended, scraping sides as needed. Arrange zucchini shells, cut side up, in a shallow baking dish. Spoon pureed mixture into shells, mounding slightly (mixture may be spooned into a pastry bag fitted with a large tip and piped into shells). Sprinkle with remaining 2 teaspoons cheese. Place shells in conventional oven, and broil 3 minutes or until tops are lightly browned, if desired. Serve immediately. Yield: 4 servings.

FRESH BLACK-EYED PEAS

2 pounds fresh black-eyed peas
3 slices bacon, coarsely
  chopped
1¼ cups water
1 medium onion, chopped
¾ teaspoon salt
¼ to ½ teaspoon red pepper
1 bay leaf
Green onion fan (optional)

Shell and wash peas (about 4 cups); drain. Combine peas and next 6 ingredients in a 2-quart casserole, mixing well. Cover with heavy-duty plastic wrap and microwave at HIGH for 4 minutes. Stir well. Reduce to MEDIUM (50% power); cover and microwave for 35 to 40 minutes or until peas are tender, stirring every 5 minutes. Let stand, covered, 5 minutes. Remove and discard bay leaf; garnish with a green onion fan, if desired. Yield: 4 to 6 servings.

Most vegetables are ready to eat when they are crisp-tender. However, corn, peas, and potatoes should be cooked until they are completely tender to eliminate their starchy flavor.

Green Peas With Pearl Onions

1 pound fresh green peas
1 cup peeled pearl onions
2 tablespoons water
2 tablespoons butter or
  margarine
1 teaspoon sugar
½ teaspoon salt

Shell and wash peas (about 1½ cups); drain. Combine peas, onions, water, and butter in a 1-quart casserole. Cover with heavy-duty plastic wrap and microwave at HIGH for 5 minutes. Stir in sugar and salt. Cover and microwave at HIGH for 1 to 2 minutes or until peas and onions are tender. Serve immediately. Yield: 4 servings.

Snow Peas With Red Pepper

½ pound fresh snow pea
  pods (about 2 cups)
1 large sweet red pepper,
  cut into strips
1 teaspoon sesame seeds
1 teaspoon soy sauce
1 teaspoon vegetable oil
1 teaspoon sesame oil

Wash snow peas; trim ends, and remove strings. Combine snow peas and remaining ingredients in a 1½-quart casserole, stirring gently. Cover with heavy-duty plastic wrap and microwave at HIGH for 4 minutes or until vegetables are crisp-tender, stirring after 2 minutes. Serve immediately. Yield: 4 servings.

Pepper And Carrots Jardinière

2 medium-size green peppers
2 medium-size sweet red
  peppers
1 pound medium carrots,
  scraped and cut into
  julienne strips
1 tablespoon lemon juice
2 small zucchini, cut into
  julienne strips
1 tablespoon butter or
  margarine
1 teaspoon dried whole basil
⅛ teaspoon salt
⅛ teaspoon pepper

Cut peppers into ¼-inch strips; set aside. Combine carrots and lemon juice in a 3-quart casserole. Cover with heavy-duty plastic wrap and microwave at HIGH for 6 minutes, stirring after 3 minutes. Add pepper strips; stir well. Cover and microwave at HIGH for 3 to 5 minutes or until crisp-tender. Add zucchini; stir well. Cover and microwave at HIGH for 3 to 4 minutes, or until vegetables are tender, stirring after 2 minutes.

Add butter, basil, salt, and pepper to vegetable mixture. Toss to melt butter. Let stand, covered, 2 minutes. Serve immediately. Yield: 6 to 8 servings.

Preparing baked potatoes in the microwave oven illustrates an important microwave principle—cooking time increases as the number of potatoes increases.

BASIC MICROWAVED BAKED POTATOES

Medium baking potatoes

Wash potatoes, and pat dry. Prick each potato several times with a fork. Arrange potatoes 1 inch apart on a layer of paper towels in microwave oven. (If microwaving more than 2 potatoes, arrange in a circle.) Microwave, uncovered, at HIGH according to the following times, turning and rearranging potatoes halfway through cooking time. Let stand 5 minutes. (If potatoes are not done after standing, microwave briefly; let stand an additional 2 minutes.)

MEDIUM POTATOES	TIME AT HIGH
1	4 to 6 minutes
2	7 to 8 minutes
3	9 to 11 minutes
4	12 to 14 minutes
5	16 to 18 minutes
6	20 to 24 minutes

PARMESAN-POTATO FANS

⅓ cup grated Parmesan cheese
1½ teaspoons dried parsley flakes
¼ teaspoon garlic powder
¼ teaspoon onion salt
¼ teaspoon paprika
6 medium baking potatoes
¼ cup plus 2 tablespoons butter or margarine
Lemon slices (optional)
Fresh parsley sprigs (optional)

Combine first 5 ingredients in a small bowl; set aside. Wash potatoes, and pat dry. Cut each potato crosswise into ¼-inch-thick slices, cutting to, but not through, bottom of potato. Allow potatoes to stand in ice water 10 minutes.

Place butter in a 1-cup glass measure; microwave, uncovered, at HIGH for 1 minute or until melted. Drain potatoes, and pat dry. Arrange potatoes, cut side up, in a 13- x 9- x 2-inch baking dish. Brush top and sides of potatoes with butter. Cover with heavy-duty plastic wrap and microwave at HIGH for 20 to 24 minutes or until tender, rearranging potatoes every 5 minutes and brushing with remaining butter. Sprinkle potatoes with cheese mixture. Let stand, covered, 5 minutes. Garnish with lemon slices and parsley, if desired. Serve immediately. Yield: 6 servings.

Plain potatoes get a jazzy new look when you slice them into Parmesan-Potato Fans or toss them with fresh herbs for Herbed New Potatoes (page 244).

Cheesy Bacon-Stuffed Potatoes

4 large baking potatoes
6 slices bacon
⅓ cup chopped green onions
1 (8-ounce) carton commercial
  sour cream
¾ cup (3 ounces) shredded
  sharp Cheddar cheese
¼ cup milk
3 tablespoons butter or
  margarine
½ teaspoon salt
¼ teaspoon pepper
Paprika

Wash potatoes, and pat dry; prick each potato several times with a fork. Arrange potatoes 1 inch apart in a circle on a layer of paper towels in microwave oven. Microwave, uncovered, at HIGH for 16 to 18 minutes or until tender, turning and rearranging potatoes after 8 minutes. Let stand 5 minutes. Cut each potato in half lengthwise; scoop out pulp, leaving ¼-inch-thick shells. Mash pulp in a large mixing bowl; set aside.

Place bacon on a rack in a 12- x 8- x 2-inch baking dish. Cover with paper towels and microwave at HIGH for 5 to 7 minutes or until crisp. Remove bacon, reserving 3 tablespoons drippings in baking dish. Crumble bacon, and set aside. Add onions to drippings; microwave, uncovered, at HIGH for 1 to 2 minutes or until tender. Add onions and drippings, bacon, sour cream, cheese, milk, butter, salt, and pepper to potato pulp; mix well. Stuff potato shells with pulp mixture; sprinkle with paprika. Arrange stuffed shells on a 12-inch round glass platter. Microwave, uncovered, at HIGH for 5 minutes or until thoroughly heated. Serve immediately. Yield: 8 servings.

Herbed New Potatoes

2 pounds medium-size new
  potatoes (about 12)
2 tablespoons water
¼ cup butter or margarine
2 tablespoons minced fresh
  parsley
1 tablespoon lemon juice
1½ teaspoons minced fresh
  dillweed or ½ teaspoon dried
  whole dillweed
1 teaspoon chopped chives
Sprigs of fresh dillweed
  (optional)

Wash potatoes, and pat dry. Prick each potato twice with a fork. Place potatoes in a 12- x 8- x 2-inch baking dish; add water. Cover with heavy-duty plastic wrap and microwave at HIGH for 8 to 11 minutes or until tender, stirring after 4 minutes. Let stand, covered, 3 minutes. Drain.

Place butter in a 1-cup glass measure; microwave, uncovered, at HIGH for 55 seconds or until melted. Stir in parsley, lemon juice, 1½ teaspoons dillweed, and chives. Pour butter mixture over potatoes, coating thoroughly. Garnish with sprigs of dillweed, if desired. Yield: 6 servings.

Whipped Sweet Potatoes

2 pounds medium-size sweet
   potatoes (about 4)
½ cup whipping cream
1 egg
½ cup firmly packed brown
   sugar, divided
¼ cup chopped pecans

Wash potatoes, and pat dry; prick each potato several times with a fork. Arrange potatoes 1 inch apart on a layer of paper towels in microwave oven. Microwave, uncovered, at HIGH for 12 to 14 minutes or until tender, turning and rearranging potatoes after 6 minutes. Let stand 5 minutes.

Peel potatoes; place in a large mixing bowl, and mash. Add whipping cream, egg, and ¼ cup sugar; beat at medium speed of an electric mixer until smooth. Spoon mixture into a lightly greased 1-quart casserole. Combine remaining ¼ cup sugar and pecans; sprinkle over casserole. Reduce to MEDIUM HIGH (70% power), and microwave, uncovered, for 7 to 8 minutes or until thoroughly heated. Serve immediately. Yield: 6 servings.

Sweet Potatoes With Sherried Nut Stuffing

2 medium-size sweet potatoes
   (about 1 pound)
¼ cup chopped walnuts
2 tablespoons butter or
   margarine
2 tablespoons brown sugar
1 egg, beaten
1 tablespoon plus 1 teaspoon
   sherry

Wash potatoes, and pat dry. Prick each potato several times with a fork. Arrange potatoes 1 inch apart on a layer of paper towels in microwave oven. Microwave, uncovered, at HIGH for 7 to 8 minutes or until done, turning and rearranging potatoes after 3 minutes. Let stand 5 minutes.

Spread walnuts in a 9-inch pieplate. Microwave, uncovered, at HIGH for 2 to 4 minutes or until lightly toasted; set aside.

Cut each potato in half lengthwise; scoop out pulp, leaving ¼-inch-thick shells. Combine pulp, butter, sugar, egg, and sherry in a medium bowl; beat at medium speed of an electric mixer until smooth. Stuff potato shells with pulp mixture, mounding slightly. Sprinkle with walnuts. Arrange stuffed shells on a 12-inch round glass platter. Reduce to MEDIUM HIGH (70% power), and microwave, uncovered, for 3½ to 4 minutes or until thoroughly heated. Serve immediately. Yield: 4 servings.

Fresh pumpkin doesn't always go into a pie. Try Ginger-Baked Pumpkin and find out how good it is when served as a side dish.

GINGER-BAKED PUMPKIN

1 (2½- to 3-pound) pumpkin
¼ cup water
¼ cup butter or margarine
¼ cup firmly packed light
    brown sugar
1 teaspoon freshly grated
    gingerroot
Grated lime rind

Peel pumpkin; cut in half, and remove seeds. Cut pumpkin into ½-inch cubes. Combine pumpkin and water in a 2-quart casserole. Cover with heavy-duty plastic wrap and microwave at HIGH for 10 to 11 minutes or until tender. Let stand, covered, 2 minutes; drain.

Combine butter, brown sugar, and gingerroot in a 1-cup glass measure. Microwave, uncovered, at HIGH for 1 minute or until butter and sugar melt. Pour butter mixture over pumpkin, tossing to coat. Cover and microwave at HIGH for 3 to 4 minutes or until thoroughly heated. Sprinkle with lime rind, and serve immediately. Yield: 6 servings.

Spiced Pumpkin Puree

1 (2½- to 3-pound) pumpkin
2 tablespoons brown sugar
2 tablespoons butter or
  margarine
½ teaspoon salt
¼ teaspoon ground mace
Dash of pepper
2 tablespoons half-and-half
Ground nutmeg (optional)

Peel pumpkin; cut in half, and remove seeds. Cut pumpkin into ½-inch cubes. Place pumpkin in a 2-quart casserole. Cover with heavy-duty plastic wrap and microwave at HIGH for 10 to 11 minutes or until tender. Let stand, covered, 2 minutes; drain.

Position knife blade in food processor bowl. Combine pumpkin and next 5 ingredients in food processor; process 10 seconds or until smooth. With processor running, add half-and-half through food chute in a slow stream. Process until smooth. Spoon mixture into serving dishes; sprinkle with nutmeg, if desired. Serve immediately. Yield: 4 servings.

Sweet-And-Sour Rutabagas

2 medium rutabagas (about 1¾
  pounds)
1 large onion, chopped
¼ cup water
2 tablespoons bacon drippings
¼ cup cider vinegar
1 tablespoon sugar
½ teaspoon salt
¼ teaspoon pepper
¾ cup chopped green onions

Peel rutabagas; cut into ½-inch cubes. Combine rutabaga, 1 large onion, water, and bacon drippings in a 2-quart casserole. Cover with heavy-duty plastic wrap and microwave at HIGH for 16 to 20 minutes or until tender, stirring every 4 minutes.

Add vinegar, sugar, salt, and pepper to rutabaga mixture; stir well. Cover and microwave at HIGH for 8 to 9 minutes or until thoroughly heated and sugar is melted, stirring after 4 minutes. Stir in green onions. Let stand, covered, 2 minutes. Yield: 6 to 8 servings.

Lemon Steamed Spinach

1 pound fresh spinach
½ cup butter or margarine
1 teaspoon grated lemon rind
1 tablespoon lemon juice
¼ teaspoon salt
¼ teaspoon white pepper

Wash spinach; tear into bite-size pieces. Place spinach in a 3-quart casserole; cover with heavy-duty plastic wrap and microwave at HIGH for 2 to 3 minutes or until spinach reaches desired degree of doneness. Drain well.

Place butter in a 1-cup glass measure. Microwave, uncovered, at HIGH for 1 minute or until melted. Stir in rind, juice, salt, and pepper. Pour over spinach, tossing gently. Serve immediately. Yield: 4 servings.

Spinach With Bacon And Onion

1 pound fresh spinach
2 slices bacon
1 small onion, thinly sliced
1 tablespoon grated Parmesan
　cheese

Wash spinach; tear into bite-size pieces, and set aside. Place bacon on a rack in a 2-quart casserole. Cover with paper towels and microwave at HIGH for 2 to 3 minutes or until crisp. Remove bacon, reserving drippings in casserole. Crumble bacon, and set aside.

Add onion to drippings; microwave, uncovered, at HIGH for 1½ to 2 minutes or until tender. Add spinach, tossing well. Cover with heavy-duty plastic wrap and microwave at HIGH for 2 minutes or to desired degree of doneness. Sprinkle with bacon and cheese; serve immediately. Yield: 4 servings.

Yellow Squash Toss

8 medium-size yellow squash
　(about 2 pounds)
1 (2-ounce) jar diced pimiento,
　drained
2 tablespoons water
2 tablespoons butter or
　margarine
¼ teaspoon garlic powder
¾ teaspoon minced fresh basil
　or ¼ teaspoon dried whole
　basil
⅛ teaspoon pepper
¼ teaspoon salt
Sprig of fresh basil (optional)

Wash squash, and cut into ½-inch-thick slices. Combine squash, pimiento, and water in a 2-quart casserole; dot with butter. Sprinkle with garlic powder, ¾ teaspoon basil, and pepper. Cover with heavy-duty plastic wrap and microwave at HIGH for 11 to 12 minutes or until squash is crisp-tender, stirring every 4 minutes. Sprinkle with salt; garnish with a sprig of basil, if desired. Yield: 6 to 8 servings.

Zucchini-Yellow Squash Flower

¼ cup olive oil
¼ cup tarragon wine vinegar
1 (2-ounce) jar diced pimiento,
　drained
2 teaspoons dried whole
　tarragon
1 teaspoon dried whole
　oregano
½ teaspoon garlic powder
½ teaspoon salt
Pinch of ground nutmeg
4 small yellow squash (about
　¾ pound)
3 small zucchini (about ¾
　pound)
¼ medium-size purple onion,
　thinly sliced

Combine first 8 ingredients in a 2-cup glass measure; microwave, uncovered, at HIGH for 3 minutes, stirring after every minute. Set aside.

Cut yellow squash and zucchini into ¼-inch-thick diagonal slices. Arrange largest slices of yellow squash and zucchini alternately around outer edges of a 12-inch round glass platter, allowing slices to overlap. Arrange medium slices in the same fashion inside the outer row of squash; arrange smaller slices in the center. Cover with heavy-duty plastic wrap and microwave at HIGH for 5 to 6 minutes or until crisp-tender, rotating a half-turn after 3 minutes. Let stand, covered, 1 minute.

Separate onion into rings; arrange over squash. Stir pimiento mixture, and spoon over squash. Serve immediately. Yield: 6 servings.

Both Yellow Squash Toss and Greek Zucchini Squash
(page 250) practically glow with freshness. Garlic and
basil complement the flavor of each dish.

CHEDDAR-SQUASH BAKE

4 slices bacon
1 tablespoon butter or
    margarine
¼ cup fine, dry breadcrumbs
4 medium-size yellow squash
    (about 1 pound)
⅔ cup chopped onion
¼ cup water
2 eggs, separated
½ cup commercial sour cream
2 tablespoons all-purpose flour
¼ teaspoon salt
¼ teaspoon onion powder
¼ teaspoon pepper
1½ cups (6 ounces) shredded
    sharp Cheddar cheese

Place bacon on a rack in a 12- x 8- x 2-inch baking dish. Cover with paper towels and microwave at HIGH for 3½ to 4½ minutes or until crisp. Crumble bacon, and set aside. Place butter in a 1-cup glass measure. Microwave, uncovered, at HIGH for 35 seconds or until melted. Stir in breadcrumbs, and set aside.

Cut squash into ¼-inch-thick slices. Combine squash, onion, and water in a 1½-quart casserole. Cover with heavy-duty plastic wrap and microwave at HIGH for 7 to 8 minutes or until tender, stirring after 4 minutes. Drain.

Beat egg yolks in a medium bowl until thick and lemon colored; add sour cream, flour, salt, onion powder, and pepper, beating with a wire whisk. Beat egg whites (at room temperature) at high speed of an electric mixer until stiff peaks form; fold into yolk mixture.

Layer half each of squash, egg mixture, cheese, and bacon in a lightly greased 1½-quart casserole. Repeat layers with remaining squash, egg mixture, and cheese. Reduce to MEDIUM HIGH (70% power); cover and microwave for 6 minutes, rotating a half-turn after 3 minutes. Sprinkle with breadcrumb mixture. Cover and microwave at MEDIUM HIGH for 2 to 3 minutes or until thoroughly heated. Let stand, uncovered, 2 minutes; sprinkle with remaining bacon. Yield: 6 servings.

GREEK ZUCCHINI SQUASH

1½ tablespoons butter or
    margarine
1½ tablespoons olive oil
2 cloves garlic, minced
½ teaspoon dried whole basil
¼ teaspoon salt
Dash of pepper
2 large zucchini, grated (about
    1½ pounds)
1 teaspoon lemon juice
Lemon slice (optional)
Zucchini slice (optional)
Pimiento twist (optional)

Combine butter, oil, garlic, basil, salt, and pepper in a 1½-quart casserole. Microwave, uncovered, at HIGH for 2 minutes. Add zucchini, stirring well. Cover with heavy-duty plastic wrap and microwave at HIGH for 4 to 5 minutes or until tender. Let stand, covered, 3 minutes. Sprinkle with lemon juice, tossing gently. Garnish with a slice of lemon, zucchini, and a pimiento twist, if desired. Serve immediately. Yield: 6 servings.

Glazed Acorn Squash Rings

2 medium acorn squash (about 2 pounds)
3 tablespoons butter or margarine
⅓ cup maple syrup
¼ teaspoon ground cinnamon
⅛ teaspoon salt

Pierce each squash 4 or 5 times with a fork, and place 3 inches apart on paper towels in microwave oven. Microwave, uncovered, at HIGH for 9 to 10 minutes or until soft to the touch, rearranging after 5 minutes. Cut squash crosswise into 1-inch-thick rings, discarding ends and seeds. Overlap rings in a 12- x 8- x 2-inch baking dish.

Place butter in a 1-cup glass measure. Microwave, uncovered, at HIGH for 50 seconds or until melted. Add maple syrup, cinnamon, and salt, stirring well; pour over squash rings. Cover with wax paper and microwave at HIGH for 4 to 5 minutes or until thoroughly heated, basting and rearranging squash rings after 2 minutes. Serve immediately. Yield: 4 servings.

Acorn squash is easy to prepare in the microwave oven. Maple syrup, cinnamon, and butter give Glazed Acorn Squash Rings a sweet taste.

GOLDEN FILLED ACORN SQUASH

2 small acorn squash (1 to 1½ pounds)
2 medium carrots, scraped and cut into ½-inch cubes
2 tablespoons butter or margarine
½ cup golden raisins
¼ cup maple syrup

Pierce each squash 4 or 5 times with a fork; place 3 inches apart on paper towels in microwave oven. Microwave, uncovered, at HIGH for 6 to 9 minutes or until soft to the touch, rearranging after 3 minutes. Cut squash in half lengthwise; remove seeds. Place squash, cut side up, in a 12- x 8- x 2-inch baking dish.

Combine carrots and butter in a small bowl. Cover with heavy-duty plastic wrap and microwave at HIGH for 2 minutes. Stir in raisins and syrup; cover and microwave at HIGH for 2 minutes. Fill each squash half with carrot mixture. Cover with heavy-duty plastic wrap; microwave at HIGH for 2 minutes. Let stand, covered, 2 minutes. Yield: 4 servings.

BUTTERNUT SQUASH PUREE

1 small butternut squash (1½ pounds)
¼ cup white grape juice, divided
1 teaspoon lemon juice
¼ cup butter or margarine
¼ cup firmly packed brown sugar
¼ cup chopped pecans

Peel squash; cut in half lengthwise, and remove seeds. Place squash and 2 tablespoons grape juice in a 1½-quart casserole. Cover with heavy-duty plastic wrap and microwave at HIGH for 6 to 8 minutes or until tender. Let stand, covered, 2 minutes. Drain.

Position knife blade in food processor bowl. Place squash, 2 tablespoons grape juice, lemon juice, butter, and brown sugar in processor; process until smooth. Spoon into serving bowl.

Spread pecans in a 9-inch pieplate; microwave, uncovered, at HIGH for 2 to 4 minutes or until lightly toasted. Sprinkle evenly over squash. Yield: 4 servings.

Pierce spaghetti squash with a fork and microwave until soft. Cut the squash in half, removing seeds. Separate strands with a fork.

HERBED SPAGHETTI SQUASH

1 medium spaghetti squash (about 3 pounds)
2 tablespoons olive oil
1 clove garlic, minced
1 tablespoon minced fresh basil or 1 teaspoon dried whole basil
1 tablespoon minced fresh oregano or 1 teaspoon dried whole oregano
½ teaspoon salt
⅛ teaspoon pepper
2 tablespoons grated Parmesan cheese

Pierce squash 6 to 8 times with a fork. Place squash on a layer of paper towels in microwave oven. Microwave, uncovered, at HIGH for 15 to 18 minutes or until squash is soft to the touch, turning squash over every 5 minutes. Let stand 5 minutes.

Combine oil and garlic in a large bowl. Microwave, uncovered, at HIGH for 1½ to 2½ minutes or until thoroughly heated. Stir in basil, oregano, salt, and pepper.

Cut squash in half, and remove seeds. Using a fork, remove spaghetti-like strands. Combine squash strands and oil mixture, tossing gently. Sprinkle with cheese. Yield: 4 to 6 servings.

Garlic-Sautéed Swiss Chard

1 pound Swiss chard
1 tablespoon olive oil
2 cloves garlic, minced
2 teaspoons lemon juice
¼ teaspoon salt
Coarsely ground black
  pepper to taste

Remove chard leaves, discarding stalks. Wash leaves thoroughly. Drain leaves, and cut into strips; set aside.

Combine oil and garlic in a 1½-quart casserole. Microwave, uncovered, at HIGH for 1 to 2 minutes or until thoroughly heated; stir in chard leaves. Cover with heavy-duty plastic wrap and microwave at HIGH for 4 to 5 minutes or until crisp-tender. Let stand, covered, 3 minutes. Sprinkle with lemon juice, salt, and pepper; toss before serving. Yield: 4 servings.

When preparing Swiss chard, remove the leaves from the stalks, and cut into strips.

Zippy Baked Tomatoes

3 medium-size firm tomatoes
1½ tablespoons spicy brown
  mustard
⅛ teaspoon pepper
2 tablespoons butter or
  margarine
⅓ cup fine, dry breadcrumbs
2 tablespoons chopped fresh
  parsley
¼ teaspoon salt-free herb
  seasoning blend
Fresh parsley sprigs (optional)

Wash tomatoes. Cut each tomato in half crosswise. Arrange in a circle on a 12-inch round glass platter, cut side up; set aside.

Combine mustard and pepper in a small bowl, stirring well. Spread mustard mixture over cut surfaces of tomatoes. Place butter in a 1-cup glass measure. Microwave, uncovered, at HIGH for 45 seconds or until melted. Stir in breadcrumbs, chopped parsley, and herb seasoning blend. Pat breadcrumb mixture over tops of tomatoes.

Cover tomatoes with wax paper; microwave at HIGH for 4 to 5 minutes or until thoroughly heated, rotating a half-turn after 2 minutes. Let stand, covered, 2 minutes. Garnish with parsley sprigs, if desired. Yield: 6 servings.

Parslied Turnips And Carrots

4 medium turnips (about 1¼
  pounds)
2 cups diced carrots
¼ cup water
½ teaspoon chicken-flavored
  bouillon granules
¼ cup butter or margarine
2 teaspoons sugar
¼ teaspoon salt
¼ teaspoon coarsely ground
  black pepper
3 tablespoons minced fresh
  parsley

Peel turnips and dice (about 3 cups). Combine turnips, carrots, water, and bouillon granules in a 1½-quart casserole. Cover with heavy-duty plastic wrap and microwave at HIGH for 10 to 12 minutes or until vegetables are tender. Drain.

Add butter, sugar, salt, pepper, and parsley to turnip mixture; toss gently. Let stand, covered, 3 minutes. Yield: 6 to 8 servings.

MICROWAVE VEGETABLE CHART

VEGETABLE	AMOUNT	PROCEDURE
ARTICHOKES	4 medium	Clip tips of outer leaves. Combine artichokes and ½ cup water in a 12- x 8- x 2-inch baking dish; cover and microwave at HIGH for 10 to 15 minutes or until leaves pull out easily. Drain.
ASPARAGUS	1 pound	Remove tough ends of lower spears. Combine spears, stem ends towards outside, and ¼ cup water in a 10- x 6- x 2-inch baking dish. Cover and microwave at HIGH for 6 to 7 minutes or until crisp-tender. Drain.
BEANS GREEN/WAX	1 pound	Wash beans; trim ends, and remove strings. Cut into 1-inch pieces. Combine beans and ½ cup water in a 1½-quart casserole. Cover and microwave at HIGH for 14 to 15 minutes or until tender. Drain.
LIMA	1 pound, shelled (2 cups)	Combine beans and 1 cup water in a 1½-quart casserole. Cover and microwave at HIGH for 5 minutes. Reduce to MEDIUM HIGH (70% power), and microwave for 25 to 30 minutes or until tender. Drain.
BEETS	1 pound	Wash and trim beets, leaving 1 to 2 inches of tops. Combine beets and ½ cup water in a 1½-quart casserole. Cover and microwave at HIGH for 12 to 14 minutes or until tender. Drain and cool to touch. Peel.
BOK CHOY	1 pound	Cut stalks and leaves into thin slices, and place in a 1½-quart casserole. Cover and microwave at HIGH for 4 to 5 minutes or until tender. Drain.
BROCCOLI	1 pound	Remove tough ends of stalks, and divide into spears. Combine spears, stem ends towards outside, and ½ cup water in a 12- x 8- x 2-inch baking dish. Cover and microwave at HIGH for 7 to 8 minutes or until tender. Drain.
BRUSSELS SPROUTS	1 pound	Cut a shallow X in stem end of each sprout. Combine sprouts and ¼ cup water in a 1½-quart casserole. Cover and microwave at HIGH for 6 to 8 minutes or until tender. Let stand 3 minutes. Drain.
CABBAGE GREEN/RED	1¼ pounds	Shred cabbage. Combine cabbage and ¼ cup water in a 12- x 8- x 2-inch baking dish. Cover and microwave at HIGH for 11 to 13 minutes or until tender. Drain.
CHINESE	1 pound	Shred cabbage; place in a 2-quart casserole. Cover and microwave at HIGH for 6 to 9 minutes or until tender. Drain.
CARROTS	1 pound	Slice carrots. Combine sliced carrots and ¼ cup water in a 1-quart casserole. Cover and microwave at HIGH for 9 to 10 minutes or until tender. Let stand 2 minutes. Drain.
CAULIFLOWER	2 pounds	Break into flowerets. Combine flowerets and ½ cup water in a 1½-quart casserole. Cover and microwave at HIGH for 10 to 11 minutes or until tender. Let stand 2 minutes. Drain.
CELERY	4 cups, sliced	Combine slices and ¼ cup water in a 1½-quart casserole. Cover and microwave at HIGH for 10 to 12 minutes or until crisp-tender. Drain.
CORN KERNELS	2 cups	Combine kernels and ¼ cup water. Cover and microwave at HIGH for 9 to 10 minutes or until tender. Drain.

MICROWAVE VEGETABLE CHART

VEGETABLE	AMOUNT	PROCEDURE
CORN (*continued*)		

ON COB IN HUSKS (large ears)	1 ear
	   3 to 5 minutes
	2 ears
	   6 to 9 minutes
	3 ears
	   9 to 12 minutes
	4 ears
	   12 to 16 minutes
		Pull down husks and remove silks. Rinse corn; pull husks back over corn. Arrange unhusked corn on paper towels. Microwave at HIGH for time indicated. Remove husks.

ON COB WITHOUT HUSKS (large ears)	1 ear
	   2 to 4 minutes
	2 ears
	   5 to 9 minutes
	3 ears
	   7 to 12 minutes
	4 ears
	   8 to 15 minutes
		Remove husks and silks. Wrap each ear in heavy-duty plastic wrap (or place in a tightly covered baking dish with ¼ cup water). Microwave at HIGH for time indicated. Drain, if necessary.

CUCUMBERS	4 medium	Peel, if desired. Cut into thin slices. Place slices in a 1½-quart casserole. Cover and microwave at HIGH for 3 to 4 minutes or until crisp-tender. Drain.
EGGPLANT	1 pound	Peel eggplant, and cut into cubes. Place cubes in a 12- x 8- x 2-inch baking dish. Cover and microwave at HIGH for 6 to 8 minutes or until tender. Drain.
KOHLRABI	1 pound	Trim ends and stems. Peel kohlrabi, and cut into thin slices. Combine slices and ¼ cup water in a 1½-quart casserole. Cover and microwave at HIGH for 12 to 15 minutes or until tender. Drain.
LEEKS	2 pounds (6 medium)	Trim leeks. Split leeks lengthwise, and cut into 1-inch slices. Place leeks in a 2-quart casserole. Cover and microwave at HIGH for 7 to 8 minutes or until tender. Drain.
MUSHROOMS	1 pound	Wipe mushrooms clean. Combine mushrooms and 2 tablespoons water in a 1½-quart casserole. Cover and microwave at HIGH for 4 to 5 minutes or until tender. Drain.
OKRA	1 pound	Cut okra into thin slices. Combine okra and ¼ cup water in a 1-quart casserole. Cover and microwave at HIGH for 9 to 10 minutes or until tender. Drain.
ONIONS	1 pound	Peel onions; cut into quarters. Combine onions and 2 tablespoons water in a 1-quart casserole. Cover and microwave at HIGH for 6 to 8 minutes or until tender. Drain.
PARSNIPS	1 pound	Scrape parsnips, and cut into thin slices. Combine slices and ¼ cup water in a 1½-quart casserole. Cover and microwave at HIGH for 6 to 7 minutes or until tender. Drain.
PEAS		
BLACK-EYED	2 pounds, shelled (4 cups)	Combine peas and 1¼ cups water in a 2-quart casserole. Cover and microwave at HIGH for 4 minutes. Reduce to MEDIUM (50% power), and microwave for 35 to 40 minutes or until tender.
GREEN	1 pound, shelled (1½ cups)	Combine peas and 2 tablespoons water in a 1-quart casserole. Cover and microwave at HIGH for 6 to 7 minutes or until tender. Drain.
SNOW PEA PODS	1 pound	Trim ends, and remove strings. Combine peas and 2 tablespoons water in a 1½-quart casserole. Cover and microwave at HIGH for 3 to 4 minutes or until crisp-tender. Drain.

MICROWAVE VEGETABLE CHART

VEGETABLE	AMOUNT	PROCEDURE
PEPPERS	2 medium	Cut peppers into thin strips. Combine peppers and 1 tablespoon water in a 1-quart casserole. Cover and microwave at HIGH for 4 to 5 minutes or until crisp-tender. Drain.
POTATOES **BAKING/SWEET** (Medium Potatoes)	1 potato 4 to 6 minutes 2 potatoes 7 to 8 minutes 3 potatoes 9 to 11 minutes 4 potatoes 12 to 14 minutes 5 potatoes 16 to 18 minutes 6 potatoes 20 to 24 minutes	Pierce scrubbed potatoes with a fork. Arrange in a circle on paper towels. Microwave at HIGH for time indicated. Let stand 5 minutes.
NEW POTATOES	1 pound	Scrub and peel, if desired. Pierce each potato with a fork. Combine potatoes and ¼ cup water in a 1½-quart casserole. Cover and microwave at HIGH for 8 to 10 minutes or until tender. Drain.
PUMPKIN	2 to 3 pounds	Peel pumpkin; cut in half, and remove seeds. Cut pumpkin into ½-inch cubes. Combine cubes and ¼ cup water in a 2-quart casserole. Cover and microwave at HIGH for 10 to 11 minutes or until tender. Drain.
RUTABAGAS	1½ to 2 pounds (2 medium)	Peel rutabagas, and cut into cubes. Combine rutabaga cubes and ¼ cup water in a 2-quart casserole. Cover and microwave at HIGH for 16 to 20 minutes or until tender. Drain.
SPINACH	1 pound	Wash spinach, and tear into bite-size pieces. Place spinach in a 3-quart casserole. Cover and microwave at HIGH for 2 to 3 minutes or to desired degree of doneness. Drain.
SUMMER SQUASH **YELLOW/ZUCCHINI**	1 pound (4 medium)	Cut squash into thin slices. Combine squash slices and ¼ cup water in a 1½-quart casserole. Cover and microwave at HIGH for 7 to 8 minutes or until tender. Drain.
WINTER SQUASH **ACORN**	2 pounds (2 medium)	Pierce squash with a fork, and arrange on paper towels. Microwave at HIGH for 9 to 10 minutes or until tender. Cut in half, and remove seeds.
BUTTERNUT	1½ pounds (1 small)	Peel squash. Cut squash in half lengthwise, removing seeds. Place squash and 2 tablespoons water in a 1½-quart casserole. Cover with heavy-duty plastic wrap and microwave at HIGH for 6 to 8 minutes or until tender. Let stand 2 minutes.
SPAGHETTI	3 pounds (1 medium)	Pierce squash several times with a fork. Place on paper towels and microwave at HIGH for 15 to 18 minutes or until soft to touch. Let stand 5 minutes. Cut in half, and remove strands with a fork.
SWISS CHARD	1 pound	Remove stems, and cut leaves into strips. Place leaves in a 1½-quart casserole. Cover and microwave at HIGH for 4 to 5 minutes or until tender.
TOMATOES	4 medium	Peel, seed, and chop tomatoes. Place in a 1½-quart casserole. Cover and microwave at HIGH for 3 to 4 minutes or to desired degree of doneness.
TURNIPS	1¼ pounds (4 medium)	Peel turnips, and cut into cubes. Combine turnip cubes and ¼ cup water in a 1-quart casserole. Cover and microwave at HIGH for 10 to 12 minutes or until tender. Drain.

MICROWAVE COOKING CHART

FOOD ITEM	AMOUNT	TIME	PROCEDURE
BEVERAGES			
Boiling Water (for tea)	½ cup	1½ to 2½ minutes	Place in a glass measure and microwave, uncovered, at HIGH until boiling.
	1 cup	2 to 3½ minutes	
	2 cups	4 to 5½ minutes	
Hot Milk (for cocoa)	½ cup	1 to 2 minutes	Place in a glass measure and microwave, uncovered, at HIGH until thoroughly heated (do not boil).
	1 cup	2 to 3½ minutes	
	2 cups	4 to 5 minutes	
CONVENIENCES			
Toasting Almonds, Peanuts, Pecans, Walnuts	¼ cup	2 to 4 minutes	Spread in a pieplate and microwave, uncovered, at HIGH until lightly toasted.
	½ cup	3 to 4 minutes	
	1 cup	4 to 5 minutes	
Toasting Coconut	½ cup	2 to 3 minutes	Spread in a pieplate and microwave, uncovered, at HIGH until lightly toasted (will darken upon standing).
Melting Chocolate Morsels	1 cup	3 to 3½ minutes	Place in a glass measure and microwave, uncovered, at MEDIUM (50% power) until softened. Stir well.
CHEESE AND BUTTER			
Melting Butter or Margarine	¼ cup	55 seconds	Place in a glass measure and microwave, uncovered, at HIGH until melted.
	½ cup	1 minute	
	1 cup	1½ to 2 minutes	
Softening Cream Cheese	3-ounce package	30 to 40 seconds	Place in a glass measure and microwave, uncovered, at HIGH until softened.
	8-ounce package	45 seconds to 1 minute	
FISH AND SHELLFISH			
Fish Fillets	4 (4-ounce)	5 to 8 minutes	Place in a baking dish. Cover and microwave at HIGH until fish flakes easily when tested with a fork.
Shrimp, peeled	1 pound	3 to 5 minutes	Place in a baking dish. Cover and microwave at HIGH until tender and pink.
MEAT			
Ground Beef	1 pound	5 to 8 minutes	Place in a baking dish. Cover and microwave at HIGH until no longer pink.
Bacon	2 slices	2 to 3 minutes	Place on a bacon rack. Cover with paper towels and microwave at HIGH until crisp.
	4 slices	3½ to 4½ minutes	
	6 slices	5 to 7 minutes	
Frankfurters	1 link	25 to 30 seconds	Pierce each link with a fork. Place in a baking dish. Cover and microwave at HIGH until thoroughly heated.
	2 links	30 seconds to 1 minute	
POULTRY			
Whole Broiler-Fryer	1 (3-pound)	40 to 50 minutes	Place on a rack in a baking dish. Cover and microwave at MEDIUM (50% power) until drumsticks are easy to move.
Cut-up Broiler-Fryer	3 pounds	18 to 20 minutes	Place in a baking dish. Cover and microwave at HIGH until tender.

MICROWAVE DEFROSTING CHART

FOOD ITEM	AMOUNT	TIME	PROCEDURE
FISH AND SHELLFISH			
Fish Fillets	4 (4-ounce)	6 to 8 minutes	Place in a baking dish. Cover and microwave at MEDIUM LOW (30% power) until partially thawed. Let stand 10 minutes.
Shrimp, unpeeled	1 pound	6 to 8 minutes	Place in a baking dish. Cover and microwave at MEDIUM LOW (30% power) until thawed.
MEATS			
Beef			
Roasts		5 to 6 minutes per pound	Place in a baking dish. Cover and microwave at MEDIUM LOW (30% power) until partially thawed. Let stand 10 minutes.
Steaks		7 to 8 minutes per pound	Place in a baking dish. Cover and microwave at MEDIUM LOW (30% power) until partially thawed. Let stand 5 minutes.
Ground Beef		7 to 8 minutes per pound	Place in a baking dish. Cover and microwave at MEDIUM LOW (30% power) until partially thawed. Let stand 5 minutes.
Pork			
Roasts		7 to 8 minutes per pound	Place in a baking dish. Cover and microwave at MEDIUM LOW (30% power) until partially thawed. Let stand 10 minutes.
Chops		7 to 8 minutes per pound	Place in a baking dish. Cover and microwave at MEDIUM LOW (30% power) until partially thawed. Let stand 5 minutes.
Lamb			
Roasts		5 to 6 minutes per pound	Place in a baking dish. Cover and microwave at MEDIUM LOW (30% power) until partially thawed. Let stand 10 minutes.
Chops		7 to 8 minutes per pound	Place in a baking dish. Cover and microwave at MEDIUM LOW (30% power) until partially thawed. Let stand 10 minutes.
POULTRY			
Whole Broiler-Fryer	1 (3-pound)	20 to 25 minutes	Place in a baking dish. Cover and microwave at MEDIUM LOW (30% power) until partially thawed. Let stand 30 minutes.
Cut-up Broiler-Fryer	3 pounds	15 to 17 minutes	Place in a baking dish. Cover and microwave at MEDIUM LOW (30% power) until partially thawed. Let stand 15 minutes.
Cornish Hens	2 (1- to 1½-pound)	12 to 15 minutes	Place in a baking dish. Cover and microwave at MEDIUM LOW (30% power) until partially thawed. Let stand 30 minutes.
Whole Turkey	1 (10-pound)	30 minutes	Place in a baking dish or on a 12-inch round glass platter. Cover and microwave at MEDIUM LOW (30% power). Let stand 30 minutes. Repeat procedure until thawed.

RECIPE INDEX

Subject Index